e-Schooling

e-Schooling
Global messages from a small island

**Roger Austin and
John Anderson**

LONDON AND NEW YORK

First published 2008
by Routledge
2 Park Square, Milton Park, Abingdon, Oxon, OX14 4RN

Simultaneously published in the USA and Canada
by Routledge
270 Madison Ave, New York, NY 10016

Routledge is an imprint of the Taylor & Francis Group, an informa business

© 2008 Roger Austin and John Anderson
Note: The right of Roger Austin and John Anderson to be identified as the authors of this work has been asserted by them in accordance with the Copyright, Designs and Patents Act 1988

Typeset in Stone Serif by
HWA Text and Data Management, Tunbridge Wells
Printed and bound in Great Britain by
TJ International Ltd, Padstow, Cornwall

All rights reserved. No part of this book may be reprinted or reproduced or utilised in any form or by any electronic, mechanical, or other means, now known or hereafter invented, including photocopying and recording, or in any information storage or retrieval system, without permission in writing from the publishers.

British Library Cataloguing in Publication Data
A catalogue record for this book is available from the British Library

Library of Congress Cataloging-in-Publication Data
A catalog record for this book has been requested

ISBN10: 1–84312–380–0

ISBN13: 978–1–84312–380–4

Contents

	Acknowledgements	vi
	Introduction	1
1	The state of schooling in Northern Ireland and its capacity to change	8
2	An integrated strategy for ICT in schools	19
3	Teacher development for e-schooling	38
4	Transforming learning within early teacher education	59
5	An e-curriculum for an e-school?	77
6	Connected learning for citizenship	97
7	Special and inclusive learning	111
8	Enterprising education	132
9	Leadership for quality in an e-school	153
10	Global messaging	169
	Notes	184
	Index	198

Acknowledgements

The authors acknowledge the enormous credit owing those innovative educators, in this small island and beyond, who have made outstanding contributions to rethinking and improving education, accelerated through technological change, in Northern Ireland over the past thirty years.

We are indebted, beyond repayment, for the encouragement and forbearance of our wives and families.

All errors and omissions remain our own.

Introduction

The idea for this book began when we were trying to answer two key questions; what are the key functions of a school in the twenty-first century and what part does and should ICT play in ensuring that education meets the millennial needs of learners? Around the world at international conferences, many were looking at the impact of ICT on teaching and learning but we wanted to take a wider focus on the purposes of ICT in education. For example, what values are attached to ICT? There didn't seem to be much discussion around what we felt was a central issue and on our doorstep, in Northern Ireland, it looked like we had a promising place to examine these questions.

As we analysed what was happening in Northern Ireland and in other countries round the world, we began using the concept, e-schooling, to describe a process in which schools were using ICT to accelerate change and we started to identify the conditions in which e-schooling seemed most likely to occur. But first, we need to spell out how we define e-schooling.

What is e-schooling?

The most common use of the term relates to the commercialisation of distance learning courses sold online. One of the few academic studies of 'e-schooling' defines it as the 'use of the World Wide Web as an extension of the school's educational and organisational infrastructure'.[1] In this book, we have developed a much broader concept. For us e-schooling is a process in which the entire schooling system uses ICT to transform learning in a way that links what schools do with key social *and* economic goals. We argue that a knowledge-based economy and society demands that e-schooling is the best way to ensure that *all* children are helped to become good citizens, with skills and knowledge to find employment and nurture their interest in life-long learning.

This concept of e-schooling has four other important characteristics. First, it sees schools as 'learning organisations' with as strong a commitment to the education of its staff and those in the community as its children. By definition, then, the school plays a critical role in the wider community by providing a wide range of learning opportunities. But the 'community' is not only the geographical locality of the school; the Internet and video-conferencing mean that schools are part of a global community. This experience is meaningful for the students, who learn what it takes to work with people across the world whom they may never meet face to face. Furthermore, David Hargreaves[2] argues that for teachers to meet the twenty-first century needs of learners, then 'rapid transformations' are needed in their practices; piece-meal innovation will not do. The challenge for teachers today is that their sense of self-definition comes from the classroom, and their sense of community from the staffroom. To be open to change, they have to work in learning communities wide enough to encompass the entire teaching force: this they can only do online.

Second, e-schooling requires an *alignment* of policy and technology. This works at two levels. At the macro-level, there needs to be an alignment between broad government policy, for example in terms of promoting social inclusion and decisions about investment in ICT in education. The same can be said for economic policy; there is little point in investing heavily in ICT infrastructure in education unless there is clarity about how this relates to the needs of the economy. At a micro-level there needs to be alignment between the goals of the curriculum, assessment, teacher professional development and the place of ICT. All arrows need to point in the same direction.

Third, e-schooling depends on *sustainability*; we use this term in two ways. Globally, one can see examples where investment in educational ICT has been made as a politically opportune 'silver bullet'. We argue that investment in ICT infrastructure needs to be seen as a commodity, as fundamental as buildings, electricity and telephones. It has to be built into core funding to enable hardware and software to be regularly refreshed to ensure that learners' use of ICT (children, teachers and other adults) keeps pace with the rapidly changing technological landscape. In Chapter 2 we examine a fully operational public–private partnership model in Northern Ireland.

We also use the term 'sustainability' as defined by Alan McCluskey in 2004.[3] He claims that for schools to become 'sustainable learning organisations', we need to focus on renewing people and the organisational context in which they work. We concur entirely with the view that no amount of technology will improve learning without the right level of teacher commitment and expertise in the use of ICT. We have drawn on McCluskey's work where he looks at 'human resources' in the teaching force in terms of the depletion of scarce natural resources – specifically the costly and 'hard to renew' resources of trust, confidence and motivation in the teaching force. He argues that both structural/organisational change and professional development are needed in schools. Short term, usually expensive, bursts of energy to embed ICT in practice cannot be sustained without whole-school improvement. Most important of all is the quality and nature of leadership in schools – not just by the few, but as a means of empowering all teachers, including not only principals, middle managers and those in training but library staff, classroom assistants and technicians. We analyse these issues further in Chapters 3, 4 and 9.

Finally, e-schooling for us implies a particular view about *learning*; there is no point in spending very large sums of money on ICT and ensuring that there is perfect alignment and sustainability unless the use of ICT is making a real difference to learning. We argue in the book that a narrow measure of the impact of ICT only in terms of public test scores misses two critical matters. The first relates to the views associated with Alan November[4] who suggested that we look at ICT and learning as a continuum. In some cases, ICT merely 'automates' learning; there is little added value and the learning could have been done just as effectively using other means. Further along the continuum, November suggests we can observe ICT 'enhancing' learning and at its best, it can be seen as 'transforming' learning. In the book we provide some examples from Northern Ireland where ICT transforms learning, making something possible that could not otherwise have been achieved.

Our final point about learning is that ICT not only promotes cognitive achievement and skills; it can also support the development of attitudes and behaviours.

We agree with McCluskey that any innovative development without values, or which does not explicitly address the issue of values, is questionable and think that there has been insufficient public debate about the values attached to ICT. Austin (2004)[5] challenges the notion that ICT is value-free, arguing that every application of ICT for learning carries with it a set of, often unstated, values; the decision, for example, to use ICT to link with another school, which is in our view, a crucial central plank in any attempt to provide young people with an education in citizenship, implies a willingness to be open to cultural difference and diversity, a point we develop in Chapter 6.

The capacity of ICT to link schools together in e-partnerships is, we believe, one of the most interesting stories to emerge from our analysis of the role of ICT in Northern Ireland.

e-Schooling – re-schooling and de-schooling

Readers may already be familiar with the terms de-schooling[6] and re-schooling; we offer here a brief account to explain how we think e-schooling relates to these two concepts.

As our research for this book unfolded we found ourselves attracted to the idea of 're-schooling' which was developed by David Istance (2001, 2003 and 2004).[7] Istance and his colleagues in the Organisation for Economic and Cultural Development (OECD) were interested in what schools of the future might look like. He described three broad clusters of scenarios:

Maintaining the bureaucratic *status quo*

Maintaining the bureaucratic *status quo* is characterised by teachers working as they do at the moment, largely in isolation and fearful of what change might mean for their status; in extreme circumstances a 'meltdown scenario' may occur when an extreme shortage of teachers through loss of morale is coupled with an inability to recruit sufficient numbers of young graduates, who have a wide range of alternative career options.

Re-schooling

Re-schooling may occur as schools become core social centres – the key social and community institution. School walls come down and a substantial variety of community activities take place within the school. Alternatively, the school may focus on learning as its rationale, 'revitalised around a strong knowledge agenda in a culture of high quality, innovation, experimentation and diversity'. Teachers become part of a wider local, national and global community, aided by the opportunities created through digital networks and linking the school to further and higher education. There is a high premium on teacher professional development to justify the use of the term 'focused learning organisations'.

De-schooling

Schools are no longer central to the education of young people and government plays a less important role compared to a range of religious and commercial providers. In effect, market forces drive the shape of educational provision and schools, as we know them, cease to exist. While this may seem an apocalyptic vision to many, the gradual death of schools as we know them is being openly talked about at conferences[8] where the benefits of online learning communities, supporting home-tutored academic achievement and social skills, are contrasted with the alleged failings of traditional schools. It is reported by Collins *et al.* (2002),[9] for example, that as many as 40 per cent of primary school age children in Northern Ireland claim to have been bullied at school. This makes uncomfortable reading for those who assert that schools play a key role in the development of the social and emotional well-being of all children.

We were particularly attracted to Istance's cluster of 're-schooling' scenarios, seeing this as a powerful vision for predicting the future and wished to investigate more fully the place of ICT. We see e-schooling as 're-schooling' through ICT; and while schools are often seen as conservative organisations, we believe that ICT could accelerate the rate of transformative change on a system-wide basis.

Questioning the impact of ICT on learning

As we refined our understanding of e-schooling, we were also aware that there is a degree of scepticism, even hostility, about how effective ICT is in improving learning. Cuban (2001)[10] and Conlon and Simpson (2003)[11] have argued that the high level of public and private sector investments in ICT have made relatively little difference to teaching style, the quality of pupil learning or measurable improvements in standards. Conlon and Simpson (2003) comparing the use of ICT in Scotland with the work of Cuban in America, commented that

> children typically encounter computers only seldom and their impact on learning experiences must be extremely limited ... when students do use computers in the classroom the activity is often peripheral to the learning process. ... Teachers mostly employ the technology to sustain existing patterns of schooling rather than to innovate.

Cuban's critique is that the introduction of ICT into schools

> ... has achieved neither the transformation of teaching and learning nor the productivity gains that a reform coalition of corporate executives, public officials, parents, academics and educators have sought.

When we came to analyse the reported effects of ICT on learners in Northern Ireland, we wondered if we would be coming to the same dismal conclusion. On balance however, we have a much more positive and surprising set of conclusions, which are gathered together in Chapter 10; but this begs a very important question. What is the Northern Ireland story and what makes it relevant beyond these shores?

The Northern Ireland experience and its global significance

The analysis offered here explores the historical and political context which has bequeathed Northern Ireland a schooling system that is both segregated along religious lines and based on academic selection at the age of 11 but which is now in a period of considerable, and at times unpredictable, change.

With a populace of 1.6 million, 340,000 pupils in compulsory education, attending 1,242 schools and taught by 21,000 teachers[12] this is not one Northern

Ireland story, but many. These schools and teachers are at different stages of what one might call the 'Alan November continuum' and in that sense we draw upon evidence in the book to argue that the embedding of a common ICT infrastructure and a coordinated approach to teacher development is narrowing the gap between the ICT 'haves' and 'have-nots'.

The approach to ICT planning and implementation adopted in Northern Ireland has sometimes been called centralist but is certainly integrationalist; it is one of the reasons why we maintain that a close understanding of what emerges here provides lessons well beyond the north-east corner of the island of Ireland. But, Northern Ireland makes a compelling case study for a number of other reasons.

The first of these is cost; how does a region or country resolve the major issues of affordability and sustainability of infrastructure and broadband connectivity? What are the respective roles of government and the private sector in this process? What are the benefits of a centralised approach to ICT infrastructure? Is there a price to pay in terms of loss of teacher or school contribution, or can choice and control be balanced? In other words, is a 'top-down' process more likely to provide quality learning than one which is mainly 'bottom-up?' We examine this issue in Chapter 2.

Another reason why Northern Ireland is an illuminating case study is because of the steps that have been taken to provide professional development in ICT for teachers, in initial teacher education, in continuing professional development and in leadership training. We reflect in Chapters 3, 4 and 9 what has been done in this area and what remains to be done, particularly in terms of building capacity for e-learning for all teachers and educators. How can teacher professional development be given the status it needs?

A third reason for suggesting that Northern Ireland's story has resonance beyond the Irish Sea is in our analysis of the links between ICT, the curriculum, pedagogy and the core purposes of schooling in a changing society; it seems to us that unless there is clarity about the links between ICT and enterprise, ICT and creativity, ICT and social inclusion and overall about the relationship between the values embedded in ICT and those embodied in the curriculum, the potential of ICT will be severely limited. We have, therefore, examined in Chapters 5 and 7 the changing curriculum in Northern Ireland and analysed the ways in which ICT is being developed to support all children, including those with special learning needs. But because of Northern Ireland's particular history of separate schooling for children from different cultural and religious backgrounds, we have considered, in Chapter 6, the role that e-schooling can play in promoting both local and global citizenship.

This is not to suggest that the main reason for sustaining ICT is its contribution to cross-community relations; elsewhere, in Chapter 8, we consider the question of how far the ICT skills in schools are relevant to a knowledge-based economy. We offer a critique of how enterprise, by which we mean creativity, innovation and risk taking are reflected in the type of ICT work that young people experience in schools and in colleges of further and higher education.

Bob Pearlman, a strategic planning consultant familiar with Northern Ireland, who can see the presence of all of these components, sums up the value of a case-study approach.[13]

> In social and economic development, 'less advanced societies' are not condemned to pass through all the gradual stages of development, but often adopt and adapt the best practices of the 'advanced' societies and leapfrog forward.
>
> Since 1997 Northern Ireland has embarked on an Educational Technology Strategy that holds clear lessons for other nations and regions. By studying closely the much earlier large scale implementations from leading nations like the US and Australia, NI has avoided costly errors and adopted and adapted the best practices of those forerunners. Key elements of the NI strategy which have made a difference include:
>
> - Focus on technology to support learning in all subjects, not a separate technology skills curriculum such as England
> - Technology for teachers (laptops) from the start, combined with intense professional development and ICT training, in-person and online. Other countries led with students, got a quick bang, and then sustained little as the teacher facilitators of learning did little to exploit the technology for student learning
> - Managed service network infrastructure to deliver content and provide a collaborative learning environment for all students and teachers, not restricted to traditional education
> - Systematic school-based networks and broadband connectivity
> - Fostering a network of practitioners and sharing online the best practices in ICT implementations for learning
>
> NI started way behind other formerly leading nations. By implementing a systematic and thoughtful Educational Technology Strategy that adopted and adapted the best practices of others and leveraged the collaborative internet and network tools of the late 90s, NI has caught up with the leaders and now makes a significant contribution to the global implementation of ICT in education.

These core messages appear throughout the book and we return to them in the final chapter; but first, some scene-setting is required. What kind of schooling system does Northern Ireland have and what forces have shaped it to be the way it is?

The state of schooling in Northern Ireland and its capacity to change

In this chapter, we make the case that Northern Ireland, like almost every other society, has a schooling system that has been shaped by some very powerful and often conservative forces that drive schools to protect and reproduce existing culture rather than to enable culture to change to meet new needs.

The forces in Northern Ireland are historical, political, moral and religious and, as in any other country, schools are also shaped by the economy, both in terms of what can be afforded and how schools might prepare young people for further study and work. In this short analysis we indicate how schools have emerged in their present form and indicate that many of the assumptions about their present organisation have been coming under question, particularly since the late 1990s.

The shadow of history and the influence of politics

Why is it that some 95 per cent of learners attend schools in Northern Ireland which are either predominantly 'Roman Catholic' in their ethos or where most of the learners are non-Catholic? And why is the curriculum in schools somewhat different to what would be found either in England and significantly different to the curriculum in the Republic of Ireland? Answers to these key questions require a brief look into the past.

We have alluded to this in previous work (Austin and Anderson, 2006)[1] and underline here the salient points. England had effectively controlled Ireland since the sixteenth century but, with some reluctance, agreed to independence for 26 out of the 32 counties of Ireland in 1921. The six counties that were excluded were those in the north-east of the island which made up part of the ancient province of Ulster, counties with a predominantly Protestant population, the majority of whom wanted to remain part of Great Britain. The creation of the Republic of Ireland and Northern Ireland at this time solved an immediate problem but left a legacy of suspicion on both sides and, for many nationalists on both sides of the border, a sense that there was unfinished business. In effect since 1921, the status of Northern Ireland

and the issue of whether there should be a reunification of the island have shaped the structure of political parties and divided opinion on both sides of the border in Ireland.

For the purposes of this book, it should be noted that since 1921, the education and schooling systems in Northern Ireland and the Republic of Ireland differ significantly in terms of control, organisation and curriculum.

The political divisions

The divisions in Northern Ireland are both reflected and reinforced through the political party structure in Northern Ireland; all of the four main political parties in Northern Ireland draw their support mainly from one side of the community or the other. Though there are parties that seek to cut across these traditional groups, they have been unable to attract significant levels of support in elections.

Despite being part of the United Kingdom, the Conservative, Labour and Liberal Democrat parties that make up the bulk of the Members of Parliament in the House of Commons in London play a very minor role in local elections in Northern Ireland. Only the Conservative Party fields candidates in some of the constituencies in Northern Ireland. Electors in this part of the United Kingdom are invited to vote for parties that do not represent standard 'class' or 'ideological' differences; instead they are canvassed on different versions of loyalty to the union with Great Britain or different degrees of support for the idea of a united Ireland. Since 1968, the date usually seen as the start of 'the Troubles', local politicians had been unable to form a devolved administration for any sustained period of time, except for the period between 1998 and 2002. Britain stepped in and took over the administration of Northern Ireland, while seeking to help local parties reach a consensus on how Northern Ireland should be governed.

Religious and cultural affiliations

The issue of political identity has a significant overlap with religious affiliation, with the 44 per cent of the population describing themselves as 'Catholic' more likely to think of themselves as Irish and those who regard themselves as 'Protestant' inclined to associate themselves with Great Britain. The schooling system in Northern Ireland reflects these differences with over 95 per cent of schools effectively segregated along denominational lines. Only five per cent of children attend 'integrated' schools where children of different religious affiliation are educated together. The vast majority of the rest of the school population attend either 'maintained' schools which are managed by representatives of the Catholic church or 'controlled ' schools which are officially 'state' schools but where the interests of the Protestant churches are officially recognised.

This level of segregation is in some respects exacerbated by housing patterns; in a housing census in 2001, 18.6 per cent of the population was recorded as living in publicly owned housing. Most of such properties are in housing estates where the display of either loyalist/Protestant or republican/nationalist identity through wall murals, flags and painted curbstones is highly visible. While there is no reliable data on the extent of 'mixed' housing in the private sector, cultural differences between young Catholics and Protestants are often expressed though preferences for different sports and support for different sporting teams. Since 1969, paramilitary activity in the cause of a united Ireland or in opposition to this has claimed well over 3,000 lives.

Although the level of violence has reduced significantly since the 'Good Friday' agreement of 1998, Northern Ireland is still recovering from its legacy of suspicion and mistrust. It is in some respects a rather conservative society where church attendance would be higher than in England, 'ordinary' crime levels are lower and where extended family networks remain strong. Compared to other parts of the world which are emerging from a long period of inter-communal tension and overt violence, Northern Ireland is relatively calm and even during the worst of the 'Troubles' schools were often seen as islands of relative peace. But this was frequently a peace based on a retreat into safe sanctuaries with like-minded co-religionists, sometimes with walls in the most dangerous neighbourhoods to provide protection. In other words, the need for self-preservation reinforced socio-cultural differences and schools were part of this process.

When we pull together these overlapping historical, political and religious factors, we can observe a schooling system that is subject to deep-rooted and invasive conservatism. So when we ask whether ICT-enabled re-schooling can bring about change that is more than cosmetic, this is a very tall order since it will have to address far more than purely academic concerns. For example, what kinds of attitudes and behaviours might e-schooling promote both in terms of community relations within Northern Ireland and indeed between Northern Ireland and the Republic of Ireland? We consider this question in detail in Chapter 6. But next we must consider what the Northern Ireland school system looks like in 2007.

The Northern Ireland school system

Any discussion of what e-schooling might mean needs to take account of what is already in place; what are the most significant characteristics of the education system in Northern Ireland? There are 917 primary, 164 non-selective secondary and 71 grammar schools, and 50 special schools[2] and, of these, all except for the special schools are designed to offer denominational choice. Unlike a number of other countries, fee-paying private schools are extremely rare in Northern Ireland. All children, except those with severe learning difficulties, attend primary schools from age 5 to 11 and most then take an externally set examination (the 'transfer test) at the age of 11 to determine whether they will attend an academic 'grammar' school or a non-selective school. While the term 'post-primary' is used in Northern Ireland to refer to the set of both non-selective schools and selective grammar schools, we use the more familiar term 'secondary' throughout this book.

So, while we have a small education service, there are many diverse types of schools. Any market town has a range of small schools often with limited and duplicated curriculum choice. Students may leave school at 16 but many choose to continue their studies until the age of 18 either at their secondary school where they take academic/general or vocational examinations or by transferring to one of the six Colleges of Further and Higher Education which offer vocational courses. These colleges are all 'mixed' in terms of gender and religious affiliation. College and school students may apply for places at University at the age of 18: the number of young people from Northern Ireland progressing to Higher Education was 36 per cent in 2003–4, an increase of 6 per cent since 2001–2 and with a rising number drawn from families whose income was below the national average.

The curriculum, compulsory for all learners between 5 and 16, is currently shaped by the Council for the Curriculum, Examinations and Assessment (CCEA), which also plays a statutory role in assessing attainment and providing public examinations. From 1989 until 2007, it could be said that the curriculum had a strong 'subject' focus, particularly for learners aged 8 and above; up to the age of 11, learners in primary schools are taught most of their work by a single teacher and in this sense there is some flexibility about how subject knowledge is embedded within broad themes such as literacy and numeracy. There is, however, a strong focus on the core subjects of mathematics, English and science which have been assessed at the ages of 8 and 11. At the age of 11, however, when students transfer to a post-primary school, their day is timetabled on the basis of 'subject' disciplines, with periods of time, ranging from 30 minutes to an hour for each lesson.

At the age of 16, most students are entered for high-stakes examinations, the General Certificate of Secondary Education (GCSE). Those who continue their studies after 16 take either the General Certificate of Education at Advanced level or more applied vocational qualifications. The Department of Education in Northern Ireland recently commissioned an Independent Strategic Review of Education (2006)[3] which showed that academic performance at 14 and 16 was at least as good if not better than elsewhere in the United Kingdom. It also noted that those who leave schools with no qualifications, 3.5 per cent of their age group, is smaller than other countries within the United Kingdom. However, the report notes that 'the legacy of underachievement is such that the current overall working-age population of Northern Ireland has a much higher proportion (24 per cent) of people with no qualifications than England (13.6 per cent) or Wales (17 per cent)'. Over 20 per cent of the working age population has difficulties with the essential skills of literacy and numeracy.

The mainly segregated character of schooling is reinforced by the arrangements for initial teacher training; some 50 per cent of all those who enter teacher training in Northern Ireland attend either a mainly Catholic university college or a university college whose student body is predominantly Protestant. The remaining 50 per cent of places are in 'mixed' university courses.

So, in summary, the Northern Ireland school system is at present deeply segregated along lines of denomination and academic ability. Like many schools around the world, teachers provide an education that is generally believed to be 'good' by a majority of parents and employers. But does the system have the capacity to adapt to a new world, where some fundamentals in the economy and in society are starting to shift radically?

The Northern Ireland economy

Northern Ireland's economy has historically been based on farming with shipbuilding and the linen industry providing employment in the greater Belfast area and beyond. Even before the start of civil unrest, unemployment was high, often running at 30 per cent of the adult working population. 'The troubles', covering the period 1968–97, made a difficult situation even worse, discouraging investment and diverting significant resources into the public sector. It is estimated that in 2005, some 60 per cent of employment in Northern Ireland is still in the public sector. More worryingly, Northern Ireland has a relatively low level of new business start-ups compared with our neighbours in the Republic of Ireland.

But it is changing; under the banner headline 'Ulster set to reap peace dividend', a newspaper report[4] in 2005 highlighted both Northern Ireland's over-reliance on government money and public sector employment, and the challenge of promoting an entrepreneurial culture. It noted that Northern Ireland has a highly educated workforce and that 'the province is … the only place in the world where all schools are linked up to broadband'. The same report noted that in the last 10 year period, 1995–2005, Northern Ireland has a job market which outstrips the UK average.

There is also evidence of the growing significance of ICT within the UK economy. An authoritative IT Insights report in 2004,[5] showed a relationship between ICT investment and productivity; this source also shows that 80 per cent of all jobs in the UK need some ICT skills and that the ICT sector is increasingly seeing the job market as split into three broad categories. There are those who will require 'IT user skills', a second group who can be classified as 'IT practitioners' working, for example, in the software industry, and finally a third group who need 'IT business and management skills' and whose leadership role requires them to understand how ICT impinges on their organisations. It noted that women were severely under-represented in the IT workforce, with only 20 per cent in this sector. A later report in 2006[6] noted that 'just under one in five employers reported skills gaps for employees who use technology in their everyday work – the highest level since the end of 2004'.

It is also claimed in a recent annual report of the global digital divide that 'the use of ICT contributed close to 50 per cent of the total acceleration in US productivity in the second half of the 1990s'.[7] Further, that:

> industrialized countries, with only 15 per cent of the world's population, are home to 88 per cent of all internet users. Internet access on its own does not ensure economic growth and prosperity; nevertheless it seems clear that those without connectivity and skills will be disadvantaged from participation in the information society.

Barber (2001)[8] has claimed that one of the functions of education is to meet the needs of a knowledge-based and global economy. This point has a particular significance for Northern Ireland, part of an island situated on the geographical edge of western Europe; this location means that all manufactured goods for export carry additional transportation costs. In contrast, services provided online from offices that are less expensive than in economic hotspots can be delivered at competitive rates, provided there is a skilled labour force with higher than average ICT capabilities.

It is within this context that questions are being asked about the appropriateness of the ICT experience of young people in schools and colleges in Northern Ireland. The Insights Report (2004) noted that:

> Government and its agencies will play key roles as enablers of change. This will require new strategies, changes to policies predicated on traditional industry models, and increased focus on improving interlock between employers and educators.

The Northern Ireland administration has started to take steps to address this problem. Their strategy is to encourage a much more vigorous entrepreneurial dimension in the economy with a particular emphasis on tourism and an ICT-based service sector.[9] Information processing and data distribution using a skilled workforce and twenty-first century communications are thought to offset any disadvantages due to geographical location.

According to Uhomoibhi (2005),[10] 'Northern Ireland's knowledge-based economy is recorded as the fastest growing regional economy in the United Kingdom'. He refers to available labour, affordable cost and world-class research in its universities as the explanation for the 45 per cent increase in the presence of multinational companies. The role of Higher Education in Northern Ireland is a highly significant element in any discussion about the complex links between the purpose of schooling and the economy. Given the lower costs of labour in India and China for manufactured goods, there is added pressure on schools in Northern Ireland to educate a workforce that can identify and exploit niche markets in the global knowledge economy. In the context of the kind of ICT experience that schools need to provide young people, it should also be noted that an increasing number of undergraduate degrees provided by Higher Education in Northern Ireland include a significant element of self-directed e-learning.

Uhomoibhi argues that it is the combination of skilled labour, university-led research and affordable costs that have acted as a catalyst for the regional development of the 200 so-called 'Hi-Tech' firms which produce £2bn in revenue. ICT, software and e-business account for most of the foreign investment, which was measured at 88 per cent in 2001–2. The same author notes that an e-Government initiative is steadily growing and affecting the ways that government departments handle information. We consider in Chapter 8, on enterprise education, how far the ICT experience of young people in schools and colleges is giving them the appropriate skill set.

Political changes and their influence on education

Just as the economy is changing and making new demands on schools, can we expect any significant change to the political landscape that might influence what happens in schooling? There are plans to try to restore a devolved administration in 2007 and there has been evidence of movement towards an accommodation. But any agreement will leave intact the current main political parties, elected in the same way and subject to the same local electoral pressures which we see as being essentially driven by retaining the status quo. If there is an agreement, this may be accompanied by a short term financial peace dividend that could be used for significant infrastructural development, including further investment in a knowledge-based economy.

All we can safely say at this stage is that it will require formidable political leadership to overcome present levels of distrust and take the bold and difficult decisions that are needed to sustain the emerging change agenda we outline below.

Changes in curriculum, school organisation and administration

Given that technology's appropriate role is to *support* the achievement of mainstream policy directions, we consider how well the school system itself is adjusting to change.

One of the ways that the school system is beginning to address vocational need is to reshape the curriculum to provide a far broader mix of academic and vocational courses for all learners. This will involve greater cooperation between schools and the colleges of further and higher education, which have a specific remit to address essential skills shortages and to provide vocational education. There has also been a marked increase in the number of students taking 'business studies' as an optional programme of study at school and in the further education sector. Also understood is the notion that the development of an enterprise culture requires far greater attention to the place of creativity in learning, with a stronger recognition that this involves risk-taking and innovation. Allied to this is the principle that sustainable enterprising economies can only survive where they are underpinned by a commitment to the principle of lifelong learning.[11]

Province-wide, there are a range of drivers for change in education policy, including investment in capital building, the integration of young people with disabilities in mainstream classrooms and the reviews of initial (pre-service) teacher education and of continuing professional development. These are all geared to achieve the Department of Education's goals of providing flexible learning opportunities to meet the varying needs and abilities of all young people, to raise their attainment, to foster creativity and to provide them with the knowledge and skills for life, employment and further learning. Of all of the changes, four major policy initiatives will dominate resources and action for at least the next eight years: curriculum reform, secondary school reorganisation,[12] the implications of 'A Shared Future' policy and the restructuring of school administration arising from the Review of Public Administration. We consider each of these in this final part of the chapter.

A revised curriculum

The current revision of the Northern Ireland statutory curriculum puts skills and competence development at its core. The move is to view the curriculum as subjects which act as contexts in which common core skills, competences and processes fit for life and work in the twenty-first century are developed across the school.[13] There is a marked increase in the use of the language of *learning* which may prove to be a more appropriate currency than the vocabulary of *curriculum* to describe what we want to achieve, and to use technology to support.

The statutory requirements of the curriculum will be reduced significantly in order to give teachers more freedom to focus their teaching on the needs of the learners. There are plans to reduce compulsory summative testing at 8, 11 and 14 significantly. Schools will report to parents on the development of a range of competencies and skills for life and work through formative assessment for learning and a pupil profile which provides a whole picture of an individual's progress, aptitudes and interests. While one expects to find literacy, numeracy and ICT at the heart, children are also expected to develop personal capabilities and critical and creative thinking skills, the ability to engage in problem-solving, to work in teams, and to be more individually self-reliant in learning.

Perhaps even more significant is the planned move, by 2008, away from academic selection at the age of 11 with future transfer arrangements based on informed parental and learner choice to enable parents and learners to choose the type of school that best meets the individual's educational needs, and the introduction of a curriculum entitlement, at the age of 14, where every learner is entitled to a choice from a menu of 24 courses, at least one-third of which must be vocational or applied, and one-third academic or general in nature. At the age of 16 that menu must have a choice of at least 27 courses, with flexibility for the introduction of additional courses to suit individual schools.

The ending of academic selection and the re-organisation of post-primary schools

Northern Ireland is one of the few remaining countries to maintain academic selection at 11-years-old to determine the type of schools learners attend. A number of factors plead for the abolition of this selection and the reorganisation of secondary education, amongst which growing dissatisfaction of learners, parents and future employers is a key element. For various reasons, the selection system and the lack of flexibility in course provision result in educational underachievement on the part of a large number of young people. To empower learners and their parents to make informed choices of the widened range of learning pathways which are envisaged, a pupil profile is to be introduced and advice is to be provided about choices and possible learning and career options. Work on the pupil profile is currently being carried out by the CCEA. The deadline for the abolition of the transfer test (the old '11 plus examination') is fixed for 2008. It will come into law unless a reconstituted local assembly established before that date takes a different view.

A strategic plan for the school estate

Given the nature of the school system, described earlier, and especially the majority of small schools, few could deliver a full, reformed curriculum on their own, so they will need to cooperate with schools in their neighbourhood, and their local college(s) of further education to form partnerships. Schools may also develop specialisms, for instance in science and technology, or in the performing arts, or in agriculture, or in languages. It is anticipated that by working together, schools will be able to share their particular expertise across the learner range that exists in all the schools in the partnership.

In addition, the demographic downturn in the province (by 2010 there will be about 12,600 fewer learners in post-primary education) coupled with strong competition between schools for enrolments raises questions about the future viability of an increasing number of post-primary schools.

In response to this, the Department of Education commissioned and accepted the main proposals of the Bain Report (2006)[14] which examined the funding of the education system, in particular the strategic planning and organisation of the schools' estate, taking account of the curriculum. Bain argued that declining pupil numbers in schools would require far closer cooperation between schools to deliver the broader curriculum.

This key objective supports the potential for social cohesion and minimises the costly effects of division, whether these come from duplication of small denominational schools to the separateness that comes from academic selection at the age of 11. This objective also extends to the need to integrate children with special educational needs fully into mainstream schooling.

Technology is expected to support distance learning through email, text- and video-conferencing and applications-sharing facilities on a common e-learning platform. Such provision could, for instance, allow a subject specialist teacher in one school to work with teachers in other schools to deliver a much broader range of courses than would have been the case in the past. Through a combination of approaches, traditional and innovative, it might therefore be possible to sustain some relatively small schools, supporting their local community, but working together to provide a richer curriculum diet than is now the case. But how might we attain a level of technology access and availability to make the dream a reality? This is a question we discuss in Chapter 2.

A shared future?

In addition to the conventional academic and economic purpose of schooling, there have been various attempts to address the problems which have arisen from the nature of schooling in a deeply divided society. A range of initiatives, some identified with the Department of Education, were summarised by Hagan and McGlynn (2004).[15]

They point to the generally limited impact such initiatives have had, with the exception of the integrated school movement which, according to other research, (McGlynn, 2004),[16] has had a 'very significant' long term effect on the ability of 55 per cent of those who attended such schools to mix with people of a different background to their own. In 2005 the Northern Ireland administration published 'A Shared Future',[17] a key policy document which acknowledged the extent of community polarisation and proposed a series of measures across all areas of government policy to increase social cohesion through a shared society based on partnership, equality and mutual respect. We look at the implications of this in Chapter 6 in the context of how e-schooling can help promote local and global citizenship.

A new administrative structure

To support these significant changes in school structure and the curriculum, the Department of Education announced in November 2005, a Review of Public Administration, designed to 'streamline' administration by merging the five Education and Library Boards, together with other employer organisations which are responsible like Local Educational Authorities in England for school support. They will become part of a new Educational and Skills Authority which will also have responsibility for the curriculum, assessment and examinations in 2008, curriculum support, leadership development, ICT and the school estate. The decision to press ahead with what is one of the biggest structural re-organisations of education in Northern Ireland reflects the seismic shifts we have noted in this chapter.

Conclusion

The schooling system in Northern Ireland has been shaped by some powerful forces and there remain strong advocates who argue that the best features of the schooling system should be retained; this is particularly true for those who say that Northern Ireland should retain its 'grammar' schools with a strong academic ethos or who assert that parents should have the right to send their children to schools with a clear denominational character.

What we say is that the changed curriculum in schools, the prospective ending of the transfer test and academic selection, the provision of children with special needs in mainstream schools and a more hopeful political climate all point to the potential for schools working more closely together and being enabled and transformed through ICT. In other words, we believe that there is a convergence of factors that all highlight the potential for e-schooling, in other words re-schooling supported by technology, to take off.

An integrated strategy for ICT in schools

Providing ICT for schools

Securing sustainable and affordable access to digital services in schools is a fundamental, yet intractable step into the twenty-first century for any national school education service. No education plan for an e-school can be sustained without connected infrastructure. An e-school needs enough reliable networked devices, with high speed Internet connection, to enable teachers to make technology their personal, professional tool and for learners to have equal ease of access for significant times during the school day. No plan, no matter how visionary, to deploy technology in addressing goals, improving learning and building economic resilience, can move forward until that foundation is in place.

Curricular and administrative/management computer-based systems, which often grow in isolation from each other, need to be integrated on a common network. They need to conform to common standards for communicating and for exchanging information about learners and learning. And it makes economic sense for schools to reduce their costs by benefiting from collaborative approaches to procuring and maintaining those services.

Starting point: aims and methods

The goal of sustainable provision for the UK was articulated, as a 'leap of faith,' in the Stevenson Report[1] back in 1997 and became the main plank of the National Grid for Learning Policy (NGFL) published by the Labour Government a year later. Stevenson saw an NGFL managed service solution as a way of resolving the major issues of access, reliability, consistency, affordability, sustainability and value for money.

Yet eight years later, the English Department for Education and Skills (DfES)[2] reported that the goal of securing 'a common digital infrastructure to support transformation and reform' remained one of the six priorities to be addressed – an indication of just how difficult a goal it is, and especially in a largely decentralised education service.

DfES's current policy is to harness technology in support of learning by providing a coherent national education broadband service with access for every school thus ensuring that every learner has appropriate access to technology, in school and beyond the normal school day, through a common systems framework based on common data, technical and interoperability standards. Only when a common system is in place can realistic plans be laid for developing efficient and effective technological means of delivering educational services, courses and resources.

In Northern Ireland, the Department and the Education and Library Boards responded to the same challenges by adopting a *managed service* approach for all schools. With no comparable approach for all of the publicly-funded schools in a single jurisdiction anywhere else, Northern Ireland has been described as one of the most complete implementations of a managed ICT service and a case study of considerable interest to other education services, regionally, nationally and internationally.

Roger Blamire, innovation manager of European Schoolnet, who is familiar with developments in all European countries, can see both the advantages of a holistic approach to policy alignment in Northern Ireland and also the gains which have come through a solution to sustainability.

> ICT developments in schools in Northern Ireland have aroused considerable interest amongst policy-makers in Europe through European Schoolnet's peer to peer policy and practice (P2P) project. Northern Ireland's schools compare favourably to other countries in terms of ICT integration, ICT leadership and teacher confidence. A number of features make the integration of ICT into teaching and learning successful: a relatively small population, a holistic approach by education authorities in planning and implementing change and adequate financing of ICT. Of particular interest to other countries has been the partnership with the private sector and the outsourcing approach to ICT provision and maintenance, freeing schools to concentrate on teaching and learning – successfully in view of the recent examination results. This has led to high levels of resourcing and efficiency gains that are the envy of others, as school leaders taking part in P2P visits discovered.[3]

The first microcomputers

On a blustery April day in 1978, the first two microcomputers for use in schools – a Commodore Pet 2001[4] with an integral cassette-tape drive, a tiny 9" green monochrome screen, an even tinier keyboard and an upgraded 8K of memory – were delivered to the Educational Computing Laboratory, the first in the UK,[5] located at the Education Centre of the (then) New University of Ulster (NUU) at Coleraine, near the world-famous Giant's Causeway and the Bushmills Whiskey Distillery on the

Antrim coast. NUU was hosting the only educational computing project in schools (CAMOL: Computer Assisted Management of Learning) in Northern Ireland, part of the National Development Programme for Computer Assisted Learning (NDPCAL). Harry McMahon, a respected science educator, directed an innovative project using mainframe ICL computers, programmed through 'truth tables' to 'manage learning' by giving each student a detailed personalised print-out of feedback and tutorial advice about what they should revise based on their results in computer-based diagnostic tests. The truth tables were programmed on punch-cards and the students completed their quizzes on forms scanned by a mark-sense reader. The science classes were taught at Methodist College, Belfast by Dr Martin Brown and a recently qualified Dr Richard Naylor.[6] Student teachers enrolled at the Education Centre also learnt how to write 'computer-assisted learning' programs in Commodore's 'PILOT' language taught by one of the authors. Many are now teachers, principals and senior educators in Northern Ireland and beyond.

Microelectronics Education Programme (MEP)

Mass production of relatively low-cost microcomputers led to a flurry of educational experimentation, but without any clear goals, until the establishment of the Microelectronics Education Programme (MEP) in 1980.[7] When the programme ended six years later, with a spend of £23 million at 1980's prices (worth about £60 million in 2006), a path had been cleared and a start made on defining and demonstrating 'enhancement' of learning through information technology (IT). The Coleraine Educational Computing Laboratory became the regional centre for MEP, connected in a pioneering online network to 13 similar centres in England and Wales. Educators in other Northern Ireland institutions, including Stranmillis College, the Ulster Polytechnic, schools and teachers' centres, supported the wide range of MEP's work in primary education, special education, and in computer-assisted learning, computing, microelectronics and in 'communications and information skills', a far-sighted definition of a new competency which is even more relevant today. In 1986 a committee of the Northern Ireland Council for Educational Development (NICED) defined the pathway for Northern Ireland[8] and some 12,000 Northern Ireland teachers – almost half of the teaching force – attended some 600 short in-service education courses in 20 related curriculum areas and topics.

The economic imperative

MEP aimed to promote the understanding of technology amongst children by encouraging teachers to incorporate IT in their practice to improve the quality and relevance of their teaching. A multiplicity of different policy goals (economic recovery, industrial modernisation, raising education standards, equality of opportunity) reflected the interests of the various branches of government. Different goal definitions still drive government investment. However, at least the Northern Ireland Economic Council (1989[9]) had a clear grasp of the connection between these goals.

> The impetus ... has come from two sources. The first has been the desire of educationalists to exploit the potential of this technology as a teaching medium. Reinforcing the strictly educationalist approach to IT, however, has been the realisation that the UK needs to restructure its economy to face increasing competition in world markets. The educational sector is seen as having a central role in this process at several levels. Firstly, by providing courses specifically directed towards IT, the skills and abilities of young people entering the workforce can be improved in a way which is directly relevant to the needs of the economy. Secondly, importing IT products and processes into the teaching of subjects which are not themselves IT related can serve the dual purpose of improving the level of teaching and generating a greater degree of IT literacy. Finally, the education sector can itself be a source of new ideas and innovations in the IT area which may be of direct benefit to the economy. This economic rather than educational perspective on the need for IT in education would appear to have particular relevance for regions such as Northern Ireland which remain heavily dependent on traditional and declining industries. (para 5.3)

At the time (in 1989) at which Information Technology (IT) was being defined and introduced as a 'cross-curricular theme' in the new statutory national 'Northern Ireland Curriculum', the Northern Ireland Economic Council was sounding alarms about the importance of IT skills development for the economy of the province and the inadequate response of the education sector to address the skills gap.

> Failure to embrace new technologies, particularly those linked to IT, and an inability or unwillingness to adopt the processes and working practices dictated by these technologies will, it is argued, undermine policies aimed at re-generating the economy. (para 5.3)

> Many young people still appear to be leaving school with very little experience of using IT equipment. (para 7.4)

> There is significant evidence of a shortage of skills in IT in the Northern Ireland economy and a need for a greater degree of integration between the IT strategies being pursued by the education and training organisations. (para 7.4)

The Economic Council put their finger directly on one of the major obstacles, the absence of a common approach to infrastructure and they made a far-sighted recommendation (eight years before the Stevenson Report picked up the same issue across the UK).

DENI and the Education and Library Boards should investigate the scope for coordinating IT purchases between Further Education Colleges and schools with the object of improving compatibility in equipment and software. (para 7.6)

The need for a consistent approach

Their proposal opened the door to the Computerised Local Administration of Schools Systems (CLASS) Project in 1991, which became, in 1997, Classroom 2000 (and, in 2001, C2K) which was set up under the Western Education and Library Board, acting on behalf of all five Boards.

The Northern Ireland Economic Council criticised the lack of equity of provision and access, arguing for a consistent set of performance measures in relation to the uptake of IT and insisting that future levels should 'fully reflect the importance of this technology for the education system' noting that:

> In the case of the Belfast Area Board, for example, the pupil/computer ratio in secondary schools varies between 14:1 and 82:1. Different Boards place greater or lesser emphasis on IT development according to their priorities and the same is true at the individual school level. (para 5.9)

As well as inequity, infrastructural diversity was another major inhibitor to progress. Across the five education and library Boards there were BBC-branded computers from Acorn Systems, various MS-DOS based systems and Apple computers – there were even some Tandy and Sinclair systems – all in incompatible flavours. *Times Education Supplement* (*TES*) freelancer, Jack Kenny,[10] looking back over the experience of one school, illustrated the undesirable results in a primary classroom where the teacher had five computers in her classroom – each incompatible with the others. If a pupil started writing on one computer, the work could not be finished on any of the others. And while there were three printers, two had not worked in a long time. The teacher explains:

> When I came here seven years ago we had a mish-mash of equipment in classrooms. You had to have a different set of software for each machine. It wasn't cohesive.

Without a coordinated approach, investment fluctuated wildly, resulting in inequalities in the educational experience for young people depending on where they lived and which school they attended. Nor was it possible to imagine a plan for systemic change in how ICT could support educational priorities. There was a clear need to improve reliability, establish value for money, and resolve sustainability in an affordable way. A single solution was needed. The *TES* reported the primary teacher's welcome for the consistency which the C2K managed service approach subsequently provided.

C2K is giving every child and teacher similar hardware and software. This entails the heads and teachers losing some autonomy. 'The advantages of this far outweigh the disadvantages' says the teacher. 'With software there is a good range. There are over 80 titles.'

The economic analysis of Northern Ireland's prospects for recovery in the digital and global economy was a strong policy driver to introduce a consistent strategy for education technology. The alarms were ringing that 'ICT must be the top priority for economic growth in Northern Ireland'[11] and that teachers still had a way to go to close the skills gap identified in 1998.[12]

There are great variations among schools regarding how much ICT is incorporated into teaching. In some cases, the limiting factor is not a lack of computers, but a lack of knowledge on the part of the teachers themselves. This has ramifications for the ability of the workforce to be effective in an ICT-driven community.[13]

So, as well as the need for dramatic improvements in infrastructure and connectivity it was clear that teacher and curriculum development also required a consistent and coordinated approach. An integrated strategy was called for.

An integrated strategy for education technology

Computer provision grew gradually from one computer in each school, as a result of the 1983 Department of Trade and Industry's 'Micros in Schools' initiative led by Minister Kenneth Baker, to a school combination of standalone machines and computer suites with a handful individually connected by dial-up access to the Internet. If schools were to embed ICT in classroom practice, they needed machines in every classroom, not just in a specialist laboratory, so that learners could use them when they needed, without the teacher having to timetable a single lesson, months in advance.

The notion of *resourcing the learner* rather than *resourcing the school* with computers was counterintuitive for those who believed computers should be concentrated in computer laboratories – teachers of computing as a specialism were, unsurprisingly, the keenest advocates. This thinking reflected the pedagogy of the time, when lessons *about* the science and technology of computers – taught by a computer specialist to whole classes – were much more common than lessons in which any teacher made use of computers as an aid to teaching in any subject. We have to remember that this was the time when it was common to hear the hope expressed that computers were just an educational fad – language labs, televisions and overhead projectors were often compared – which would pass, leaving classrooms as if unchanged from the previous century.

Inspection evidence throughout the decade of the 1990s (DENI: 1999) indicated that, while there was some use of computers in teaching across the curriculum, it was relatively patchy, never continuous, and often tokenistic. Use had reached a relatively low plateau from which it did not progress, notwithstanding some excellent and exciting innovation in practice.

> The provision in ICT continues to be disappointing and presents a challenge not only for primary schools but also for those charged with the responsibility of supporting their work.[14]

Economists were impatient with this, and even before Classroom 2000 had begun to be implemented in schools, the Foresight eBusiness Report[15] recommended that the school-focused objectives for the project should be stretched

> to include community access, private sector partnership and local creative capacity to reach the widest possible audience.

The view that there was an 'ICT Curriculum', which could be improved to close the software skills gap, was reinforced by the Leapfrog economic analysis, while the inspectorate took, and still takes, a broader integrationalist view about the embedded use of ICT as a tool for teaching and learning across the whole curriculum, involving all teaching staff.

A Department of Education survey at the time[16] documented the obstacles:

- more than 70 per cent of computers in schools were 'old';
- most could not support any multimedia;
- only 1 per cent of primary schools had computer networks;
- and when teachers listed the main constraints for them, the top items were:
  - poor access to appropriate technology provision in their classroom
  - their own weak competence and confidence in ICT generally
  - lack of training and support
  - the financial constraints under which their school operated.

Building on the local economic analysis, the inspection and research evidence, the Stevenson Report and the 1997 Labour government's NGFL policy the Department commissioned an Education Technology (ET) Strategy (1998)[17] and secured the financial support for an integrated approach. The decision to take a managed service route to curricular ICT across the entire sector responded to the shortcomings in a fragmented approach and built on the advantages in the single, province-wide approach adopted to provide computer-based administrative systems in schools through the CLASS project.

The ET Strategy set out to ensure that young people would be well prepared for life and work in the information economy of the twenty-first century, and that ICT would be used to raise standards. Some 50 targets relating to the competence of teachers, the entitlement of pupils, the provision and use of ICT in teaching and learning and for the integration of ICT into the curriculum were declared:

- *Learners and their ICT skills* – targets in standards of pupil competence, curriculum integration, accreditation and assessment for learners, homework policy, special education needs and policy on acceptable use of the Internet;
- *Teachers and learners* – targets for teacher competence in ICT, the use of ICT in the professional development of teachers, quality assurance by the schools' Inspectorate, the role of the senior management in schools and access to personal computers for teachers;
- *Schools and resources* – targets dealing with links between school libraries, the home, the community and expectations for accommodation and equipment needs;
- *Implementation and support* – targets to resolve issues of finance, levels of expected use, technology refresh, communication and network tariffs, and user training and support.

Classroom 2000 was responsible for the targets related to infrastructure and connectivity, and the education service – mainly the curriculum advisory and support services, the initial teacher education institutions, and the Council for Curriculum, Examinations and Assessment were responsible for the targets related to teacher education, curriculum and assessment respectively. At the same time all four UK government education departments jointly published *'Open for Learning; Open for Business'* which challenged the ICT supply industry to improve value for money by putting forward proposals for a National Grid for Learning (NGFL), which included a new 'competing managed ICT services' model for supplying ICT to schools and offering curricular, training and administrative facilities.

The competing managed services to which schools or, more critically,

> ... joint LEA (local education authority) purchasing groups would subscribe, would meet the majority of schools' ICT needs: installing and maintaining the hardware, providing access to the Internet and search engines to navigate it, and developing high-quality software accessible on the grid. These managed services would generally need to be provided by consortia combining the facilities offered by individual commercial companies.[18]

The NGFL approach held out the promise of resolving major issues of access, reliability, consistency, affordability, value for money and sustainability and capitalising on the advantages of high-speed infrastructure and large-scale data-storage across all authorities.

The resulting strategy committed the Department of Education and the education and library boards 'to consider how the various elements of ICT, curricular and administration/management systems could be brought together as a coherent whole'.[19]

It recognised that re-generation in an economy under duress, depends, amongst other things, on the effective exploitation of ICT in education. It represented a challenge, managed in a way described by Gordon Topping, Chairman of the ET Strategy Management Group and Chief Executive of the North Eastern Education and Library Board, as 'centrally coordinated and locally delivered'.

Classroom 2000 became that 'joint purchasing group' and set out to procure a single managed ICT service solution. Given the relatively small number of schools in the province, it was essential that all take part in the managed service in order to achieve the economy of scale and make a significant difference to costs. While commentators sometimes say that this solution could only be adopted in small-scale jurisdictions, it would only take groups comprising some 3.0 per cent of all of the schools* in the UK to form a joint procurement group and to achieve the same economies of scale as those achieved here.

C2K as a 'managed service'

The stated aim of Classroom 2000 (C2K) is to provide a learning technologies service to support the Northern Ireland Curriculum, school administration and management and the professional development of teachers. Its strategic role is to provide a fully distributed infrastructure across all 1,224 schools in Northern Ireland, connected in a networked environment and resource the service with up-to-date content relevant to the curriculum.

C2K is technically a PPP (private-public partnership) initiative in which private industry funds the up-front costs and the government contracts the service, paying the provider for accountable deliverables. The industry owns and is responsible for the hardware, and ensures that a reliable and working service is available to the classroom teacher. Up front costs are spread over the lifetime of the project, which is built into government funding through a ten-year outline business case which enables the system to be refreshed on a regular basis, keeping up to date with technological developments (such as wireless) on a three to five year basis. A main purpose of a managed service is to transfer the range of technical risks, for which the government pays, based on performance – in other words, the delivery and availability of the service determines the payment – where it is judged that the private sector is better able to manage that risk. In the case of computer-based

---

* The Barnett formula of 2.87 per cent is generally used as the ratio to calculate the Northern Ireland economic share in the context of the UK programmes as a whole.

services, the technology management is often better left with industry, which has the expertise, and the educational change to the education service, where the expertise lies. It is essential to get the right balance of risk and reward. Too much risk carried by the private sector can result in poor value for money as the provider protects himself from the risks through possible loss of performance payments. The costs can be reduced by retaining more risk within the public education service; however, the effectiveness of the service may be reduced if the public sector is not able to secure the effective embedding of ICT into the curriculum and does not develop adequate teacher competence to use ICT effectively.

Specifications for the ICT service are drawn up and collectively agreed by the project Board, on which the Department of Education and the major stakeholders are represented. The Board governs the project and the service continues to evolve and innovate to meet changing needs and circumstances. Productive partner relationships, constrained within the requirements of the performance-based contract, are developed with the range of commercial companies in the private sector which provide the managed services. Detailed management arrangements deal promptly and effectively with any issues as they arise; the co-location of the private sector delivery team with the public sector 'intelligent customer', in the Belfast data-centre (from where the helpline services also operate), is a significant factor in dealing promptly with challenges and risks to the service.

Another challenge in providing a single managed service, from the centre, is to balance the guarantee of a mission-critical, industry-standard, reliant service against the importance of retaining the right of choice for the teacher over the educational resources which they decide to use in their classroom. But what was 'choice' to be about, the technology or the content? 'Curriculum content and titles, or the colour of the (computer) box and shape of the go-faster stripe on the side?',[20] as Tom McMullan, a former teacher and the director of procurement for Classroom 2000 put it. There are three different ways in which teachers can run their own choice of curriculum titles on the network, assuring them that while the system is centrally managed, it has not 'locked them down' nor removed choice over content from their hands.

The managed service approach minimises the problem for the customer of coping with several different IT companies supplying the hardware, software and content; management responsibility for the total integration of the solution lies with the prime contractor for each contract. School leaders no longer have to make difficult decisions about technology purchases on limited information. In the educational world, dozens of companies supply educational titles; the service provider has the expertise and is responsible for integrating these and ensuring that they work. While a few schools may, most are unlikely to have such expertise. And, as C2K works with a wide range of private and public sector partners, it can deliver an integrated and supported service, installed, maintained and upgraded by specialist providers.

Furthermore, many of the curriculum titles are supported by specialist consultants – expert teachers employed locally by the software companies.

Award of high-stakes service public sector contracts conforms to demanding legal requirements, including EU procurement law, as well as stringent formal government control and reporting mechanisms, both prior to implementation and during and after each phase. Bidders, for instance, are subject to pre-qualification rounds which examine the financial, technical and experiential viability of the bidding company or consortium. Qualifying bidders, with considerable experience supplying to large IT projects, especially in the public sector, are subject to close scrutiny and scoring on criteria (including financial, technical and match of solution to need) to produce a short-list. Detailed risk analysis and management, dependency analysis, gateway reviews and post-benefit evaluations are some of the formal project management methodologies carried out by consultants, legal advisers, accountants and by government procurement advisers. All of these protections are centrally assured; it is highly unlikely that schools could individually afford the same safeguards.

A high standard of service availability of 98 per cent is set for C2K – working computers and networks must be almost as reliable an experience as getting a dialling tone on your phone network. In practice, service availability sits consistently at and above 99.6 per cent. Technical problems are normally remedied remotely online or within hours by a visiting engineer. As a consequence, project delivery of ICT in Northern Ireland schools lives up to the highest expectations and teacher satisfaction remains high.[21]

Finally, the Department funds the core ICT service, at no cost to schools' own local budget accounts, which frees money in each school to spend on extending the core service in a way that meets local, individual needs. For example, government provides, at no cost to the school, core ratios (computer:pupil) between 1:5 and 1:12, depending on the type of school. Additional investments by the school to improve the ratio are realistic, as NI schools, unlike schools elsewhere, are not meeting the cost of the core service. The costs of £43 million per annum are on average under £135 per pupil roughly 1.5 per cent of the annual cost of schooling a pupil each year. For instance, for a school of 600 pupils to service the core provision on their own would cost some £80,000, annually.

Schools can rely on the service and know that the technology will be updated and refreshed regularly over ten years, which will enable it to take advantage of technological innovation in an affordable way. For example, a future wireless infrastructure could support a range of mobile devices/smart phones that young people use to access their learning anytime and anywhere.

In summary, C2K is a large-scale, wide-ranging and highly complex project and all of the associated targets are, accordingly, very demanding. C2K's responsibility has been to take the risk out of technology in schools and to resolve the biggest problems of effectively embedding technology in teaching, which are those of reliability and sustainability of the service over time. C2K continues to meet its objectives and as a consequence, many government targets for ICT provision in schools (such as LANs and broadband) were provided to schools in Northern Ireland ahead of time.

The C2K service

At no cost to themselves, grant-aided schools receive, based on pupil numbers, a core entitlement comprising:[22]

- an infrastructure of 55,000 networked computers with broadband connection to the Internet which, linked to schools' existing hardware, brings the computer/pupil ratios close to 1:4 in post-primary schools and 1:8 in primary schools;
- 14,000 laptops for teacher user (a ratio of two for every three teachers);
- access to a wide range of content and services to support the Northern Ireland Curriculum and teachers' professional development – including 200 centrally licensed curriculum software titles;
- an integrated suite of services for school administration and management;
- broadband connection of schools' networks into a single wide-area education network, connected directly to all of the public libraries in the province, to the UK's higher and further education network (JANET), to the National Education Network (NEN) for schools across England, and to GLOW, the Scottish network;
- e-learning tools to facilitate the development of online teaching and learning – including online curriculum content;
- first line support through a central help desk.

The final piece of the managed service jigsaw, Learning NI,[23] a new online learning environment serviced and maintained by the private sector, will aim to provide:

- all teachers and pupils with personal, secure email and Internet access;
- digital resources, including some subscriptions to online curriculum content;
- online tests and formative assessment tools;
- collaboration and sharing in online classrooms, text and video conferencing;
- access to learning resources and personal work files from inside and outside the school network;
- personal home web pages and calendars for teachers and pupils;
- a flexible means of setting and submitting homework;

- tracking, recording and reporting the use made of the content by individuals;
- one-to-one feedback between pupil and teacher;
- access to the school's administration system.

Some initial curriculum content is licensed from educational publishers. Over time, schools, teachers, advisers, librarians, professional officers, assessors, examiners and anyone who creates content, resources, services and courses will to able to develop and publish local content and services, and be able to work collaboratively. Online activities can take place in a safe environment.

Chapter 5 describes the progress being made to use communications technology to bring experts online to teach specialist subjects as a common resource.

A comprehensive initial training programme, focused on how to use the service, was provided by C2K for teachers as it was rolled out to each school (not because of perceived resistance, but because this is good practice). Evaluation evidence is that this programme has been very welcome. Further pedagogic training is the responsibility of the curriculum advisory and support services and it is up to the local curriculum advisory and support service to ensure that teachers get the best from the service in their own classroom practice. Chapter 3 examines progress in more detail.

C2K has achieved a much-needed coherence across the whole infrastructure which now enables schools to think about the longer-term advantages of wide-area services. It is now possible to imagine how teachers might jointly develop school curriculum development plans by working online together and how they might personalise learning for children because the system will in future allow the tracking of the learner, create diagnostic reports on performance and help the teacher to plan teaching for individuals in a way which is differentiated on the basis of relevant information.

The gains, in terms of value for money, are worthwhile at the school level, but are potentially even greater across the whole service, because all stakeholders have a common platform on which they can base development of advisory and support services, leadership and curriculum development programmes, programmes of study, lesson plans and professional support programmes and through which management information can be derived. This is already starting to happen in support of the roll-out of the revised curriculum and is likely to accelerate when the stakeholder organisations come together into one single Education and Skills Authority for Northern Ireland in 2008. Innovative service-wide programmes of teacher support can be put in place cost-effectively. Collectively, they can accelerate programmes of change because the infrastructure is reliable and dependable. There is now enough technology in Northern Ireland's schools for users to realise that change is not about technology; instead they can begin to think about the real issues of new approaches to learning and teaching and behavioural change in the process of education.

Student-teachers, at the very start of their careers, are being inducted into a digitised world, expected to communicate with their peers and tutors during their periods of school placement and to reflect on their professional development through the creation of personal e-portfolios. The application of international standards means that those entering the teaching profession will be enabled to carry their e-portfolio of reflective evidence into induction, early professional development and continuing professional development. In the most innovative cases, they are already becoming part of a growing community of practice which is explored further in Chapter 4.

Achievement of the strategy targets

In 2002, five years after the launch of the ET strategy, the stakeholders collectively undertook a review of the extent to which targets had been achieved and a discussion paper on the future of e-learning was published. The results indicated that about 85 per cent of the targets had been wholly or largely met.[24] C2K had overcome the major challenges regarding infrastructure and connectivity.

Chapter 3 explores the gains made on the teacher education front, where 94 per cent of teachers voluntarily and successfully undertook a national teacher education programme which focused on the pedagogic use of ICT in their classroom teaching. Over 90 per cent of participants reported a relatively good experience in their training, while the learning experience of others was not without its difficulties. For many, it was a first step, even for those whose ICT technique was not well developed, and a psychological barrier was broken. As a result all teachers should have a personal action plan for their continued development needs, even though those needs are highly differentiated. Online professional development is now a required component of the Professional Qualification for Headteachers.

Chapter 5 explores the gains on the curriculum and assessment front. A large number of post-primary schools offer their 14-year-old pupils an ICT accreditation introduced by the Council for Curriculum Examinations and Assessment (CCEA), with a similar level of uptake in a primary schools scheme for 11-year-olds. Entries to accreditation schemes had risen rapidly to 20,000. In most lessons pupils display consistently high levels of interest and enjoyment and there is evidence of good home use of computers. The use of ICT to support learning more effectively continues to increase gradually in many schools.

CCEA, the Curriculum Council, also responded to the urging of strategy to explore the role of online high-stakes examinations through a 'Paperless Examination Project' and a computer-based adaptive testing pilot which has far-reaching implications for online assessment and examinations.[25]

Yet, in many schools impact was limited, for example, pupils' information handling skills were still weak. More opportunities were needed to provide for more creative use of ICT by pupils. Home–school links had not been enhanced by taking advantage of communications technologies and links with pupils in other countries were limited. There was also a need in almost all schools to promote a more consistent approach to the development of ICT within and across the curriculum.

It was time to change up a gear into a new strategy.

A renewed strategy – *Empowering Schools*

A focus on learning

The Education Technology Strategy Management Group (ET SMG) took a vigorous consultative approach, organising 38 events involving over 900 stakeholders, with online consultation bringing in a further 1,300 participants and published a new strategy – Empowering Schools[26] which the Minister, Barry Gardiner MP, signed off just before Christmas 2004. He underlined:

> the need for good coordination and wide ranging partnerships both between the two government departments (the Department of Education and the Department for Employment and Learning) as well as with all the stakeholders, including industrial partners.

Recognition of the strategic importance of ICT came when the strategy was identified as one of government's four strategic priorities for education and was embedded into the main education priorities through the government programme 'Entitled to Succeed'.

The overarching goal stated that all young people should use digital and online technologies to acquire knowledge, to practise skills and develop competencies as individuals, as contributors to society, as contributors to the economy and as lifelong learners. The strategy calls for a more unified and coordinated approach to e-learning across all education and training sectors including schools, teacher training, further and higher education, libraries, museums, youth activities and continuing education. It also requires a systemic approach seeking a system-wide understanding and coordination of the process through strategic partnerships and team working.

> This process demands careful work on evaluation and quality control and above all is firmly grounded in the recognition that success depends on the ability to build the human, institutional and technical capacity needed. The further integration of ICT in education proposed by the Empowering Schools strategy is seen as being in the service of changes undertaken or planned by the different institutional actors.[27]

> The Empowering Schools strategy is integrated, but it is not yet unified ... there is still a parallel strategy for further education and another for libraries. ... All the strategies are going in the same direction, but they are not connected.[28]

An important difference between the 1997 and the 2004 strategies lies in the content. The first strategy was largely about technology, its provision and its introduction to teachers. It found an answer to the question of provision: a managed service solution. While that provision has its strengths and weaknesses, it resolves the challenges of standardisation, economies of scale, value for money, affordability and sustainability. The second strategy is mainly about practice: changing the experience of teaching and learning and developing the skills needed for lifelong learning. The new strategy aims to make sure that educational benefits flow from the technology investment by centering on a more unified approach to personalisation.

Expected outcomes

A belief is expressed that young people should be able to use digital online technologies appropriately, effectively and creatively to acquire knowledge, to practise skills and to develop competencies in a way that supports the revised curriculum:

- as individuals
  to be creative, self-aware and able to communicate with and work well with others;
- as contributors to society
  to act in informed and responsible ways as citizens;
- as contributors to the economy
  to be economically aware and active, and to be excellent employees and employers in the twenty-first century global knowledge economy;
- as lifelong learners
  to identify, address and meet their learning needs in formal and informal education settings, working both individually and with others, locally, and at a distance from school.

The renewed strategy comprises over 50 milestones grouped into sets of actions impacting on the learner, the teacher, the school leader, the professional support community and on the opportunities for innovation with the technology itself.[29]

The central set of actions addresses the need for enhanced practice for the learner, resulting in young people using technology to achieve independence in their learning earlier than is traditionally expected, attain high standards, work creatively, and develop broad, transferable competencies for employment and lifelong learning.

It is envisaged that technology can be used to offer a broad curriculum, which offers greater diversity, and improved choice of courses which can be adapted flexibly to meet the developing needs of young people. Curriculum support is matched with assessment for learning opportunities, which will track and record progress, providing pupils, teachers and parents with detailed diagnosis of need and enabling learners to be given personalised support.

The strategy sets out to develop team working, through which pupils learn to work collaboratively, within and beyond their school, and are rewarded for it, and where they can observe their teachers, who model collaboration and cooperation in the way they too work. The curricular expectations for the service are explored in Chapter 5.

ICT is expected to play a key role in enabling school leaders to lead transformation for a self-improving school, where technology provides the management information to support leadership decisions which raise standards, and where administrative burdens are eased for all staff.

The goal is to develop online institutions, which use networked communications to collaborate with each other and share, collegially, in curriculum provision and professional development and to enable schools to develop their community role, where networked access and provision extends how the school serves, and is served by its community, and especially its parents.

Government fully recognises that developments in modern communications and advances in ICT combine to make the world ever more accessible. New skills and new relationships must be fostered if Northern Ireland is to compete in international markets where industry and commerce are increasingly knowledge based. Technology can enhance the school curriculum, school management and professional development for teachers. In addition, there is recognition that modern communication technology has much to offer in terms of social cohesion – equally important for the shared future in Northern Ireland.

Global messages

A number of key messages for e-schooling about technological sustainability and alignment between educational policy and technological investment arise from the Northern Ireland experience.

- Putting an effective, mission-critical technology service into schools can be driven with political will. The message is that a corporate solution, such as C2K, delivered through a centralised approach, provides equitable access to up-to-date technology and can ensure that educational goals are addressed.

- Leveraging change requires the introduction of a central plan, revenue-funded, quality-assured, affordable, sustainable, providing value for money, locally implemented, strategic, integrated, and target-driven approach, which is directly linked to the needs of the country's economic strategy.

- A central investment by government in ICT services reduces considerably the inequity inherent for pupils whose access to ICT was previously dependent on highly variable local spending decisions, and also removes pressures on school budgets. It does not guarantee total equality, however, as schools are encouraged to enhance the core, centrally funded service, and such decisions rightly remain local and varied, depending on vision, commitment and spending power. However, it does ensure, as far as the rising tide is concerned, that all ships start out by riding on a high tide.

- A common, single standard solution can offer efficiencies and economy of scale. Value for money is extracted more effectively in single contractual negotiations through an aggregated approach for services, for licensing, for tariffs and for products than is possible through scattered and diverse purchases. Public and private partnerships can be successfully developed, tailoring to meet local needs.

- A centralised approach to ICT services can be wrapped in legal, contractual, financial protections not normally afforded by schools. It is more realistic for a single, powerful customer to negotiate demanding penalty-based performance measures for an industry-standard, reliant managed service and hold the provider accountable for the availability of the service, than it would be for individuals or even a range of smaller customers.

- A corporate approach need not run counter to the delegation of autonomy and responsibility for school management, a feature, to a greater or lesser extent, in many school systems. Even in the most decentralised of school systems, it remains possible to rationalise a corporately managed and shared ICT service as the most effective approach without the risk of it being the thin end of a wedge of greater centralisation.

- A consistent, fully integrated solution supports the curriculum and assessment, as well as continuing professional development and training and school management and administration, while protecting user choice over content and at the same time freeing up teachers, principals and schools to concentrate on – and to remain accountable for – using ICT effectively to meet their own educational goals of providing high quality education.

- An integrated strategy can, however, have the effect of setting milestones and targets to ensure that the same direction of travel is taken by all of the stakeholders.

- Looking back, and in a different environment of local educational organisation than was the case at the start of the project, one might have considered the merits of transferring educational/pedagogic ICT support for teachers to the control of the managed service project. In a different technological environment than was the case at the start, one would, of course, be able to refine and advance the technological solution. In a different political climate than was the case at the start, one might be able to achieve, earlier, a more unified approach across the sectors – as indeed we now aim to do through the new strategy – Empowering Schools.

Teacher development for e-schooling

Teaching the teachers

As Douglas Adams wrote in *The Salmon of Doubt*[1]

1   Anything that is in the world when you're born is normal and ordinary and is just a natural part of the way the world works.
2   Anything that's invented between when you're fifteen and thirty-five is new and exciting and revolutionary and you can probably get a career in it.
3   Anything invented after you're thirty-five is against the natural order of things.

It's at the heart of the digital divide between teachers and taught in schools; a divide which needs to be bridged in an e-school.

In this chapter we look first at how the UK's largest single ICT teacher education exercise was managed to achieve the maximum effect: a step-change in ICT competence for all serving teachers and school librarians. The national lottery-funded teacher education scheme (1999 to 2002) identified, rightly, the need for training in the pedagogic skills and knowledge related to using ICT in the classroom. It, again rightly, identified classroom skills of an order higher than mastering basic techniques of computer operation. However, a major problem encountered by the approved trainers was the very unevenly distributed baseline of expected core skills across the teaching force. Many teachers needed a crash course in coping with computer crashes before they could even load the pre-training CD ROM.

No matter how successful or unsuccessful the first step on the ladder for teachers, the challenge was always how to follow it up. Most teachers agreed that their top priority was to improve their own competence to use technology[2]. They also agreed on the most commonly given reason for not doing so: *'not enough time'* – not enough time to become masters of the teaching tools and the educational software with which they had been provided. However, when time is cited as an obstacle, the underlying issue is that the goal is not a sufficiently high priority. And, if it was not a priority for teachers in 1999, did this mean that technology was seen then as peripheral to their main concerns in the classroom? If technology was perceived as peripheral to the main business of teaching, is that because it was regarded as an add-on without recognition or reward?

Teachers face a number of dilemmas. First, they lack confidence that ICT adds value which is rewarded through promotion and/or salary and recognised through summative assessment and examination of their pupils. And when most teachers lack sufficient technique to be able to prepare teaching which uses learning technologies, they are not motivated to take the extra time needed for training. This is one of the reasons why it is hard to see anticipated time savings in a teacher's workload being achieved.

This is a 'Catch 22' in the creation of an e-school and we explore here five strategies with the potential to break its grip:

- Make ICT competence a measure, that can be reported annually to parents alongside literacy and numeracy;
- Embed ICT centrally in whole school-improvement;
- Provide experience of online professional learning for teachers;
- Provide online professional development in a holistic way, rather than just training teachers to teach ICT competence directly to pupils;
- Review the implications of this approach for the provision of teacher education as a whole.

The Northern Ireland approach

As we explain in Chapter 5, the revised curriculum intends to establish ICT as a *measurable*: ICT competence for pupils will be treated on a par with literacy and numeracy, reporting progress annually to parents. This is a high-risk tactic: the danger lies in schools responding with direct teaching of ICT skills through specialist courses. Such a response would have an unintended consequence if it relieved some of their perceived obligation to embed ICT in their teaching. Containing this risk requires parallel changes in the examination specifications of subjects to ensure that ICT is fully incorporated in teaching. Take mathematics as an example: it ought not to be possible, for instance, to obtain top grades in examinations, unless an ability to use a spreadsheet competently to demonstrate aspects of mathematical mastery can be demonstrated.

Next, an approach to professional development needs to establish the embedding of ICT in the curriculum as central to whole e-school improvement. Any twenty-first century educational reform not capitalising on the driving force of ICT is flawed. It is no accident that the schools which reported the most effective benefits from the lottery-funded ICT training were those which organised the training on a team basis, such as subject department or key stage. Such collegiality reinforced the embedding of ICT effectively through organisational groups. The strategy adopted in Northern Ireland aims to extend ICT capacity by casting change in terms of organisational development.

Another effective means of compensating for teachers' lack of experience with learning technology can provide them the personal experience of an online learner by delivering elements of continuing professional development through an online environment. Continuing professional development can be addressed holistically, covering all approaches to teaching, including the effective use of ICT resources. A clear distinction is made between professional development in a digital age on the one hand and training teachers to teach ICT competence to pupils on the other.

The intention in Northern Ireland is broader; as Barry Gardiner, Minister responsible for Education, indicated when approving the Empowering Schools strategy: 'e-learning needs to become part of the professional competence of all educators'.[3]

Finally, we cannot examine ICT strategy in isolation from teacher education as a whole. If a lack of experience with learning technologies is an issue for teachers, so must it be a challenge for those intermediaries, who train, support, advise and guide them. We assess proposed changes in continuing professional development against the challenge posed by David Hargreaves in his paper 'Education Epidemic'.

When teachers model collegiality and professionalism by using e-learning as a vehicle for developing reflective practice, they will demonstrate their personal commitment to lifelong learning, trustful sharing and partnership, especially when that mutual learning takes place in areas of scarce expertise. Such an approach blurs the traditional notions of 'deliverer' and 'receiver' prevalent in non-technology based models of in-service education.

Mind the skills gap

We identified earlier a problem encountered in the lottery-funded national scheme with the uneven base of ICT core techniques across the teaching force.

Pupil familiarity with ICT

In many school systems the skills gap between teachers and taught continues to be a major element in the digital divide. A main finding of Becta's IMPACT 2 study[4] is the widespread personal use of ICT by children. Primary pupils spend three times longer on ICT at home compared with the time spent on ICT at school and, in 2001, over half had personal e-mail addresses. Older pupils spend four times longer using ICT at home and over two-thirds had their own websites. Furthermore, the degree of access to computers and the Internet and quality of use at home are strongly related to socio-economic status. Children in less well-off homes are deterred from using information technology to its fullest potential, while those in better-off families are able to enhance their learning with a wealth of online information at their fingertips. Building on this base, those who use computers at home use them both more frequently and confidently at school, yet ICT is not being used to its full potential to transform learning and teaching. Inspection evidence[5] indicates that schools still teach pupils basic ICT skills which they already know and do not give discretion about when, how and why to use ICT in lessons. Furthermore, the way in which ICT is used in lessons is often neither motivating, enriching nor developing higher level reasoning or creativity.

Much hangs, therefore, on raising the 'sufficient competence' of the teaching force as a whole, and not just to show that technology investment is worthwhile.

Teacher competence with ICT

The original 1998 Northern Ireland Education Technology strategy[6] established a level of 'sufficient competence' for ICT while at the same time clarifying a useful distinction between different levels of 'skills' which are needed and which remain valid today.

It describes teacher competence at three levels:

- Personal competence in the use of specific ICT tools;
- Subject competence in the integration and evaluation of educational technologies in the teacher's main subject specialism(s) or area of teaching;
- Teaching competence in planning, preparing, teaching, assessing and evaluating lessons which make significant use of ICT.

It said that teachers needed to show some general competences pervading all three levels of competence, namely:

- Positive attitudes to education technology – the confidence, open-mindedness, flexibility and vision to explore the potential of ICT and its applications to the wider world;
- The ability to evaluate the use of education technologies – the ability to take a critical view of the personal use of ICT and the educational use of technology, of use by others, and an understanding of what constitutes appropriate and effective use.

Personal competence can be specified in terms of the use of word-processors, clip art, databases, spreadsheets and electronic communications at the core, with a range of optional tools depending on the nature of specialist teaching required such as, for example, CAD/CAM for technologists, art packages for artists and GPS and mapping models for geographers.

The 1998 strategy called on teachers to use ICT personally, as well as understanding how ICT changes approaches to learning and teaching, which includes being able to make judgements about the ICT standards which learners display when they use ICT. They also need to understand enough about progression to help students make the appropriate choice of ICT tool for a task – especially difficult when teachers may feel that the pupils are more knowledgeable of how ICT works than they are themselves.

By 2004 the relevance of these skills sets had not diminished. The Empowering Schools strategy found it necessary to redefine the professional ICT competence needed by all staff ('all staff' including classroom and learning assistants, those who work in libraries and technicians, who should be able to support teachers with ICT) and the application of those skills to enhance teaching and learning in the classroom.

The strategy called upon schools to have a continuing professional development (CPD) action plan built upon teachers' individual action plans with targets for the school and for individuals. It is recommended that progress needed to be monitored regularly and planning revised in light of developments.

The plan should:

- cover the knowledge and skills needed to:
  - choose and integrate digital resources/content effectively in their teaching schemes;
  - organise the pupils for ICT-based work, managing the classroom effectively;
  - use digital resources to enhance practice in the classroom.

- extend the teachers' ICT skills, and the appropriate skills of other support staff, especially in the use, where relevant, of:
  - digital curriculum resources;
  - assessment software;
  - tools for online communication;
  - presentation software;
  - multimedia software;
  - tools for publishing locally-authored digital resources/content;
  - software for modelling;
  - control technology resources.

There is now sufficient access to computers and other electronic devices in schools to allow staff to improve their productivity and to reduce administrative and bureaucratic burdens. Processes for routine educational administration, information gathering and information giving, planning and documentation should now be brought online and streamlined, wherever possible, to avoid duplication and to reduce bureaucracy.

For example, the Empowering Schools strategy indicates how professional efficiency and productivity should be improved, by using technology to reduce bureaucratic burdens.

Raising teacher competence with ICT should help to ensure that teachers have enough skills to use ICT tools to be more efficient and productive across a wide range of educational tasks, including:

- finding appropriate lesson resources;
- planning and preparing lessons;
- presenting information to pupils and others;
- assessing and marking; recording and reporting;
- organising time, activities and resources;
- registering pupils and keeping attendance;
- sending messages; communicating online;
- responding to the information needs of school managers, parents, Boards, the Department and the Inspectorate;
- seeking and getting advice and support from elsewhere.[7]

Closing the gap

Achieving these gains in any e-school system requires systematic action by government so that all educational administrative and information functions are moved online to meet e-government targets. It requires an active coordination at the institutional level to advance computerisation of administrative tasks, including the dissemination of practices and case studies in the effective use of ICT which reduce bureaucratic burdens.

Yet, paradoxically, while many teachers are able users of the Internet and of email in their personal lives – emailing relations living abroad, downloading and attaching digital photographs, making holiday arrangements, buying insurance, booking flights and hotels online, banking online, ordering books, gifts, tickets online and using e-Bay[8] – these same skills are not often deployed in a way which achieves savings in teacher workloads.[9]

According to PWC, savings of over nine hours a week per teacher can be achieved on administrative tasks, including lesson planning, lesson resource preparation, teaching, assessment of pupil progress, recording of assessment and reporting. But, there are seven identifiable obstacles to achieving these savings.

In Northern Ireland the first five obstacles have been resolved through the C2K provision described in Chapter 2:

- variations in computer network provision;
- variations in the teachers' email service;
- lack of a common infrastructure;
- lack of a universal broadband;
- the effectiveness of technical support.

The two remaining obstacles:

- confidence and competence of practitioners;
- a focus in the school's ICT strategy, aimed at addressing workload issues

remain targets in the current strategy.

The survey warns however, that overcoming these hurdles will take an initial investment of time and that the tasks will initially, and paradoxically, take longer as teachers climb through an 'implementation dip' as they develop new competences.

To add to this challenge, we are also trying to hit a moving target. In Chapter 8 we describe the highly creative Dreamlab project, set up as a response to concerns that the very speed of ICT advance means there is a widening gap between the ICT skills of teachers (and those they develop amongst their pupils), and the digital skills needed for employment today and tomorrow. Schools may successfully provide generic skills; yet the pace of industrial change leaves school leavers unable to capitalise on new employment opportunities in global markets. In the longer term, re-professionalisation of teachers is the only way that e-schools can keep pace with the needs of their learners.

The New Opportunities Fund (NOF)

ICT training programme for teachers and school librarians

In 1998, £208 million of lottery income administered by the UK agency called (at that time) the New Opportunities Fund (NOF) was allocated, in the largest national teacher education exercise anywhere, for training in the use of information and communications technology (ICT) for teachers and school librarians; £10.8 million went to Northern Ireland.

The programme was criticised in its implementation, especially in England.[10] We look here at how the programme was approached and managed in Northern Ireland to achieve its maximum effect – a step-change for teachers and school librarians.[11]

The programme's main aim was to raise the standard of pupils' achievement by developing the expertise of serving teachers and school librarians to a level in the use of ICT then expected of newly qualified teachers. However, the programme revealed a deeper chasm of need for training in basic ICT techniques than had been commonly believed. The lack of access to resources hobbled the provision of basic skills training regarded as the entry level to the programme.

The programme was based on a detailed statement of expected outcomes which envisaged that teachers, taking account of their pupils' ages and phase, as well as their prior learning, should know:

- how ICT can be used in teaching the whole class, groups, or individuals within carefully planned lessons;
- when, when not, and how to use ICT in teaching particular subjects;
- how ICT can be used for planning, as well as for preparing and organising resources;
- how to assess pupils' work when ICT has been used;
- how ICT can be used to keep up to date, share best practice and reduce bureaucracy.

Although the training model was pedagogically sound, it was a significantly new training experience for the majority of teachers, who were used to out-of-school, centre-based, face-to-face in-service training. However, participation rates in Northern Ireland were the highest in the UK, with 21,164 teachers and school librarians enrolling and 94 per cent completing the programme by March 2003. The response of Northern Ireland teachers to quality assurance factors of competence, confidence, motivation and satisfaction showed the highest UK scores.

Preparing for success

Three factors contributed to the success of the programme in Northern Ireland. Where the programme worked best, there was a clear commitment by the principal and senior management to make training a priority. Second, there had been sufficient advance notice of the national programme for the five education and library Boards to run a local scheme to prepare the ground in advance. An ICT advisory team from the Boards, led by a recently-retired ICT adviser, ran a 'Connecting Teachers to the Internet' programme to provide five intensive days full-time training for one teacher-leader from each school – over 1,200 in total. The concept of 'teacher-leader' was coined specifically for the purpose of the programme in response to the request of principals who wanted to broaden the base of expertise in their school. Many schools had a teacher designated as 'ICT coordinator', often a paid post of responsibility. Teachers were more usually selected on the basis of their technical ability, knowledge and expertise to carry out duties as 'system managers'. Many principals wished to identify an additional teacher with strengths in professional development and change leadership. A centrally agreed job description placed a strong emphasis on 'people' skills, notably communication and leadership. While some schools placed the same individual for both roles, the distinction between the two roles and two remits, and the differentiation of essential skills was, and remains today, an important one.

Each 'teacher-leader' was equipped, through their training, with a laptop with Internet connectivity, loaded with a selection of educational software titles which were later provided on the C2K systems in classrooms. The teacher leader was asked to develop a small cohort of no more than 6 or 7 staff. A modest budget to enable them to take part in local support network meetings was provided. Each cohort member was, in turn, provided with a laptop. The cohorts formed an effective advance party of teachers with enough knowledge and skills to encourage their colleagues through the NOF programme.

A delay in contractual negotiations over Classroom 2000, described in Chapter 2, provided an opportunity to equip the teaching force with some 14,000 laptops to share, on a basis of two for every three teachers. This resource was a significant component in the success of the NOF training.

Where school principals supported the programme, participants' progress against the expected outcomes was good. Schools were encouraged to adopt a collegiate model of mutual support for the NOF programme, modelled through the 'Connecting Teachers' programme. Where 'Connecting Teachers' had been effectively implemented it worked well, and those schools benefited from the NOF programme.

Successful results summarised

Increased levels of ICT activity, covering personal use, lesson planning and use of ICT with pupils during lessons, were noted.

> This has been the biggest change in the curriculum in recent years. It has been the best use of time and has resulted in teachers becoming more confident and more competent in the use of ICT in the classroom. (Primary teacher)

> The programme has been a great confidence builder ... there is a great sense of partnership between pupil and teacher. In this situation the teacher is not necessarily the expert ... the programme has helped staff in their professional development and it has also helped the overall unity of the staff. (Primary teacher)

> This programme has inspired and ignited teachers. (Post-primary teacher)

... a psychological barrier has been crossed which leaves the path open to continuing professional development. (ELB adviser)

The integration of ICT into classroom practice was most successful in primary schools where teachers seized the opportunity substantively. In this sector, the vast majority of teachers generally had greater confidence and were more enthusiastic in the use of ICT than their counterparts in secondary schools. The integration of ICT with classroom teaching was more variable in the secondary schools, yet as a result of their training, the teachers became more aware of the relevance of ICT to classroom teaching. Teachers were beginning to include ICT, even if tentatively, in departmental schemes of work and individual teaching plans. An Inspectorate report summed up the situation as follows:

a majority of schools, however, need to integrate ICT further into the curriculum and ensure continuity and progression in the development of children's ICT skills.[12]

Teachers as learners

The learning experience of some participants was not without its difficulties. The online, supported self-study aspects of the training were largely unfamiliar to many. The extent of individual commitment required was not well understood; nor were many teachers ready for a critical, reflective focus on their classroom practice. These problems were exacerbated by inadequate infrastructure and connectivity, particularly in the secondary sector. Local advisory staff took time to build up their own expertise with this new mode of training. The quality of external support was often inconsistent, particularly in the case of subject areas.

Despite some initial teething problems, most teachers reported a relatively good experience. Motivation was often high, mainly due to the sustained enthusiasm and hard work of the lead teachers. Most teachers talked about the greater collegiality, cooperation and mutual support within and beyond their own schools through professional contacts and networking, as well as the sharing of ideas and materials. On the other hand, where support at school level was inadequate, poor motivation was almost inevitable, with consequent low commitment. Since the success of any training programme depends to a great extent on the commitment of school principals and senior management teams, it was important that their involvement included a focus on quality assurance. In some cases insufficient time and resources were allocated for training; in others the role of the school organiser was poorly understood and inadequately supported, leading to a loss of focus and an absence of clarity about the requirements. This was exacerbated by initiative overload in school development plans, where the programme was not given appropriate priority, perhaps because of poor communication with schools in the early stages. In general, principals and senior management in primary schools were more successful in remaining close to the spirit and requirements of the programme than those in secondary schools.

Stress was laid on the importance of online communication and conferencing as an integral part of the training. However, possibly because of limited access, some schools did not have a culture of using email for communication; similarly the online conference facilities provided were not much used for sharing ideas and practices. One teacher association instructed its members not to engage in ICT training 'outside directed time', which sometimes made it more difficult for trainers to convince teachers of the value and importance of developing their skills, and of learning how to embed ICT in teaching and learning.

Despite the difficulties, the advent of C2K hardware and connectivity coincided fairly closely with the NOF training in primary schools, but its delay in the secondary sector was a disincentive. Finally, the conservative nature of school culture presented a particular challenge to those charged with managing and supporting the programme.

While there was ample evidence that the programme developed the expertise of serving teachers and school librarians in the use of ICT, it is much harder to say how much it raised the standard of pupils' achievements, and almost impossible to show any causal link. Nevertheless, evaluations with principals, key contacts and school organisers indicated a remarkable degree of confidence in the outcomes.

Commenting on success

> The ... programme has had demonstrable success in meeting NOF's ultimate aim – improving learning experiences and raising the standards of pupils in the classroom.

> The ... course was a means of developing ICT in school, with all staff progressing together, as we worked through the programme. It has provided us with a shared understanding of how to deliver ICT throughout the school. It has also proved highly motivating for all staff and is beginning to show positive results in the classroom.

> NOF training has had a substantial and positive effect on the use of ICT throughout the school. The training ... has been well received by the majority of staff who have been trained. [There is] much more use of ICT by all departments across the school and by individual teachers for administration and preparation of resources.

> NOP, the independent polling organisation, surveyed 25 Northern Ireland primary principals, with the following results:

> The quality of teaching and learning has improved greatly. The children are more enthusiastic. ... Teaching now has more depth, class management has improved, group work is encouraged.

Table 3.1 Results of NOF Programme

Statement	%agreeing with the statement
The programme was fairly or very successful in terms of the expected outcomes	100
Teachers seem more confident and competent in the use of ICT since the programme began	97
The programme had an impact on work in the classroom	94
The programme had an impact on pupils' work	90
The programme had an impact on continuing professional development	94
Principals were satisfied or very satisfied with the support from CASS	93

There has been a very significant impact on both teaching and learning because of the programme. Teachers are willing to experiment and to ask for help amongst each other to ensure a good ICT experience for the pupils. There is much evidence of sharing of expertise and resources among the staff.

Key players judged the impact of the training on achievement in primary schools to be significant, but were split on its impact in secondary schools. In individual Boards, contacts variously said:

The overall view is that the vast majority of primary schools show a significant improvement, some show very significant improvements.

The change in post-primary schools is very patchy. Some schools and some departments show significant changes, others much less.

A significant number of schools maintain a view that the impact on pupils' achievement cannot reliably be measured in such a short period of time. However almost all post-primary schools do report an improvement across the subjects with respect to increased pupil motivation, teacher confidence and motivation, resource production tailored to the particular needs of the pupil and use of Internet.

Value for money

Judging the value for money of the NOF programme can only be done very roughly. If a systemic step change in the overall competence of the teaching profession for 21,000 teachers cost £10.8 million (roughly equal to the cost of providing local advisory support to all schools for three months) then the programme was good value for money. If it meant that teachers are one measurable step closer to being able to make effective use of a multi-million investment in infrastructure, connectivity, content and services, then the expenditure was essential. It is perhaps more straightforward to consider where Northern Ireland might be in terms of its chance to compete effectively in the global information economy were it not to invest significantly in ICT in education.

The most significant impact of this programme was to shift the professional knowledge base to a point where using digital technologies to support learning, teaching and professional practice had come to be seen as the new norm for all, with ICT no longer seen only as a select subject for specialists and some pupils.

After 2003, it was possible to say confidently that 'no teacher any longer thinks that ICT is not for them', but, in as much as this was the first rung on the ladder for many teachers, competence generally needs to be raised further for every member of staff. Continuing professional development in an e-school, based closely on individual needs, is required. The challenge is – what is the next competent step upwards?

The Teacher Education Partnership: early professional development

The first of several next steps lies in initial teacher education where the right kind of foundation for fundamental long-term change can be laid: we examine this in the next chapter. While such professional rebuilding, from the ground floor, can change the profession, it is essential to get it right, for it is the longer haul and it does not replace the need to bring about behavioural change among serving teachers.

The right 'next step' appears to be similar to the development of the concept of Early Professional Development in Northern Ireland. In this compulsory programme, beginning teachers are required to demonstrate how they embed ICT in their practice during their second and third years of teaching after qualifying to teach.

Since 1998, it has been a requirement for newly-qualified teachers to undertake a self-managed set of professional development exercises, moderated by a more experienced senior teacher acting as a tutor. The teachers are expected to engage in critical self-evaluation, producing a portfolio of reflective journals, accompanied by the teaching materials used and assessed samples of pupils' work and showing how ICT is incorporated in some way *to support learning*. This approach to early professional development, now common in the UK, was pioneered in Northern Ireland.

The *Teacher Education Partnership Handbook*[13] describes the process as one of

> encouraging beginning professionals to develop their critical, reflective practice in order to improve their teaching and the quality of the pupils' learning. As the beginning teacher grows in competence, the focus of development shifts progressively from learning how to teach, to thinking about teaching, and finally, to thinking

about learning. Such reflective practice is characterised by an open, informed, critical dialogue amongst all the partners, combined with support from experienced practitioners.

This is a good, working articulation of the need for a professional community for an e-school, but, to be successful, it requires more opportunities for communication and dialogue than a teacher, traditionally ensconced behind a desk and closed away from other teachers for the large part of the day, has the chance to develop.

The General Teaching Council for Northern Ireland (GTCNI) has promoted proposals for all teachers to work towards 'chartered teacher' status as a mid-career target,[14] similar to plans already operating in Scotland, where the award of a Master's degree in education is seen as the best guarantee of quality for the award of 'chartered teacher'. The design of Masters Programmes reflects GTCNI's competence framework for continuing professional development, including the expectation that all teachers will gain the experience to make increasingly sophisticated judgments about how ICT can promote learning at classroom and whole school level.

It would hardly be surprising if many were to feel that the *opportunity* for collegiality and cooperation would be a fine thing. How can technology help?

Building professional communities online

David Hargreaves, in his paper 'Education Epidemic' for the think-tank Demos,[15] sets out a startling challenge for the education world to respond by making 'rapid transformations' so that e-schools can meet the twenty-first century needs of learners. He believes that no less than transformation is required and that the piece-meal, unevenly distributed innovation which characterises schools today will not fit the bill.

In any case, he argues, traditional expectations of transferring 'best educational practice' from site to site are conceptually flawed, and, even if they did work, would take too long – leaving schools even more dysfunctional in the future.

Quoting Donald Schon[16] he says:

> We must ... become adept at learning. We must become able not only to transform our institutions, in response to changing situations and requirement; we must invent and develop institutions which are 'learning systems', that is to say, systems capable of bringing about their own continuing transformation.

Hargreaves argues for an e-school to survive and prosper by becoming *a learning organisation*, with a rate of change matching change in the world outside schools. Put bluntly, he argues that schools and teachers are not fast changing enough to stay relevant.

Hargreaves shows how, with the right kind of leadership and governance, the formation of networks combining collaborative and competitive endeavour play a vital role in creating world-class, adaptive public services. The advantage of a network is that change does not need to trickle slowly down 'from the top' with all the misinterpretations and simplifications which that implies, but can spread out and disseminate rapidly, like an illness does through a neural network, because of the multiplicity of sideways connections. In Hargreaves's terms a combination of vertical-central 'initiatives' and lateral-local innovation networks is needed.

Government is challenged to ensure that the conditions are in place to facilitate an 'epidemic' of change, the rapid lateral infection and infusion which are created when like-minded professionals have the opportunity to come together to tease out issues and create 'best practice' solutions. 'Community-built' solutions offer a different model from the arid 'transfer' notion of posting packages of 'best practice' from one place to another, where, out of context, it is highly unlikely that a 'practice' will 'take'.

Michael Fullan[17] echoes this approach when talking about 'lateral capacity building', that is to say, the development of competence through peer-based learning. He identifies several successive steps in lateral capacity-building: the realisation that capacity-building is important; vertical capacity-building using external trainers at a regional level; and lateral capacity-building across peers.

In his review of approaches across European communities to embedding ICT, Alan McCluskey[18] points out that the UK is relatively unusual in placing an emphasis on the need for teachers to continue to learn.

> Depending on the subject being taught, there are varying pressures on teachers to keep up-to-date in their area of expertise. New technologies and innovative methods also require some learning on the part of teachers. In addition, in their daily practice, many teachers experiment to some degree or another, but it is extremely rare to find an organised, collective 'learning-experience'.

As Hargreaves put it, the challenge for teachers is that the way they define themselves is located in the classroom, and their sense of community in the staffroom. The challenge is to build wider professional identities and learning communities that encompass the entire teaching force, oriented towards innovation and improvement.

And, if we aspire to learners having experience of *global* learning in the curriculum to prepare them for living and working in the 'global village' then we must aspire to a self-defining experience for their teacher.

Hargreaves's lessons for a 'global' community, such as Northern Ireland, are to capitalise on the existing investment in online networks to build social, peer-to-peer, networks. While online environments can sustain online communities, they are not adept at creating them where they do not already exist. An advantage of a small province is the variety of informal networks which already exist, often created during initial teacher education. Lateral online networks can enable education leaders to enhance their organisational and social capital, mobilising the intellectual capital for innovation across schools.

Through C2K, and our strategic approach, we have achieved just this. We have recognised the nature of the challenge in terms of providing access to networks, and through programmes of action we are building the capacity for innovative educators to jump-start change.

Building capacity for organisational change

In responding to the challenge, we set out a number of steps to help an e-school become empowered.[19]

We see that development is needed on a range of fronts:

- capacity-building within the professional community;
- supporting critical reflection and sharing of instances of new practice with ICT across the service;
- reviewing teacher competence and developing teachers professionally in the twenty-first century.

We set out a number of change steps to be taken by e-schools in the context of their development plans. They need to develop:

- the school leaders' roles, supported through technology;
- professional ICT competence for all staff (which includes classroom and learning assistants, those who work in libraries, and technicians, who should all be able to support teachers with ICT) and the application of those skills to enhance and support teaching and learning in the classroom;
- the capacity to use online resources and tools to enhance teaching and learning;
- supporting professional development through collaborative online communities of practice;
- approaches to assessment and evaluation to support learning, making more use of, for example, online tests and formative assessment information;
- professional efficiency and productivity, by using technology to reduce bureaucratic burdens;
- their capacity to use online resources and tools to enhance teaching and learning and to support professional development through collaborative online communities.

Online environments will enable teachers to find and use curriculum content, from a wide range of sources, published online. As they become confident with this way of working, e-schools should be drawing up plans to develop and publish their own courses on their school intranet. In doing so, they will modify and integrate externally provided resources, such as, for example, lessons and teaching plans, course content, projects and tests.

Innovative teaching needs to be explored, evaluated and quality-assured, through research and development projects. For example:

- different ways of organising teaching (changing the duration of lessons, many of which are too short to accommodate research-based learning and for varying the size of class groupings depending upon the activity);
- the support of learning, including the blending of online support for learning with more traditional practice, both in the classroom and for professional development purposes;
- the development of online resources;
- the migration from a less subject-centred to a more integrated experience of the curriculum for learners.

Taking teachers online

First steps

Taking teachers online in a professional development process takes much more than just providing an email account. Even when, as in Northern Ireland, there is an average of four networked computers in schools for every teacher, the behavioural change in the daily habit of checking email is not commonplace.

To address this issue, email online delivery is now the only means through which communications are sent to schools. The Department of Education issues all circulars electronically, not on paper. Major decisions are announced only by email; yet the process remains slow, even when individuals lose out on opportunities advertised online, it is still common to hear technical reasons given as a cause, when it is working practices which are the matter.

Since 2001, a range of projects has tested the viability and built up the capacity to run in-service education courses online, or partly online.

The Northern Ireland eLearning partnership[20] was created as an umbrella to coordinate and advance e-learning for schools, where the needs are different from those in tertiary institutions where practices are more common-place.

The projects used *Blackboard* (an online learning platform), licensed by C2K and Granada Learning's *Learnwise* (a similar platform) to host projects demonstrating the feasibility of e-learning. The projects resulted in the production of quality guides for using online environments for teaching, for initial teacher education, for the professional development of serving teachers, Headteachers, curriculum advisers and for tutors in the professional qualification for headship provided by the Regional Training Unit.

From 2002 to 2005, the government strategy provided limited support for some 20 pilot projects over a range of curriculum topics and short in-service education courses. The partnership ensured that the projects were independently evaluated by consultants from the British Educational and Communications Technology Agency.

Online courses for teachers

The first online in-service education course for teachers was run by two advisory officers from Southern Education and Library Board (SELB) and North-Eastern Education and Library Board (NEELB), Heather Thompson and Vivian Kelly, for 30 teachers.[21] The officers were part of the cohort of 17 hand-selected educators in an online education development venture provided by the University of Ulster in collaboration with Duquesne University in Pittsburgh.

The SELB/NEELB 'Effective and e-learning' course connected current research on learning and teaching in the traditional classroom with the developing knowledge and skills of the virtual classroom. It set out to prepare participants to be the 'learning consultant' in their own schools.

The course was highly successful and aspects became mainstream in in-service education programmes for teachers. It accommodated different learning styles and provided a basis for research into online learning methodologies. An online learning experience was provided for selected primary and secondary teachers through which they developed a shared understanding of effective learning relating to the potential of e-learning in the classroom. Participants developed an aspect of effective learning within their own classrooms, sharing their professional learning and resources online.

The course led to a range of further experiments: these included courses to support professional development online between the Regional Training Unit and the SEELB working at a distance online with staff at Framingham College in Massachusetts to develop the capacity of advisory and tutorial staff to design online courses, and a course run by Granada/C2K special needs consultants with the WELB special education advisor to support special needs teachers in mainstream schools, who rarely have sufficient opportunity to meet and share solutions. The course led to more specialist provision of an online early professional development for beginning special education teachers through the *Special Needs Working Group* to provide help through an online community of sharing practitioners, especially when the problems they face with children with special needs often require a rapid, overnight, response.[22]

The course aimed to integrate ICT into teaching and learning, develop online support for new teachers, build a community of sharing practitioners and encourage reflective, critical analysis and improvement in teaching. Beginning teachers from special schools and units interacted, shared, questioned and supported each other in online forums. The mutual support helped them to reflect, analyse, share and celebrate their work with colleagues, improving their practice. Their reaction was highly positive:

> The course provided good focus, direction and support … and was very enjoyable.

Teachers' online learning

In just six weeks, more than 600 messages were posted online, with teachers sharing advice on everything from handling difficult learner behaviours to developing suitable resources. A sense of the challenges faced by the teachers can be had from just one exchange:

> Teacher 1: I have a little girl in my class who is an absolute angel in school … however the reports of her behaviour at home are quite the opposite … I get the impression from her parents that she 'rules the roost' … and if she doesn't get what she wants she resorts to throwing tantrums/violence until her parents finally give in. The boundaries were never set for her at home so she just keeps pushing. … This is only my first year in special and i [sic] was wondering is it common to have such extremes in a child's personality depending on their environment?

> Teacher 2: … I know that it's not unusual for our pupils to display very different behaviours in different settings. … I too have several pupils in my class who pose no behaviour difficulties. I've been shocked to have been contacted by behaviour nurses and social workers regarding their (violent) behaviour at home. So what's going on? … Are expectations a bit lower at home and are boundaries a little unclear? Do my (teenage) pupils 'swing the lead' at home (I accept, like most teenagers) but know rightly to abide by school standards? Nature v nurture – to what extent?

As one teacher said:

> The VLE [virtual learning environment] is a valuable source of support and encouragement for teachers who are in similar situations.

The teachers worked together to create multimedia classroom resources suited to special needs. They shared their unfinished work online; feedback and suggestions from peers helped them to fine-tune and improve their resources. The teachers learnt that, online the more you put in, the more you get back.

At times I found the course very time-consuming, but it was worth putting in the time, as I found you reap what you sow.

Based on the experience of the early professional development pilots, and in response to a request from the ET Strategy Management Group, the Regional Training Unit established a professional, accredited course, Online Teaching and Learning for Educators (OLTE) which has provided professional development in two years for over 85 professional officers from the curriculum advisory support services, and elsewhere, and continues to do so.[23]

Consequently, confidence that e-learning has the potential to improve teaching and learning in schools and support a collegial approach to professional development for teachers has been established and a small cohort of educators suitably qualified to take it forward developed. The introduction of e-learning approaches has been shown to substantially improve access to education by broadening curriculum choice, vocational access and skills. For teachers, e-learning approaches can help to build learning communities enabling them to engage in professional development with other professionals without necessarily meeting face to face every time.

Putting e-learning at the heart of educational reform

The Empowering Schools strategy sets out explicit milestones: collectively they spell out the message that an e-school, to be fit for purpose in the twenty-first century, must have ICT and e-learning at the heart of educational reform, no matter what its focus, or risk being out of step.

Hargreaves catches, succinctly, the way in which enhancements of practice using technology can build into recognisable transformation. The process depends completely on a sustainable infrastructure being in place, but the dynamic required is one of helping teachers to develop the professional confidence to see past the technology glitter and align their view of technology with their personal vision of effective teaching.

Classroom teachers do not want to become experts in the use of ICT, and most are not interested in improving their ICT skills in a general way; instead, they want to be expert teachers of physics or French, mathematics or music, and if ICTs will help them teach these subjects better, they will use them for this overriding purpose, which is at the heart of transformation.[24]

Global messages

Whereas technology provision for an e-school clearly benefits from a unified approach, as described in Chapter 2, teacher development, given all of the distinctive components – initial teacher education, in-service education, leadership development is much more of a partnership which cannot always be so easily reconciled. It requires considerable coordination, if, as is likely to be the case, a single agency approach cannot be easily achieved. In addition, technology mastery provides its own learning curve – which for many can appear daunting enough – and the effort and attention required risks masking the real need to ensure that ICT becomes an integral part of teaching and learning. Nevertheless, we can identify some important messages for teacher education.

- The coordinated timing of training and provision is important if alignment is to be achieved between technology and educational goals. The sequencing of provision is all. Teachers, like any learners, are responsive to training opportunities when they see the contingency of resources and staff development. They need to get the best of the resources when they commit to staff development. There is a strong sense of professionalism amongst teachers which leads them to want to be capable users of the tools of teaching and learning. Provided that this is recognised and supported with time and resource, they respond in kind.

- At the same time, schools do not change through the installation of hardware; e-school improvement, in terms of efficiency gains and raised standards only comes about through institutional development, that is to say, when set in the context of efforts towards whole school improvement. Isolated, stand-alone courses are themselves insufficient to make a systemic difference.

- While essential, training in ICT techniques alone is insufficient; basic techniques are important, but purpose and context are much more so. Technology is only perceived as a valuable tool when it supports valued professional goals, such as the development of collegial reflective practice and lifelong learning.

- All teachers in an e-school have an equal entitlement to professional development, whichever routes towards a chartered status they choose to follow, and there is an entitlement for some of that experience to be supported online. A competence model for career-long teacher development can provide the basis for continuing professional development to be supported online; benefits can accrue from the use of e-portfolios to facilitate reflective practice by teachers. In this way teachers can experience, first-hand, what it takes to become an online learner – thus providing them with insights about its potential to relevance as an approach for their learners.

Transforming learning within early teacher education

In the previous chapter we examined the steps that have been taken to support teachers to help them embed ICT in their approach to teaching, learning and assessment. But alignment of policy and sustainability for e-schooling mean that steps need to be in place to ensure that those entering the teaching profession have the skills and the pedagogic understanding to use ICT confidently, to become active members of the learning community of teachers and transform their practice in ways which add value to learning.

In the early 1990s, the position of ICT in initial teacher education might best be described as follows; one or two enthusiastic staff members developed interesting innovative uses of ICT with student teachers, there were relatively few opportunities for the use of ICT when students were in schools on teaching practice and there was no formal recognition or assessment of ICT in initial teacher training.

This chapter offers an analysis of how this position has been changing over a period of 15 years by examining four key issues: the provision by government to the initial teacher education providers of the same C2K hardware and software as that found in schools; second, staff development within Initial Teacher Education (ITE) institutions; third, the role played by government and professional agencies both in the promotion of innovation and in determining levels of competence in ICT from student teachers; and finally, we consider evidence of how ready student teachers are to transform learning through the use of ICT.

The structure of teacher education

In Northern Ireland, teachers are provided with initial training either through a four year Bachelor of Education degree or through a one-year postgraduate qualification following a degree. Unlike some parts of the world where there is a shortage of trainee teachers, competition for these places is intense and the overall quality of applicants is high. Initial teacher education programmes are designed for those planning to teach in primary schools or secondary education.

Northern Ireland has one other distinctive feature in terms of its teacher education framework; when student teachers complete their initial training they are required to undertake a structured period of induction, normally for one year, in their first teaching post. During this time they are supported by curriculum advisers from one of the five Education and Library Boards. After this period of induction, beginning teachers have to follow a further period of Early Professional Development (EPD) when they are required to carry out two professional development activities in the classroom. The focus of their reflective practice is negotiated between the teacher and the school. In a later section of this chapter we will return to comment on the place of ICT in this three-stage process.

The first part of this chapter examines the ICT infrastructure in Initial Teacher Education, an essential prerequisite for preparing new teachers for e-schooling.

Hardware and infrastructure

Until 2004, any hardware that student teachers had access to during their period of initial teacher education (ITE) provided by their institution could have been based on an Apple, BBC Microcomputer or PC platform. Equally, when they went to schools for teaching practice, there was not only a variety of hardware and software but the extent of provision was so uneven that there was no certainty that student teachers could use ICT in their teaching. As C2K was being planned and rolled out to schools, the providers of ITE campaigned government for matching hardware and software. They did this through a local forum of the UK-wide Universities Council for the Education of Teachers (UCET) which proved to be a very valuable means of coordinating joint action.

Initially, from 2001, students and lecturers were provided at no cost with copies of the curriculum software titles being installed in primary school systems. These titles ran on the equipment in the training institutions. This was the first significant step in integrating ITE providers within the C2K framework. But it was only by 2004 that all of the institutions that offered training for primary education were given the same systems as well as all the software environment and titles that student teachers would encounter in the schools where they did their teaching practice. By late 2005, similar facilities were provided for those who were training student teachers for post-primary teacher education.

A key lesson here, then, is the need for policy makers to ensure that in designing a managed learning environment, sufficient resources are provided for those engaged in initial teacher education. Where a principle is being adopted that all children have a right to a quality ICT learning environment, it is unwise to expect that those who provide the training for new teachers will always have the available resources to upgrade their ICT facilities to the same level as schools. Given the quality of those entering the teaching profession, these beginning teachers can quickly take a lead in promoting good ICT practice in schools, but they can only do this if their training institutions have the expertise and resources to nurture innovative ways of technology-enabled learning.

We turn next to the question of how steps were put in place to ensure that all student teachers, and not just the enthusiasts, reached levels of proficiency in ICT that have enabled them to have the skills and pedagogical judgment to make good use of the opportunities that C2K is creating.

A competence-based model of initial teacher education

Northern Ireland has adopted a competence-based model of teacher education which defines a range of competences that those in the profession are expected to acquire over a period of time. It is accepted that competence in areas such as planning, teaching and assessing of children requires continual refinement over an extended length of time through a process of critical self-reflection and professional development. The first phase of this process was introduced in 1998 when the Northern Ireland Teacher Education Committee reached agreement with all ITE providers on a framework that not only embraced a very wide range of essential competences but indicated what focus should be placed on them in three stages of professional preparation, defined as initial, induction and early professional development. This framework was revised in 2005–6 by the General Teaching Council for Northern Ireland (GTCNI),[1] a body that is independent of government, with responsibility for the teaching profession.

What place does competence in ICT have in this process and who provides quality assurance that student teachers have reached an acceptable level of competence at the end of their initial teacher education before they apply for their first teaching post? Selinger and Austin (2003)[2] compared the regulatory framework for ICT in ITE between England and Northern Ireland and noted that whereas student teachers in England had to meet 'ICT standards' through an online test, those in Northern Ireland were mainly assessed through the development of an ICT portfolio which placed emphasis not only on the students' personal competence in ICT but on their capacity to make informed judgments about the role of ICT in teaching and learning. In contrast to the high level of specification in England, the regulatory framework put into place in Northern Ireland by the Education and Training Inspectorate (ETI) was significantly more flexible. And, even more importantly, it was based on an understanding that the fast moving pace of change in ICT meant that it was better to focus on broad learning objectives enhanced through ICT than skills in particular software.

The position taken by ETI, whose staff have a statutory responsibility for inspecting the quality and performance of schools and teacher training, is continuing to evolve. While its traditional role of inspecting and making judgements remains a high priority, another approach to their role is being explored with far greater emphasis being placed on schools and educational organisations developing their own capacity for self-evaluation and quality assurance.

Judgement about whether or not a student teacher may be considered 'competent' rests with the teacher training tutors whose decisions are based on evidence from teachers in schools where students have carried out teaching practice, on their own observations and on the quality of student written work including reflection on the ways that ICT has been used in teaching and learning. ICT is not assessed as a discrete competence but is treated as part of a student's ability to make effective use of resources in the promotion of effective learning.

These arrangements regarding the place of ICT in teacher education can be further illuminated by comparing the situation in Northern Ireland with the Republic of Ireland. Here, in line with a long commitment of giving schools considerable autonomy over what best suits their ICT needs, government agencies responsible for education have allowed teacher training institutions to determine how much emphasis to place on ICT in initial teacher education. In effect, the position adopted in regulatory terms in Northern Ireland is somewhere between the tightly specified arrangements in England and the more deregulated approach in the Republic of Ireland.

A good illustration of the Northern Irish approach can be found in the 2006 version of the competences developed by the Northern Ireland General Teaching Council[3] which includes a requirement that student teachers should demonstrate 'a knowledge and understanding of how to use technology effectively, both to aid pupil learning and to support their professional role'. The statement of competence also provides an indication of 'progression' from initial teacher education through induction, early professional development and into continuing professional development. In other words, the advice from the profession provides clarity about the importance of ICT as a competence but leaves the teacher training providers with the responsibility for building an ICT curriculum that enables student teachers to demonstrate the competence.

Assessment of ICT in initial teacher education

As we noted above, ICT is clearly identified as a required competence in Northern Ireland. The most recent version of the competences from the General Teaching Council in Northern Ireland makes specific reference to the potential value of e-learning. Unlike England, however, ICT competence is not formally assessed through any online test but is treated as an integral element of teaching competence. Student teachers build up a portfolio of evidence on their personal use of ICT, use of ICT in preparation for teaching and with children. Perhaps, most significantly, it contains a reflective section in which students are required to place their own experience of using ICT in the broader context of learning. This enables them to think about whether their use of ICT was effective, was appropriate for the particular topic and children they were working with and how it might have been used to better effect. In 2004–5, a pilot scheme in one institution was run to convert the paper-based portfolio into an e-portfolio; initial conclusions from this work suggest that while students welcomed the process of compiling their e-portfolio as a means of evaluating the extent of their expertise, identifying shortfalls and locating resources, the application of the e-portfolio as a tool to plot and manage professional development activities was still underused (McNair and Marshall, 2006).[4]

The portfolio approach has the advantage of enabling tutors and students to move well beyond the mere ticking of boxes to indicate that a particular skill has been achieved to a more grounded experience which embeds ICT into teaching and learning. It also means that as expectations about ICT competence rise, the portfolio can be easily adjusted to cater for a wider range of ICT applications. Until the introduction of C2K, University tutors were uneasy about demanding specific evidence of the use of particular applications in the classroom since some schools might not have been able to offer these opportunities. The common core of hardware and software that C2K provides schools and more recently the teacher training institutions is changing this landscape; it will be far easier to require student teachers to demonstrate effective use of particular software on school placement. While there are obvious advantages in this, such as a greater degree of consistency of ICT work across all students and all training providers, there are also risks, not least in the potential stifling of the creative and imaginative work that has been a feature of ICT work in training institutions in the last five years.

The most difficult policy issue around this is the degree of regulation and control that needs to be exercised externally around the extent and depth of ICT experience required by all student teachers. The Empowering Schools strategy encouraged initial teacher training providers to provide at least part of their training courses online. Some of the providers are already moving in this direction because they see the obvious benefits of such an approach; one recent example was the development of online resources in special education needs that are available not only to all student teachers in Northern Ireland but to all teacher training students on the island of Ireland. These resources were funded through the Standing Conference for Teacher Education, North and South (SCOTENS)[5] which has also contributed to a similar resource in citizenship education. In both cases, these were identified as areas of growing importance where book-based resources would get out of date quickly as new statutory frameworks were brought into effect. Another example can be found in the teacher training course provided for those working in the Further and Higher Education sector.[6]

This example suggests that an agreement between the training providers and those responsible for ensuring that ICT and e-learning targets are met, might be the most effective way forward. At present the quality of teacher training is monitored by all providers through robust internal quality assurance procedures which include detailed annual analysis of student experience and visits by external examiners to ensure that nationally agreed outcomes and benchmarks are being met. Few would dispute the need for ICT to be an integral part of initial teacher education and a career-long e-portfolio, developed by the key stakeholders in Northern Ireland, is the focus for a development project in 2006–7. It should become the means of providing a robust account of how student teachers and all other members of the teaching profession reflect on their learning and teaching, including the key role that ICT plays in that process.

Staff development in initial teacher education

So far in this chapter we have considered the physical resources available through government to support ICT in ITE and the overall inspection framework which gives ITE providers benchmarks to take account of in the work they do. But this would all count for very little if there was insufficient capacity among higher education teacher tutors to research the use of ICT in their own practice and offer student teachers a model of what ICT could provide in terms of teaching and learning.

In this section of the chapter we reflect on the key factors that have made it possible for the teacher training providers in Northern Ireland to work both independently and collaboratively to address staff development in ICT.

In one institution, there has been a long record of innovative use of ICT going back to the late 1970s; at first, this was confined to individuals who followed promising areas of investigation into microcomputers in schools, got involved in national ICT initiatives and began exploring the application of ICT for communication between schools within Northern Ireland and outside.

From 1992, further projects supported by the Department of Education in Northern Ireland were designed to encourage the five different ITE institutions to work together. These included the use of video-conferencing between the training providers and schools and assistance with cross-border educational ICT links through a programme called 'This Island we Live on' which later evolved into the Dissolving Boundaries Project, discussed in Chapter 6. One particularly interesting feature of this programme was its link to the InTENT project which was aimed at the development of evaluative capacity in ICT. Through this and a joint MSc programme in e-learning with Duquesne University in the USA from 2001 to 2002, research capacity and leadership in ICT was systematically developed. With the advent of C2K, the Department of Education set up an e-Learning Partnership[7] which has provided both seed-corn and expertise to continue the development of e-learning across Northern Ireland. Some of these innovative developments are reviewed in Chapter 3, including a significant and on-going initiative in the use of e-portfolios which will be introduced into initial teacher education.

The external support for ICT projects encouraged institutions to initiate their own developments such as the introduction in 2002 of wireless technology into several of the teaching rooms in one institution to ensure that laptops could be more easily integrated into teaching and learning (Austin, 2003; Abbot *et al.*, 2005).[8] This flourishing of innovation occurred because of a culture of risk-taking and the readiness of the Department of Education to invest in leading-edge ICT initiatives at the right time. The cumulative effect of this has been to encourage a culture of enterprise in ICT that gradually extended beyond pools of expertise to a wider penetration of all staff. Staff development was primarily built around colleagues' demonstration of what they were doing, links to networks well beyond Northern Ireland and the evaluation and publication of their work. While there have always been 'leaders' in this enterprise, a collegial relationship between tutors has been critical to the overall development of ICT skills and ambitions. Crucially, ICT is no longer taught by a 'subject' expert; it is seen as the responsibility of all tutors to find ways to make the most appropriate use of ICT in their own interaction with students.

Impact on the students

Taken together, what evidence is there that this is making any difference to the student experience? And what is this effect? Is it transforming the way they teach and learn? Sime and Priestly (2005)[9] identify a body of research which suggests that there are five key factors in student teachers' effective use of ICT. These are:

- Opportunities to use ICT for their own learning in the university part of their training and to practise it in teaching;
- Modelling of ICT by the university tutors and teachers in their placement schools;
- The existence of a community to offer support and learning;
- Making ICT a compulsory element within the course;
- The provision of ideas and practical activities relevant to the subject/topic areas to be taught.

While this research draws on English perceptions and experience of ICT in teacher education, we believe it offers a useful template to consider the effect of

C2K provision on a cohort of student teachers in Northern Ireland. Data to explore these questions are taken from the 2005 progress report on the Empowering Schools strategy where it was reported that there had been evidence of 'enhanced curriculum and learning experiences for student teachers to prepare them to be more e-confident'.[10] More detailed evidence is drawn from a comprehensive survey of the 67 students who completed the Postgraduate Certificate of Education (PGCE) primary course at the University of Ulster in 2005 and who responded to questions about their experience of ICT both before they joined the course, while they were training in the university and while they were in school on teaching practice. This data was collected at the end of the course in June 2005.[11]

The PGCE students did three periods of teaching practice during their one year course, the first in the Foundation stage of school with children aged 3–5, then a second practice in the same school with those children aged 6–8 (Key Stage 1) and finally a third practice in a different school with children aged 8–11 (Key Stage 2). The student group was drawn from both main denominational groups in Northern Ireland, was predominantly female and their school experience took place in schools randomly distributed across Northern Ireland in all five Education and Library Boards. One set of questions in the survey sought to explore the students' prior experience of ICT; 52 per cent had little or no experience of using computers while they were themselves at school, a proportion that would be a matter for concern given the investment in technology in schools, were it not for the fact that, of this group, half were over 30 years of age. When these students then went to University for their undergraduate courses in a variety of different subjects, their experience of computers increased significantly. Only 13 per cent had had 'little or no experience' while by far the largest group, 43 per cent, said their experience was 'extensive'. Interestingly, when asked whether they had used ICT in any work situations before they started their PGCE course, 55 per cent said they had little or no experience.
In summary form, when asked to rate their ICT experience at the start of the PGCE course, 7 per cent said it was 'extensive', 30 per cent had 'much' experience, 46 per cent 'a fair amount' and 16 per cent 'little.' The survey also sought to explore what type of ICT applications the students had become familiar with; the highest scores here related to word processing, email and the Internet but taking usage to include both 'frequent' and 'sometimes' it became clear that this group of students also had some familiarity with CD-ROMS, games, databases, graphics, desk top publishing, statistical analysis and spreadsheets. The applications with the lowest figures of usage were web design, programming and educational software. Overall, compared with previous cohorts of similar students on this programme, the 2005 group's prior knowledge and experience of ICT was both deeper and broader.

Student teacher use of ICT during their training

During their PGCE course, students spend 19 weeks in the University and 19 weeks in school; each of the three teaching placements is preceded by a period of time in the university when students are given an opportunity to prepare for the practice and this includes blocks of time when students are introduced to ICT to develop their personal skills and, for the first time in 2004–5, to become familiar with the C2K software they will encounter in schools. Approximately 5 per cent of the time spent in the university is devoted exclusively to ICT skills training; all other ICT work is part of broader professional activity, such as lesson planning, designing learning resources or assessing work.

Students were asked a series of questions about their experience of ICT during their PGCE course, both within the University and in their placement schools; analysis of this data enables us to draw a number of conclusions.

First, the students asserted that their overall confidence and competence in a range of ICT applications, including the use of C2K software had significantly improved by the end of the year. Compared with only 37 per cent who thought their ICT experience at the start of the course was 'extensive' or 'much', this figure had increased to 89 per cent by the end of the year. In terms of their personal familiarity with a range of applications, there were again striking improvements; while word-processing, use of the Internet and email remained the three top applications, responses showed growing zones of comfort with spreadsheets, graphics, desk-top publishing and a variety of educational software titles. We suggest one factor in explaining this improvement is the quality of teaching on the PGCE course but a second is access to hardware whether in the University or at home; data from the survey showed that 92 per cent had their own personal computers. Furthermore, these students also had access to laptops for periods of time during their PGCE year.

The second broad conclusion concerns the students' frequency of use of ICT during their 3 periods of teaching practice; in their first practice, carried out over 4 weeks in October working with the youngest children, aged 3–5, relatively little use was made of ICT for teaching and learning; the highest number, 46 per cent said they used ICT 'sometimes' but 49 per cent said they did so 'rarely or never'. Two reasons can be advanced to explain this; the first is that this practice occurs at a very early stage of the training year when students are more preoccupied with issues to do with lesson planning and classroom management. A minority were also short of confidence in the use of ICT at this stage. The second is that students perceived that only 50 per cent of the teachers they were working with gave computers a high priority, a view which is also supported by evidence from the ETI inspection report of 2006. By the time the students did their second practice in December 2004 and January 2005 with older children aged 7–8 in the same school, usage of

ICT had increased significantly. The percentage of the students who were using ICT 'frequently' was 51 per cent, while 36 per cent did so 'sometimes'. Amongst the frequent users a third had access to a computer suite but all had at least one PC in the classroom. Furthermore, students reported that their teachers were slightly more likely to use computers and this appears to be linked to changes in how computers are used. Whereas computers are made use of at Foundation stage for games and in many cases as a 'reward' for pupils who complete work well, teachers with 7–8 year olds are more likely to want to use computers on a more systematic basis for the whole class. The students themselves commented that in their own usage of ICT in the three different school placements, they had only used them for 16 per cent of the time with the whole class at Foundation stage, compared to 27 per cent at Key Stage 1 and 41 per cent at Key Stage 2 with the older children. Sime and Priestly (2005)[9] indicate that using ICT with a whole class requires a significant change of practice, moving rooms and negotiating access to a computer suite. Our evidence indicates that there is a very important variable here. A significant number of schools have installed interactive whiteboards and this allows some teachers to use ICT for whole-class teaching without changing rooms.

So why did far more students make greater use of ICT on their second practice compared to the first? We believe there are two key factors here; the first was the growing confidence of the students themselves and the second was more intensive use of ICT in the University prior to this second practice.

Towards the end of the year in May 2005, students undertook a final practice with children 8–11 in a different school and were required to carry out a curriculum project which included the use of ICT. In this practice 92 per cent of students reported using ICT regularly. This is an important finding, not least because this took place in schools where, according to the students, only 71 per cent of teachers used ICT regularly. Some teachers (22 per cent) were reported as rarely or never using ICT. In other words, relating to the five key conditions that Sime and Priestly referred to above, our study shows that these students certainly had extensive opportunities to use ICT for their own learning and, over the year, had increasing opportunities for its use in classrooms. However, we need to add a very significant caveat; when students were asked about the factors which impeded their implementation of ICT in schools, the single biggest restricting factor was 'a lack of hardware' and this was true for all three teaching practices. It needs to be stressed that this finding relates to a context in which all primary schools in this survey had already received their allocation of hardware from C2K. What this suggests is that the early expectations of what C2K could provide are being outstripped by the ambitions of trainee teachers who have seen what they can deliver through ICT. It should be noted that one of the central features of the C2K provision is the 'refreshment' of the hardware; this is due to take place in 2007–8 for the primary school sector and will provide hardware with a much higher specification, considerably more portability and improved software provision which will maintain the overall ratio of computers to learners, without necessarily improving it.

Modelling of ICT in placement schools

How important was modelling of ICT use by tutors at university and at school? This is a question which has elicited different views; on the one hand, Simpson *et al.* (1998)[12] were critical of lecturers who expressed positive attitudes towards the use of ICT but demonstrated them only in automating already well-established practices such as the production of handouts. In that study, lecturers did not integrate software and other strategies often and therefore did not model the use of technology for students. As we have seen, Sime and Priestly (2005) believe that effective modelling by tutors is vital but Taylor (2004)[13] claims that modelling by university tutors produces unrealistic expectations of what is possible in schools compared to modelling by teachers in situ whose practice does have a great effect on student expectations. In our study, we have data which does not entirely fit the existing body of evidence. When the students were asked to rate the value of the ICT training they had received in the University, 89 per cent were positive about it in terms of developing confidence and expertise in managing ICT in the classroom, with even higher figures for its role in developing competence in handling software (particularly the C2K software) and hardware.

One other point of significance in terms of modelling is that the use by tutors of an interactive whiteboard provided a model for the use of ICT teaching which was based around whole-class instruction and demonstration. In other words, it might be seen as a model which was reinforcing conventional styles of teaching where instruction was enriched by access to Internet resources and attractive software. A model of this kind is sharply different to one which is based on student use of portable or hand-held devices.

In terms of effective modelling of ICT by teachers, some inferential data can be drawn from a question which asked students about the factors which impeded their implementation of ICT in the classroom. The factor that was ranked either third of fourth in importance in each of the three practices as a barrier to good use of ICT was a perceived 'lack of encouragement from the teacher'. In terms of overall importance, this diminished over time across the three practices and suggests that as students become more confident in their ICT-related work, they become less reliant on teacher views. However, the data does show a clear relationship between student teacher use of ICT and teacher use of ICT; the more student-teachers observe teachers using ICT, the more likely they are to replicate that practice. Interestingly, our data suggest that teacher use of ICT with older children is more likely to be based on whole-class teaching and the use of an interactive whiteboard than a model based on pupils learning at their own work stations. This is driven both by a lack of workstations and possibly by a preference among teachers for whole class tuition, seen as more manageable and less disruptive to the life of the school. We return to this issue in Chapter 9 in the context of what is required for leadership in transforming schools.

Given that initial teacher training in Northern Ireland is based on a partnership model of good cooperation between Higher Education and schools, this finding underlines the need for continued dialogue about the best ways to improve the sharing of good practice. Crucially, in the context of whether ICT is supporting existing models of learning or helping to transform models of learning, there is a need to examine the learning implications of the use of interactive whiteboards compared to other models of ICT use which focus more strongly on pupil use of hardware.

While lack of confidence by the students was cited as the second most important factor on the first practice, in both the second and third practices it was 'an overcrowded curriculum' that was cited as the second biggest obstacle. In percentage terms it was considered to be hugely more important than any of the other factors. Two observations may be apposite here; the first is that it is generally believed that preparation in primary schools for the selection exam at the age of 11 has had the effect of distorting the curriculum for pupils aged 8–11 in the sense that teachers increasingly have to focus on those aspects of teaching and learning that relate directly to the language, numeracy and science elements of the examination. A recent decision to end the transfer test in 2008 and replace it with a pupil profile may alleviate this difficulty. Equally, the recommendations by the Curriculum Council for Examinations and Assessment (CCEA) that the curriculum should become more skills based and less content driven may open new opportunities for teachers and student teachers to make greater and more effective use of ICT. A word of caution, however; 88 per cent of the students in the survey did their final practice with classes that were not directly involved in preparation for the transfer test. Although we have noted how student teacher use of ICT had increased significantly in this practice, only 55 per cent of teachers in these classes were believed to accord ICT a priority. Further research is needed on the extent to which student teachers can be agents of change in terms of ICT; there is considerable anecdotal evidence that this is the case but little is currently known about the long term influence this has on the schools where enterprising student teachers introduced innovative use of ICT in the classroom.

A second comment arising from this data is that student teachers, possibly reflecting the views of teachers in their practice schools still see ICT as an 'add-on' to the curriculum rather than a means of delivering the curriculum. This is a good illustration of the point that deep and abiding change requires action at all points of the system; student teachers are more likely to observe good models of ICT practice when they see continued professional development in action from the principal and all the staff in the school. In turn, their own ideas and innovation will find a readier acceptance.

The existence of a community to offer support

The importance of having an online community of support for student teachers has been emerging since the mid-1990s and reported on at length by, amongst others, Clarke (2002) and Lambe and Clarke (2003).[14] After a series of pilot projects, all students on the PGCE primary programme are now registered in an online environment and required to use this to take part in regular online discussions with peers and tutors. This is seen by tutors as especially important when students are on teaching practice since it allows them to locate their own school experience in the broader context of what happens in other schools and to feel less isolated from their fellow students. The process of contributing to structured discussions both within the university and on school placement is also believed by tutors to promote critical reflection on practice. In 2004–5 students used the Blackboard virtual learning environment (VLE) for these discussions and to access course materials. Given that the VLE is designed to encourage cooperation and sharing of classroom based experience, it should be noted that while participation is not required in the course regulations or in the assessment of the course, in practice, it is expected and there are no instances reported in this study of students who failed to contribute. Students were split into equal groups of 17 or 18 and each had a tutor to act as the moderator for their discussions.

Students were asked a series of questions about the use of Blackboard at the end of their course; for example, in terms of its usefulness for sharing ideas, the highest percentage, 37 per cent described it as 'very useful' with 30 per cent saying it was quite useful and 24 per cent saying it was useful. These positive views by the overwhelming majority still left 10 per cent saying that Blackboard was 'not useful'. Similar figures emerged from a question about the value of Blackboard in sharing and accessing course materials. One of the most important findings from this survey, however, concerned the value of Blackboard for enhancing classroom practice. The figures were as follows: 24 per cent found it 'very useful', 34 per cent 'quite useful' and 20 per cent 'useful'. Almost 4 out of 5 students judged this to have been valuable but 22 per cent did not find this to be the case. Further questions on the frequency of use of the VLE showed that 15 of the students used Blackboard more than once a week, while 44 students used it less than once a week; analysis of their responses showed that in nearly every area, there was a correlation between frequency of use and perceived value. The fact that one in five of the students did not find the VLE an aid to improving classroom practice is a matter of concern that deserves further comment. Some students commented that written reflection on top of what they were already expected to do on teaching practice was seen as an additional burden. We believe that this is not a reflection on the use of online discussions as such, but a more general perception by a minority of student teachers about the intensive nature of their programme.

In response to a different question, 30 per cent of this group did not find Blackboard useful for communicating with tutors and this may be illustrative of a limitation in communication of this type. Tutors are both mentors of students but ultimately assessors in that they play a key role in determining whether students successfully complete the course. We suggest that this can impose some restrictions on the nature of discourse in an online environment for a minority of students. It is an issue which the tutors plan to monitor closely in the future; they recognise that the role they play as moderators in these discussions is critical and requires continued reflection on the optimum ways to maximise student participation.

The discussion areas, based on topics that included literacy and numeracy, classroom management, special education needs, reflection of classroom competencies were all seen by students to be of value with particular support for the topics that were discussed in the final teaching practice. There is some evidence, therefore, that usage of the VLE increased over the course of the year and this reflects a growing familiarity with the VLE, increased confidence generally with ICT and possibly a developing sense of collegiality within the student body. It should be noted that since the course is competence based, students are judged to be either 'competent' or 'not competent'; the absence of marks may be an incentive for students to share ideas and resources freely in this online environment.

In spite of the caveats noted above, when asked about the value of the VLE overall on the PGCE course, 48 per cent described it as 'very useful', 27 per cent as 'quite useful' and 21 per cent as 'useful'. Only 1 per cent said it was 'not useful'. Given that these students had completed the course, filled in the questionnaire anonymously and were not in any sense under any pressure to 'please' their tutors, we believe that this data has strong validity and reliability.

One final point should be made about the operation of this virtual learning environment; teachers in schools who play a day to day role in supporting the students have not been involved in the online discussions. This decision was based on the premise that students needed some 'space' to be able to reflect on their work without it being subject to daily scrutiny by their teaching colleagues. A second factor was that the University was reluctant to add any further to the demands already being made on teaching staff by encouraging them to join in an online forum. Like every other aspect of the course, annual review requires that careful thought is given to existing practice and the need to take account of the views of the teaching profession. We believe that further reflection and discussion on this key issue is timely; it is possible that teacher involvement in such discourse could be seen as a very positive form of professional development and could lead to increased effective use of ICT by both teachers and student teachers.

ICT and perceived value in 'subject' teaching

Sime and Priestly's final point about the necessary conditions for achieving ICT success with student teachers was the provision of ideas and practical activities relevant to the subject. When the PGCE student teachers were asked about the most important areas that should be included in training, the highest percentage was for 'ICT knowledge of what to teach to meet curriculum expectations'. Overall, the third highest request was for more work on 'how to integrate ICT into lessons in subject areas'. We think the reason for this is that the single most difficult aspect of embedding ICT in everyday practice is in the pedagogical thinking that is required to transform learning through ICT. These student teachers have made a good enough start to recognise how much further they have to travel.

Part of this journey involves understanding the relationship between embedded ICT and pupil academic performance; evidence on this is starting to be more widely disseminated and understood. Data published by Becta in England in 2004 showed that 61 per cent of schools with good use of ICT in mathematics reached or exceeded standards in mathematics at Key Stage 2 as against 38 per cent of schools with unsatisfactory use of ICT.[15]

Further evidence from our case study relevant to this question comes from interview data with the tutors themselves. One tutor was trying to find a way to help his secondary level pupils learn poetry, a topic which he said often presented problems to many non-academic pupils. His solution was to ask the pupils to record their reading of a poem while combining this reading with the words of the poem presented on PowerPoint and enriched by a variety of images that the students felt were appropriate to the meaning of the poem. The students had to decide at what point in the poem the image and words projected should change. In other words, this use of ICT was not only related to a deep understanding of the meaning of the text but was also a form of creative development of the poem. The application of this approach to poetry on teaching practice was not without its difficulties; the tutor commented:

> ... this involves using a data-projector if you're going to use the PowerPoint display. Many of the students will say to me things like 'Oh well there is no data-projector in our school' or they'll say they'll mention it to the Head of Department or the teacher and they'll say 'Oh yeah, but it's gold-dust you will really have to put your name down several weeks in advance for that!' So they really do sometimes get a bit discouraged at the number of doors they will have to knock on in order to get their hands on the equipment. Plus of course I suppose to be fair these students are trying to survive

and they're fearful in some cases that if they go into anything too sophisticated, anything that breaks, not only in terms of getting the equipment but anything that breaks the kind of pattern of old traditional teaching that that might be frowned on to some extent, maybe by some members of staff but that the kids might find it quite disruptive and they might, having their chains shed so to speak, they might go wild. So while they do use it I think they do have some concerns both in terms of provision of resources from the school and also in terms of how the youngsters react. Having said that I do know that some of them used that very strategy in a more modified form and they're finding it very very helpful.[16]

The tutor went on to comment on the potential of this work for use with special needs children and expressed concerns that this type of wider digital literacy had not yet been fully embraced in schools, particularly those that took the traditional view that literacy was purely related to books and reading rather than a re-definition which incorporated visual and multi-media literacy.

Another, commenting on work done by PGCE primary students said that much of the work was enhancing current practice rather than making any paradigm shift that could be termed transformative. A key explanation she believed was that there was a shortage of good examples of what 'transformed learning through ICT' might look like in practice. In our view, the sharing of best practice online should be a major priority.

Before we conclude this chapter on the changes that have taken place in ITE, we need to consider the experience of teachers in the early phase of their teaching career. What happens when they take up their first posts in schools in Northern Ireland and seek to implement their ICT knowledge as full time teachers? Evidence for this comes in part from a report by the Education and Training Inspectorate (ETI) in 2005 on the 'Induction and Early Professional Development of Beginning Teachers'.

The beginning teacher

Beginning teachers are required to demonstrate continued professional development in their first year of teaching, their induction year. They are supported in this by tutors in school and the advisory staff from the Education and Library Boards; by the end of their first year they are required to develop a portfolio of work which shows evidence of critical reflection of work done in the classroom. The ETI report (2005)[17] shows that during 2002–4, when a wide-scale survey was carried out, no use was made of computer conferencing in this process. Beginning teachers reported difficulties in logging onto the website which had been extensively used by many of them during their initial teacher education programmes. It is important to note that this survey was carried out while C2K was being implemented in schools, a process that was not complete until 2004 and which involved a significant amount of disruption.

Interview data carried out in June 2005 with a small sample of teachers who had completed their initial training in 2001 suggests that there were two major reasons why their positive experiences of using ICT on the PGCE year were not followed through into their early years of employment. The first was that access to hardware between 2001 and 2003 was very difficult especially for those teaching subjects that were not regarded as 'core' (English, maths and science). Second, their teacher-tutors and advisors often had no direct experience of online conferencing.

On completion of their induction year, beginning teachers are required to register for Early Professional Development, a two year process in which their employing school takes the lead. Teachers are supported by mentors and expected to present evidence of their continuing professional development by undertaking two pieces of classroom-based action research. According to the ETI report, the website designed to support EPD was only used by beginning teachers to download the format for their two pieces of required work, the Professional Development Activities (PDAs). The ETI report noted that although the quality of these PDAs was often good, very little use was made of ICT except for word processing. The ETI report also commented that beginning teachers too often resented having to carry out additional professional activities at a time when they were grappling with many new professional demands.

One final comment is apposite at this point; the PGCE students who had just completed their training in June 2005 were asked whether they felt that their experience of ICT had prepared them for their first teaching post. A percentage (21) felt strongly that this was the case, 67 per cent agreed with the statement, 10 per cent were unsure and only 1 per cent disagreed. The same cohort of students was asked what form they would wish induction and early professional development to take; 84 per cent indicated that they wanted a combination of school-based support, linked to a blended model of face to face and online facilities.

Global messages

So what are the key messages that can be drawn from this data in the wider context of preparing student teachers for an e-schooling agenda? We believe that there are five which deserve special mention.

- The first is that the introduction of C2K into Initial teacher Education has had a significant effect on the frequency and use of ICT in teaching and learning. The roll-out of hardware and software to the ITE providers was a critical investment in the long term sustainability of this enterprise.

- Second, it needs to be understood that what has been provided to support ICT through C2K is not a panacea which will transform learning immediately. We need to think of this as a continuum, a stage on a journey, where the evidence suggests that at the moment, ICT is being widely used to enhance learning.

- Third, to move further along the continuum, towards ICT transforming learning, there needs to be substantial professional discourse on what transformed learning looks like and how this can be best supported across the lifetime of a teacher. The development of e-portfolios and a strengthening of online learning to improve classroom practice will need to feature strongly in this.

- Fourth, decisions about the deployment of hardware in schools and ITE are vital; in our view, a focus on interactive whiteboards at the expense of portable devices for children or student teachers would be a retrograde step. In this context the introduction of wireless capability in the refresh of the managed service will be of considerable benefit to the mobility of learning.

- Finally, building on the progress that has been measured from 1999 until 2007, and underwritten by a common competence framework for all teacher training providers, we believe that much more needs to be done to accelerate the realisation of the full potential of the technology. Securing both sustainability and alignment, two critical conditions for e-schooling, demands nothing less.

An e-curriculum for an e-school?

Transformative ICT?

What would the curriculum of an e-school look like? The answer lies somewhere between embedding ICT to serve today's curriculum, thereby enhancing today's classroom, and e-learning approaches which transform curriculum and practice tomorrow. This chapter looks critically at the evidence in Northern Ireland of the necessary conditions for change.

The Chief Inspector's report for 2002–4[1] recorded: the impact of the major investments in ICT since 1997 on the 'the significant improvement in ICT resources through the C2K initiative' in classrooms; the clear evidence that ICT is highly motivating in encouraging learners and the increasing evidence of inventive and effective usage of ICT by teachers. Nevertheless there was still evidence in primary schools of 'insufficient integration of ICT into the wider curriculum to promote greater breadth, challenge and coherence in the children's experiences', while in secondary schools, despite an 'increased recognition of the potential of ICT to improve teaching and learning' there was 'generally inappropriate teaching in timetabled ICT classes at KS3 [pupils aged 12–14] and the need for the further embedding of ICT across the curriculum'. Inspection evidence points to the greatest deficit being in the creative uses of ICT for learning.

In this chapter, we start by recalling the radical thinking from 1989 of the impact that ICT might have on education, and examine why it took 15 years before hints of enhancement promising transformation emerged. The subsequent chapters look more closely at three of the more significant dimensions for an e-school: connected learning for citizenship; inclusive learning for special education and creativity and enterprise education.

Cross-curricular information technology

At the time of the critical Economic Council report on the IT skills gap (discussed in Chapter 2) and in parallel with the new National Curriculum for England and Wales, a ministerial working party[2] produced a masterly and far-sighted report defining how Information Technology (then called) would be represented as a 'cross-curricular theme'.

The report tackled capability, not by recommending an upswing of skills courses, but by showing how the use of IT as a set of teaching tools and skills could be embedded in every subject in the school curriculum. The embedding of IT, it was argued, would develop the skills of pupils, set in the context of real and appropriate uses. These real uses in the classroom would simultaneously enable subject teachers to achieve teaching objectives supported by the use of computer packages and tools. The working party approached the development of IT skills in an educationally holistic way, securing the notion of ICT skills as integral to the skills needed for life, work and lifelong learning in an information-based society. They argued the case for embedding ICT based on an understanding of its relationships to the key cross-curricular processes (communicating, creating, researching, investigating, calculating, experimenting and testing, presenting, and so on) which are central to the curriculum, common both to all subjects and to constructivist approaches to teaching and learning.

For the first time the notion of developing IT capability was linked to the possibility of raising standards in subject achievements, while also improving the relevancy of schooling, motivating learners and transforming their classroom experience.

The report illustrated in a pedagogically cogent way what an e-curriculum could look like with IT fully embedded. Although well ahead of its time, its reflections can be seen clearly in the specification for the role of ICT in the revised curriculum 15 years later.[3] The report went on to argue that, even though IT was statutorily one of only six educational themes, it was fundamentally different from the other five (Health Education, Economic Awareness, Education for Mutual Understanding, Cultural Heritage and Careers Education) and that, as a capability it could also help learners achieve the other thematic objectives. As one commentator quipped, the report could be summed up in one sentence: 'Study the curriculum – with the help of a computer.'

In effect, the report did not make the radical difference to the subject specifications for the new subject programmes in Northern Ireland which it might have done. Only a few of the specialists working on the subject specifications had classroom experience of the 'process embedded' concept of IT and, without that knowledge and insight, working parties often lacked the confidence, missing out on a range of opportunities to lever change. Insufficient embedding of IT as educational theme in statutory curriculum and assessment arrangements when the national curriculum was introduced took a further ten years to overcome. A review of classroom experience in the early in the 1990s summed up the challenge under the heading *Coherence or Fragmentation*?

> Whether the implementation of the cross-curricular theme will result in a coherent or in a fragmented experience for pupils will depend upon success with a number of critical factors. These include the establishment of simple and effective procedures for overseeing the scattered elements of IT experience, together with a means of tackling gaps that might occur and for combining the pieces of recorded evidence of pupils' attainments in IT into useful monitoring reports to aid curriculum planning and into a summative report at the age of 16, and perhaps earlier.[4]

Responding to the challenge, some leading-edge teachers worked with far-sighted officers in the (then named) Northern Ireland Curriculum and Assessment Council and developed a popular, voluntary ICT Accreditation scheme for learners at the age of 14 (the end of Key Stage 3). In response to demand from schools, the Council followed up with a similarly popular primary scheme for 11-year-olds (end of Key Stage 2).[5]

The use of ICT is embedded in graded tasks, set in the context of a topic from a subject, at an appropriate level for the age and ability of the learner. Successful completion of a range of these ICT tasks, in a variety of subjects, leads to accreditation. While the tasks could be criticised as 'ready-meals', the scheme boosted tentative teachers, some of whom go on to create, and have accredited, additional tasks. Evidence from moderators and inspection is that the scheme makes a significant contribution to the confidence and competence of teachers, who are not generally ICT experts, and can ensure a coherent experience for the learner of the kind originally anticipated.

Recent examiners' reports[6] indicate that the competence levels reached at the end of Key Stage 2 are rising year on year to such an extent that some secondary schools are adding little value to the grades already achieved at age 11. For a voluntary scheme the very high level of uptake is remarkable.

While much innovation was to be found in embedding ICT into the curriculum, high-stakes qualifications in computing and IT at GCSE and A Level remained popular for learners interested in a specialist career in IT. GCSE Computer Studies was at one time the fifth most popular GCSE examination. However, high-stakes examinations in the specialist subject and the ICT accreditation aside, the assessment of embedded ICT as an integral part of assessment of subject knowledge and skills was not generally fit for purpose. It is one thing to learn how to teach with IT as method and tool, but subject teachers could be forgiven for seeing little purpose if subject assessment fails to measure the specific ICT-based subject knowledge, skills and understanding being developed. It takes a particularly stubborn kind of teacher to teach something for which he or she knows their pupils will not be given adequate credit.

Given a combination of educational obstacles on the one hand, and the lack of an adequate supply of technology provision, as the NI Economic Research Council report quoted in Chapter 2 makes clear, it was no surprise that a major shift in approach took place. This occurred when the chairman of the Minister's cross-curricular IT report working group and its principal architect, Tom McMullan, became director of the CLASS project and then the director of procurement for C2K from which position he could begin to address these frustrations.

ICT, the revised curriculum and the e-school

We go forward ten years to 1998 to a time when, province-wide, two major curriculum and structural reform policy initiatives were being initiated. After a five-year moratorium on change – a period of stability to give teachers a chance to embed new national curriculum practices – the debate was reopened and the Council for Curriculum, Examinations and Assessment undertook a wide debate and curriculum review:[7]

> CCEA was responding to the challenge of the global economy; technological change; the information explosion; changing patterns of work; the need for skills, adaptability, flexibility and creativity.[8]

After five years of spiralling debate (and three major consultations later) government agreed a far-reaching set of curriculum changes which aimed to clarify educational aims and values for the twenty-first century, with a focus on skills development 'for life and work'. These changes included: more flexibility for schools to decide what is best for their pupils; more emphasis on developing children's thinking skills, and their ability to solve problems and handle information; making personal social and health education a legal requirement; adding education about citizenship and employability to the curriculum; making sure that the connections between what is taught in different subjects are clearly visible where previously they have often been hidden; moving from assessment at intervals to assessment on an ongoing basis which updates a pupil assessment profile which assists the learning process. The implementation process should be completed by 2010.

The revised curriculum is competence and values-based, with learning processes and skills development at its core. It aims to improve relevance and enjoyment for young people by providing better balance, more coherence, greatly diversified provision and more choice across the curriculum offer. There is an intention to strengthen the formative role of assessment, without abandoning its summative role and, in the process, centrally embedding ICT to create a curriculum fit for an e-school.

The statutory requirements are being reduced significantly and some statutory testing is being removed in order to give teachers more freedom to teach their pupils in a way which suits the individual pupils – in short, to give scope for personalization. Schools will report to parents on the development of a range of competencies and skills through a new pupil profile. Literacy and numeracy will be at the heart as would be expected, but so will ICT, closely allied with personal competences such as critical and creative thinking, the ability to work in a team, and to be more individually self-reliant in learning.[9]

You will see some radical changes coming through in the KS3 [Key Stage 3 – for 11 to 14 year olds] review (as has been the case already for primary) – the removal of the Key Stage 3 tests of the 'big 3' (English, Maths and Science) – a much greater emphasis on assessment for learning, a big push for the development of personal capabilities (learning skills, personal and inter personal skills) and thinking skills (investigation, problem-solving and decision-making with a big emphasis on ICT as a tool for skill development). How this will all work out in practice is the challenge – shifting teachers from the emphasis on content which the current curriculum has promoted – to an emphasis on process.[10]

A reviewer of the plans for the revised curriculum commented:

The Northern Ireland curriculum framework is an intelligent compromise ... Like the English curriculum, the proposed Northern Ireland one begins with a statement of aims and objectives. But it goes further than England in two crucial respects...the traditional subjects, taken one by one, are still key building blocks in the whole structure. Art and design, music, English, Irish, geography, history, modern languages, mathematics, science, technology and design and physical education are each separable 'strands' within 'general learning areas' and have their own objectives and learning outcomes. At the same time – and here the 'idealism' comes back into play, these objectives and outcomes are not defined, as they traditionally are, by intra-subject requirements. They derive from the overall aims – and are, moreover, statutory.[11]

Complementing curriculum review, and in the context of many types of schools found in Northern Ireland as described in Chapter 1, is an even more fundamental reorganisation of secondary schooling – the intended move away from the use of academic selection tests at the age of 11 and the introduction of a curriculum entitlement, at the age of 14, where every secondary learner must have access to a choice of 24 courses, at least one-third vocational provision, as a contribution to economic regeneration, and one-third general (or academic). At the age of 16, the entitlement menu grows to 27 courses.

Although among the four educational systems in the UK, learners in NI schools fare well in national examinations, there is an acknowledgement of the fact that education fails a significant if relatively small percentage of pupils – ones who leave school without qualifications and ill-equipped vocationally.[12]

The schools which can deliver a full entitlement curriculum on their own are a minority, so the need to partner with neighbourhood schools and colleges for further education is central to broadening curriculum choice. Working together, schools will share their expertise for the benefit of all the pupils enrolled in the schools in a partnership. Added to this are the first Specialist schools in Northern Ireland which have been designated with specialisms, for instance in the performing arts, mathematics, languages, science, music or technology. Together with greater community use of schools and more opportunity for the inclusion of learners with special educational needs, school reform brings a range of practical implications for structure and organisation.

Several things are clear – technology is central to delivering crucial aspects of policy; therefore much rests on the ability of technology to be sustainable and mission-critical and on the capability of teachers to use reliable technology to deliver. It was with the aim of improving this state of affairs and addressing the need for realignment, that the Empowering Schools strategy was produced.

Empowering schools to change their curriculum

The Empowering Schools strategy[13] set out where and how government sees technology enabling learning. It delineates the dimensions of a broader curriculum, which offers greater diversity and improved choice of courses which can be adapted flexibly to meet the developing needs of young people. It holds to a vision in which technology-enabled curriculum change is matched with change in assessment – especially assessment for learning – which tracks and records progress, providing pupils, teachers and parents with detailed diagnosis of need and enabling learners to be given personalised support. And, because much more information about the continuous progress of young people is readily available in an easily manipulated form, it is a curriculum which can be delivered by self-improving schools, where technology eases administrative burdens and provides the management information to support leadership decisions intended to raise standards.

The strategy goes on to spell out the dimensions of curriculum provision most ripe for change.

> We believe that where technology is integrated effectively into the heart of education, it should:
>
> - enhance and individualise the learner's educational experience, helping them to enjoy learning, improve their performance and raise standards;
> - improve the learner's standards in literacy, numeracy and other areas of study;

- elevate the learner's creativity, developing their digital and visual literacies;
- personalise learning and teaching and improve arrangements for assessment, record-keeping and reporting;
- provide the learner with an appropriate blend of non-technological and online methods of teaching, connecting them to other learners through online networks;
- help the learner develop the skills needed to be economically active in the global knowledge economy;
- blur the boundary between learning in and out of school, extending the partnership between the school, the home and the community.

We will come later to consider how the challenge of making *tomorrow's classroom* is being addressed and what progress has been made so far, but, before we do, we need to ask what sort of job is being made of enhancing today's.

Enhancing today's classroom

The need to identify the best practice of leading-edge practitioners and support its spread is a major concern. The Sharing Excellent Practice in ICT scheme was set up in 2002 to recognise, reward and promote the best practice across the whole life and work of the school and it identified 38 award winners over a period of three years.[14] This section draws on these examples together with a series of local school portraits of successful embedding, produced by inspectorates working collaboratively across Europe,[15] to examine what might make an e-school.

We consider a relatively modern grammar school in Belfast; this is a building with two boomerang-shaped wings of study and work-areas and traditional classrooms built around a three-story, glass-roofed atrium, reminiscent of a shopping mall containing trees and plants. The centre functions like a village square as a venue for assemblies, group meetings and dining. Pupils gather in small groups sitting on its spotlessly clean, heated floor, chatting, using wireless laptops and working. Flanked on one side by a networked library, on the other by the catering service. The atrium is criss-crossed at first floor level by walkways joining up classrooms. Every classroom and study area has an interactive whiteboard and the school supplemented its C2K service to reach a ratio of at least one computer for every three learners. The learners are motivated, competent ICT users, able to talk confidently about the influence ICT has on their work. Observers note increased attention spans as the learners focus on the sustained use of interactive whiteboard during class teaching. Doing more than replicate the existing practice the whiteboards have broadened the approaches adopted. Staff collaborate in harvesting the Internet to gather together online resources, including websites and multimedia presentations, digital learning objects for teaching purposes to stimulate the learner through the use of visual imagery, short video clips, animation, colour, graphics and sound. They created a resource which learners access during and outside class teaching. In response, the learners have been seen to take more responsibility for their own learning.

> ... it is more accurate to say that (the interactive whiteboards) have helped teachers become even more innovative in the resources they can bring in front of the pupils, and pupils learn more effectively given the plethora of stimuli that is now before them. In no way have the boards stifled teaching. The software is so flexible that most, if not all, teachers can use them. If anything, they have indeed helped organise the work of the teacher.[15]

Whole class teaching is transformed by the use of personal voting devices by each learner, delivering immediate feedback on progression and visible sight of misunderstandings.

> The teacher used an interactive whiteboard to revise chemical bonding; the technology enabled several views of the concepts of bonding, including static diagrams and animations, all of which maintained the pupils' interest and levels of concentration. Through careful intervention and questioning, the teacher managed to achieve good levels of pupil interaction. The pace of the lesson was lively and challenging for the pupils. The teacher administered a test consisting of past-paper examination questions on the topic just revised. The pupils made excellent use of the [interactive voting] devices, by choosing a correct answer from a range of close alternatives. The pupils enjoyed this method of interaction and assessment and responded enthusiastically to the questions. Through the software and a graphical display on the interactive whiteboard, the teacher was able to gauge immediately the level of understanding of the pupils. As a result he was able to recap a particular concept quickly when a significant number of pupils answered a question incorrectly. The pupils were motivated and challenged throughout the lesson.[15]

ICT supports learning autonomy

Mutual engagement in learning and different learning styles has evolved, with an emphasis on study skills, throughout the school;

> ... a more collaborative culture for learning and teaching has emerged and this is seen in the growing use of group and paired work. The pupils are now involved in lesson planning activities to a certain degree. The pupils also help each other with the technology, learn from one another and [they] are keen and confident enough to assist the teachers if a problem arises.[15]

The ICT skill levels of the learners are assessed on entry through pupil self-assessment. The information is used to ensure that all are challenged by the classroom activities and learn new skills.

The way in which learners can organise their own personal and collaborative learning has observably extended their knowledge and understanding of complex concepts. For instance, 14-year-olds discussing what they already know about genetics, agree areas to research and undertake refined searches of the Internet and current, high-level scientific journals available online. Marshalling their genetics research findings, they present what they have learnt through multimedia, using appropriately selected images, animations and video clips, posted into the shared online science area on the school's intranet for the teacher to comment on. Refined in light of the feedback from the teacher, reflecting on their own learning, they use the interactive whiteboard to demonstrate their new knowledge to their peers.

Digital technology is used to maximum effect.

… digital still and video cameras record the outcomes of science experiments. In one practical lesson, the teacher used a digital video camera connected to the interactive whiteboard to demonstrate quickly to the whole class the methodology of a normally difficult investigation of photosynthesis. This worked well; the pupils asked a range of questions and all of the groups managed to, and with minimum fuss, complete successfully the experiment.

… to study parasite behaviour as part of an investigation into the effects of pollution on marine cercariae [the class] used digital video capture to record the parasites and using freeze-frame and slow motion software, the pupils analysed the digital recordings and assessed cercarial fitness.

Powerful research technologies accessible through the Internet benefit many subjects. Northern Ireland schools can take robotic remote control of one of two Faulkes telescopes built by British software millionaire, Dill Faulkes, for use by learners.[16]

Ignoring another wet and dreary Belfast afternoon, a class of 15 year olds … were totally absorbed studying the Jovian Giant, Jupiter and the Crab Nebula through their personal control of a multi-million dollar, research-quality telescope, perched on the Haleakala summit of Maui in Hawaii, which they steer around the Pacific night sky Some of the primary and post-primary maths and science projects include tracking near-earth asteroids, imaging galaxies and studying gamma-ray bursts – the most violent explosions in the Universe. According to Robert Hill, Faulkes Coordinator at the Armagh Planetarium, it is planned that schools will join up with their peers across Europe for shared investigations. 'We are encouraging pupil research links to entice our next generation into science, technology and engineering disciplines, using state-of-the-art multi-media resources'.[17]

ICT broadens learning resources

This research-based method of teaching and learning is not only appropriate in the sciences.

Learning is motivated, challenged and broadened by the range of ICT applications used. In language lessons, use of technology enabled all four language skills (talking, listening, reading and writing) to be practised, normally difficult to achieve in a single lesson. A Spanish teacher alternately displays, highlights and hides important aspects of written language on the screen and the learners enjoy working out the correct answers. In Irish, there is emphasis on grammar, with model phrases presented on the screen, and the pupils engaged in oral exercises which strengthen their grasp of key points. A language teacher will switch between live feeds from presentations and tests on his own laptop, teaching resources stored on the school intranet, to the Internet itself and to live satellite television links from European news channels as an authentic source of language.

In English learners presented their research-based character analyses from their reading of the text of *A Streetcar Named Desire* by Tennessee Williams. Multimedia is skilfully used to demonstrate their insights, by taking a design approach to a choice of digital graphics as metaphors for the behaviours of the main characters in the play. In response, the teacher demonstrated her ability to raise the thinking of the learners to an even higher level – as well as her effective lesson research and preparation – by presenting a short fragment of a movie of the play, found on the Internet. They analysed the director's intentions, testing their earlier findings against it. Creative use of digital technology offers ways of learning and raises standards in ways which are impossible otherwise.

ICT supports whole-school improvement

Across the city, in a non-selective girls' school of over 1,000 pupils, with a very different enrolment, ICT is seen as a part of whole school improvement and is embedded strongly into the learning and teaching activities of teachers across almost all departments, including autonomous use of ICT by learners reinforcing everything that they do in, for example, art, geography, English, mathematics, physical education, Young Enterprise and science and technology. With high motivation, lively participation, confidence and self-esteem the learners, including those with special educational needs, understand when and how ICT can be used.

> ... in English, [the pupils] worked well in groups to investigate various aspects of animal welfare. They retrieved relevant information from a range of sources, including e-mail contacts with appropriate interest groups. The pupils created effective and thought-provoking posters, leaflets and multimedia presentations on different aspects

of the topic. They were able to discuss confidently well-informed opinions on the range of issues concerning animal welfare.

In a year 11 [15 year-olds] geography lesson on meteorology ... the lesson started with a focus on recently taken satellite images of the United Kingdom and Europe. These were discussed at length and the pupils used the [interactive] whiteboard to highlight different weather fronts and predicted the likely impact of these fronts. The pupils then worked in small groups to create a weather forecast for a region of the United Kingdom for the day specified in the satellite image. They produced this quickly and each group presented a forecast making use of a synoptic chart on the interactive whiteboard. The teacher completed the lesson by playing a video of the actual weather forecast for that day and the pupils compared their predictions with the actual report.

In practical classes, digital video recordings and animations are evaluated, analysed and routines discussed with the teacher and other pupils to improve individual and group technique, sequence and performance: in physical education for the athletic and aesthetic performance of pupils and teams; in dance for the routine of the aerobics team as they prepare for competition; in swimming lessons to understand swimming theory through video-taped images of breathing techniques and arm movements.

ICT and the impact on standards

These are glimpses of how the revised curriculum is becoming more skills-based and more closely orientated towards employability. Curriculum policy for an e-school can now rely upon the centrality of ICT and plan to exploit it more holistically and thus accumulate the enhancements which, we argue, build towards transformation in our concept of an e-school.

It would be prudent to end on a salutary note: one may wish to see the experience of the third of a million of school-aged learners in Northern Ireland being equally as good. We know from inspection and evaluation evidence that the quality of teaching with ICT and the learning experience are improving, but it takes excellent leadership to inspire and instil the curriculum changes needed to make most effective use of technology as a powerful resource, and we need more systematic evidence about the impact on standards.

Transforming tomorrow's classroom: going online

ICT and a broader curriculum

Going online in the lesson is the first step out of today's classroom and into tomorrow's. We have seen that it may be part of directed investigation on the Internet, or to email other learners with new knowledge half-way round the world. Taking more steps means spending a greater proportion of teaching and learning time online and exercising greater autonomy in the decision to do so.

Earlier we described reorganisation as a major driver to re-engineer schools, but re-invention will not happen without the development of high quality online education provision. The Costello Report[18] on post-primary reorganisation claims that e-learning has the potential to make 'a major contribution to local partnerships of schools, which could make it possible to provide courses for small groups that would not otherwise be viable'. The report calls for further investment in facilities and teacher training 'so that they [the teachers] are comfortable with the issues related to teaching in this way' and a development path with clear targets for e-learning to secure significant gains as soon as possible.

It is recognised that technology can have a significant role to play in broadening choice through the online delivery by distance learning of courses traditionally only delivered face to face to a single class gathered in one room. To reduce the need for learners to travel between school sites during the school day, online technology can support collaboration through the communication tools of text-conferencing, audio and video conferencing and applications-sharing. And schools will need open access computer-resourced study areas for learners who come and go, throughout an extended day. Once online, courses can be accessed from elsewhere not only from home but also from public libraries.

Access beyond the school

The Electronic Libraries for Northern Ireland (ElfNI) programme in 2002 located a common network, with an average of ten computers per branch, in all 123 public and 47 mobile libraries and provided no-cost, fast, secure Internet access, personal email, multimedia storage and retrieval, videoconferencing, colour-printing, photocopying, scanning and access to the complete library catalogue for videos and audio books, as well as books. Customers use their library tickets to log-on from home and in any branch, anywhere and borrow any public library book available in Northern Ireland.

From 2005, ElfNI connected computers in schools with the systems in the public libraries through the C2K data-centre.

It's 2.45 pm on a wet Wednesday afternoon in the Spring term, and Mary logs on to a C2K computer at her school. She needs a specific book on Africa for her (already overdue) Citizenship project and the single copy in the school library is out on loan. A quick search of the catalogue in her local public library locates another copy and, with a quick sigh (which might be relief) she reserves it to borrow on her way home – and, after a moment's further thought, books a one-hour session on one of the library computers for 4 pm. She works for another 40 minutes on her own African work-file until the bell sounds, logs off the network, and is quickly on her way. Arriving at the library, she picks up the book, logs onto the People's Network and, after a few clicks, opens up the very work file she was editing an hour earlier at school.[19]

The online teacher

Online distance provision will allow an expert teacher in one school to work with generalist teachers in other schools to deliver courses to a much broader range of pupils than would be possible without networked learning. And with the greater implicit flexibility, there is more opportunity for discrimination in the roles of the teacher – specifically the development of those who coach and facilitate the learner and mentor the learning, without necessarily being the subject expert who teaches online.

Such an approach requires an enhancement of the competence of teachers to act as online educators, teachers whose competence is defined by their ability to design and develop a course and teach and assess it online. And of course, it implies a high level of basic ICT skill for all the participants.

Much is understood about the role of online courses for adult learners, but very little for learners of compulsory school age. However, through carefully targeted pilot projects, subject to independent evaluation,[20] much progress has been made over four years in understanding what it takes to deliver high quality teaching and high standards of attainment online to school-aged learners[21] with some of that provision becoming mainstream.

Over three years, by the summer of 2005, nearly 5,500 pupils, with more than 225 teachers in 200 schools, had experienced online teaching and learning as part of their curriculum. The range, across age groups from 11- to 17-year-olds, with most focusing on the more mature learners able to regulate their own learning, include: advanced vocational education courses and advanced level courses in geography, mathematics, computing, physics, chemistry and biology and senior courses in ICT. Also included was Citizenship teaching for 14-year-olds and Japanese Studies, European Studies and a range of courses conducted by linking schools from the North and South of Ireland. In the primary school science, literacy and numeracy hosted exciting examples of experimental online teaching. Several of the pilots tested approaches to the online delivery of high-stakes examinations and adaptive assessment for formative purposes. Online innovation is also an important element of professional learning and capacity building for educators as described in Chapter 3.

Much of this innovation takes place in a virtual learning environment (VLE) and a well-designed VLE programme will contain clear information about all aspects of the course: the objectives, content, assignments and expected outcomes.

Designing an online course

All of the above components were present in the first most complete 'online conversion' of a substantial part of a GCSE course taught online in Northern Ireland. The course, comprising two modules from a GCSE specification for ICT, was prepared and taught online by a former chief examiner and author of much of the syllabus, Richard Wallace, supported by several teachers and advisory staff. There were 140 pupils from five schools who undertook a detailed study of online multimedia materials which included digital texts, images, video, animations and links to external websites, covering ten theory units of the course, complete with comprehensive online assessment. The learners engaged in real-time text and video conferencing with the expert teacher, created online assignments, submitted them online, had them marked and annotated, and tracked their learning through their e-portfolio. The course director actively managed their engagement through a control panel of tracking and reporting tools.

Much of the teaching from the experts used interaction by text, by audio or by video, sometimes recorded and streamed, and sometimes live. There were online seminars and chat in limited time hot-seats and discussion areas and email where responses did not need to be in real time, but were maintained with frequency – all of this collectively creating a virtual classroom. The teacher routinely participated in five online synchronous (in real time) text-based group discussions simultaneously – with five text windows open on his screen at the same time – each discussion running for 30–40 minutes. He described the experience as being much harder than being a teacher in a classroom with five face to face group discussions running simultaneously.

As well as assignments, the course contains assessment management which provided the learner with scaffolding to correct wrong answers, and with rapid feedback on tests. A good assessment engine has the facility to allow the tutors to build up pools of questions, sort and display all the answers for essay-type questions to aid their marking and contains a grade-book for pupils, parents and teachers to access recorded achievement and to allow detailed review of engagement and progress.

In short, e-schooling is about much more than publishing course content online. It's the interactivity, the engagement, the trackability and the immediacy of feedback and the ability to act on it which makes the difference between texts published 'under glass' and e-learning proper.

We know from experience that e-schooling is fundamentally different from non-technology based courses. Detailed preparation is vital: taking much more time to prepare and teach online – the teacher cannot be just 'one page ahead'. Participants need induction to new teaching and learning methods. Learning engagement makes for longer teaching, as Richard Wallace put it (Stein and Wallace, 2004), 'pupils cannot just "click" and hope that something sticks!'[22]

In addition to the design issues there are: child protection matters; the need for accessibility of resources at all times; the need to design explicit navigation and readability throughout; the opportunity to match media types (text, visuals, audio) to some perception of the different preferred learning styles of the learners. Assessment methods must change to match the new style of learning; putting paper-based assessment on-screen is relatively easy, but is often not fit for purpose.

Given this crucial issue of online assessment, a follow-up to the GCSE project used interactive voting devices attached to an interactive whiteboard; with an extensive, newly-written bank of questions to explore further how online assessment tools can enhance learning for pupils. The course materials were also translated into Irish, and evaluated in an Irish-medium school in Belfast.

E-learning innovations are found in all areas of the curriculum and are explored in more detail in the following three chapters: here is a short selection.

Collaborative learning online

An advanced level geography decision making exercise, based on the 'A' Level geography specification, has been offered online to well over 500 pupils for more than three years. The exam task requires pupils to demonstrate higher-order reasoning skills through the study of resources related to a contentious local environmental planning issue, absorb and understand the factors, marshal the arguments and structure a professional report. The online activity has all the demands of the original paper-based activity, but adds access to video clips and a range of related multimedia resources. In addition, the online forums and digital file exchange allow collaboration between groups of four students from paired schools who work together at the heart of the project. Collaboration between students from different schools is not a normal feature of advanced level study. Learners find it stimulating and demanding in equal measure and it raises the issue of e-learning running ahead of the assessment opportunities offered in high-stakes public examinations.[23] Both the decision-making process and the collaborative product are assessed by a team of examiners and students receive individual feedback. Because it is online, explaining their arguments clearly to each other and engaging with the issue is demanding for the students – but can lead to greater understanding. A student from Ballynahinch, commented 'The fact that we were grouped with another school gave us an incentive to work hard and to complete the activity successfully.'

The discussions often display high levels of geographical skill, as well as evidence of peer mentoring and group work. Tracking shows students regularly accessing the resources at any time of day from 7.00 am to 3.00 am next morning. Another student commented 'I find the written [A level] exercise very tedious sometimes but this format was exciting and interactive.'

Their teacher, Head of Geography, agrees,

> ... our Department have seen this initiative as a wonderful opportunity for our 'A' Level students ... they have benefited from ICT skills and they have gained knowledge of how to structure a report ... it has no doubt enhanced their academic performance but the social skills acquired have also been beneficial.[24]

Extending collaborative learning online

'Moving Image Arts' is the first A level in this subject in the UK and is offered by the Council for the Curriculum Examinations and Assessment. Students study the theory and art of film-making, make their own films and develop practical skills, as part of the coursework. The students, nearly 100 from 13 schools in 2005, view movie clips online and prepare essays on screen for marking online by examiners.

Bernard McCloskey, head of education at the Northern Ireland Film and Television Commission (NIFTC) adds:

> The NIFTC are currently developing a dedicated website for students and teachers involved in Moving Image Arts at A [Advanced] Level. This will include access to material from our Digital Film Archive, which contains 55 hours of moving images covering the last century in Northern Ireland.

In all of these examples, course content is locally authored and costs can be high. It would be uneconomic to take this approach for coverage of the entire region's curriculum. The 'Scholar' pilot explored the adaptation of materials developed in Scotland for 'Highers' examinations in mathematics, computing, biology, chemistry and physics to the specifications for A level examinations elsewhere. Students interact with a range of learning materials that contain text, diagrams, and dynamic animations which provide the learners with personal progress assessment through quizzes and tests. Online assessment provides teachers with indications of progression at the end of each topic. An online discussion board supports group discussions, and the Northern Ireland pilot aimed to discover more about online tutorial support by introducing the role of one teacher as an online tutor–mentor for each subject for the students from the four pilot schools, to add value to the use of the interactive resources.

Some of the pupils welcomed the experience because it provided another rich resource that engaged them, as they prepared for a high-stakes public examination. As one sixth form pupil put it, 'It's like this; when you are studying for an A level, all the help you can get is welcome.'[25]

Others found the independence – disposition, self-regulation and perseverance – needed to study online too demanding, especially when they were more used to studying in a learning style dependent on their supportive teachers.

Changing roles – teachers and learners

The DE Research Briefing[26] indicates that teacher development will be needed in the following areas:

- skills and judgements needed to blend good traditional pedagogic practice with the integration of innovative learning contexts, in which the pupils assume much more control over how they seek and use the information that underpins their learning;
- skills of assessing and recognising pupils' progress and performance in increasingly complex learning contexts ranging from wholly individualised to wholly collaborative;
- skills needed in engaging with pupils in online feedback and support and learning outside the classroom (in existing or developing collaborative communities).

In our pilot work, we have seen rapid changes in patterns of online study. It is evident that learners prefer a mixture of evening and day-time, as well as weekend working, when they have ready access online outside the classroom, at home and in public libraries. This was always true in a non-technological world; it was simply that traditional homework has been constrained by a lack of access to study and library resources. In the online world, the opposite is true.

For the learner, the advantages are evident:

'If you can use the Internet properly you can learn a lot from it.'

'I liked the answers from the online expert because they were immediate and a lot more useful than what the teacher had to say…'

'When I was off ill I was able to do the work that others were doing in school.'

'I liked that I could ask other pupils and I didn't always have to ask the teachers …'[27]

There needs to be continuous investment in the infrastructure to ensure equality of access to resources especially outside school; easy access by staff to resources at home will also have the effect of consolidating and improving their competence.

E-assessment

Assessment is the Achilles heel of ICT embedding in e-schooling. While considerable progress has been made on reducing the obstacles of poor infrastructure and connectivity, and teacher competence and confidence are improving slowly, assessment remains unfit for purpose not only for today's ICT-enhanced classroom, but also for tomorrow's transformed one. The experience in Northern Ireland points to the need for 'radically new approaches to assessment to exploit and establish the benefit of curriculum changes and the impact of ICT'.[28]

The effective use of assessment is widely regarded as an underdeveloped skill for teachers generally. According to the Assessment Reform Group, while 97 per cent of teachers report their confidence in selecting and using appropriate resources in their teaching, only 23 per cent regard themselves as able to make effective and appropriate use of assessment.[29]

In this context, more needs to be made of online tests and assessment information – the automation of familiar approaches to assessment, such as essay-writing taking place on-screen, is not in itself enough.

At a time when online learning platforms provide online tests, as well as digital content, there is little appreciation of the value of:

- providing the learner with rapid feedback on their progress;
- enabling the teacher, and the learner, to aggregate assessment information on progress;
- easing the administrative burdens of record-keeping and reporting;
- using electronic portfolios for organising learning and collating and presenting evidence of progress.

As a result, we have seen that when innovation in online courses fails to integrate assessment, it has been flawed from an educational point of view.

We have to doubt if appropriate online assessment can be achieved when there is lack of agreement generally about the need 'to overhaul radically the system of examination and accreditation to meet the aspirations driving the modernisation of education in the UK'.[30] Take, as a case in point, the need to revise examination requirements to increase the amount of ICT-based coursework required from candidates and to use e-portfolios to keep records and evidence of achievement and to present and show case learning as part of the pupil profile.

Learners should be able to study a curriculum, into which technology is fully implemented, which is determined partly by setting individual targets and personalised testing, and completed at their own pace.

Online assessment tools, record-keeping and e-profile systems will increasingly need to be integrated with curriculum content. School staff will need professional development to help them to make effective use of assessment information from school Management Information Systems to:

- track and analyse pupil progress;
- personalise learning support;
- set and address targets;
- use performance measures;
- report on 'value-added';

and bring to life the concept of 'assessment for learning'.[31]

Global messages

Looking only at our classroom of tomorrow, what are some of our global messages concerning the development of an e-curriculum and e-assessment for e-schooling?

- When a school starts to embrace technology, teachers first become comfortable most quickly with teaching aids such as projectors and whiteboards which change neither the curriculum, nor their role. More frequent use however, does not always mean that the learner's experiences are improved, or that the experience is widely felt across the curriculum or with a wide range of technologies. It is clear that young people are capable when it comes to accessing technology, it does not follow, however, that their retrieval and use of information or their online communication is sophisticated.

- Looking to the future, the global messages for us are that the potential for e-learning to facilitate distance learning is at its most appropriate:
    - where new subjects (such as Citizenship) are being introduced;
    - where rapid expansion of provision is dictated and yet where teaching expertise is scarce such as in vocational teaching in smaller schools;
    - where regular teaching contact with specialists from outside Northern Ireland is desired (such as French teaching in primary schools and working directly with the author of the class novel);
    - where the objectives of the course foster connected learning with pupils from other countries, such as in Japanese Studies or European Studies courses or cross-border programmes like Dissolving Boundaries, described in the next chapter.

- Online teaching is about much more than publishing books online or a teacher waving his arms around on a video-conference screen. It is much more lively and interesting, but so much more demanding. It is not possible to separate an e-curriculum from the challenges of learning to teach online which we addressed in Chapter 3. We have learnt that designing and teaching online courses requires skills over and above those needed for face to face courses. The investment in time may be essential if it is the only way a pupil can access a specialist course; the investment has to be beneficial as measured by the outcome. It is not enough to be excited that the interaction took place, if the pupils could have learnt more effectively in other ways. Teachers who have taught online are beginning to understand that difference, and the change in teacher/learner role relationship that can occur online when a pupil grasps something and can explain it effectively to others. For some teachers, this is a threat to their authority and for some learners, a threat to their dependency on the teacher. The successful introduction of an online course, with expert teaching delivered online, will require a preparation of both teacher and learner based upon a good understanding of the special teaching skills and the lifelong learning competences required.

- Investment in technology provision may well be substantial, there may well be exciting innovation and clarity about its nature, but without regulatory reform in the shape of modernised curricula with suitable examinations, assessment, accreditation and accountability, we can only expect, as Alan November indicated, 'automation' of current practice. We will return to the key issue of regulatory reform in Chapter 10.

Connected learning for citizenship

The importance of education for citizenship

This chapter explores one of the most innovative areas of e- schooling, how ICT can help to make citizenship education become real for young people through enabling them to work with partner schools. This approach to citizenship education can best be described as education for citizenship, using Selwyn's[1] term (2002); we argue here that it is through working and negotiating with pupils in other schools that valuable citizenship skills are being learned which have relevance not only in Northern Ireland but elsewhere. Recent evidence highlights the difficulties of teaching citizenship well. According to a 2006 newspaper report[2] on the teaching of citizenship in England, over a quarter of the lessons were judged to be inadequate.

As we saw in Chapter 1, education for citizenship is particularly important where both cross-border suspicion and cross-community tensions within Northern Ireland have ruptured the normal flow of daily contact between young people and created particular and persistent difficulties in providing an education in citizenship. But the use of ICT for creating partnerships, both locally and internationally, has been steadily growing, with governmental endorsement[3] since the mid-1980s in many parts of the world, not just those which have a history of communal, religious or racial tension. So a key theme in this chapter is an analysis of the theoretical and conceptual models which are shaping the use of telecommunications for joint work between schools and what lessons are emerging about good practice and sustainability.

In our definition of e-schooling, we said in the preface that ICT use needed to be aligned to other government policies. The most significant current policies in Northern Ireland are 'A Shared Future' (2005) and the report of the 'Independent Strategic Review of Education' (2006). The first of these states that there is an 'economic and social imperative' in 'tackling the costs of division' and an urgent need to address 'communal polarisation'.[4] This is not the first time that the Northern Ireland administration has attempted to introduce policies designed to reduce the prevalence of sectarian attitudes that have arisen from centuries of mistrust, divided schooling and segregated housing. Austin (2007)[5] has summarised previous initiatives that were driven by efforts to promote both integrated schools, where children from different religious backgrounds would be taught together, or through the curriculum. As we saw in Chapter 5, Citizenship now occupies a pivotal position in the revised curriculum, arguably more central to learning than the previous cross-curricular themes of Education for Mutual Understanding and Cultural Heritage. A recent evaluation of the pilot work in citizenship (Niens and O'Connor, 2005),[6] reflecting the fact that citizenship education for 95 per cent of Northern Irish pupils takes place in a mono-cultural setting with pupils from a similar background to themselves, suggested that 'inter-school collaboration might be a useful tool to share good practice'.

The use of ICT to enable young people to work together in Northern Ireland may receive a further thrust from the practical working out of the Independent Strategic Review of Education Report (2006).[7] This report, commissioned and accepted by the Department of Education, sprang from a need to examine the 'school estate', the number of schools needed in Northern Ireland, at a time when the school population is in decline. This strategic review asserts that schools will need to cooperate and share resources if they are to deliver the much broader curricular choices that will be required when pupils reach the age of 14. In other words, like many other countries which are experiencing smaller family size, schools in Northern Ireland find themselves facing smaller numbers and the loss of specialist teachers. There are clearly opportunities here for elements of some courses to be provided and shared through video-conferencing and online to make best use of subject expertise.

The significance of ICT

So far, we can see that a single managed learning environment, operating in every school in Northern Ireland through C2K could provide the technical means through which significant progress might be made in providing key parts of the curriculum, including Citizenship. To understand whether or not this will happen requires a critique of research on the use of ICT for school links and whether teachers are confident to embrace the competences that are associated with inter-cultural education (Davis et al., 2005).[8] What then are the most important lessons that are emerging from the use of ICT in schools working together?

The first is the scale of work taking place, reflected in papers presented at an international conference on the role of ICT in bridge-building and social inclusion which took place in 2006[9] and in a database of such projects and programmes being developed by Hamber (2006).[10] We need to add to the data the European Union's eTwinning programme, introduced in 2005[11] which claims to have 10,000 schools registered and Unesco's ICT and education policies which are broadly framed to embed ICT in teaching and learning[12] and reduce the digital divide between the estimated 1 billion computer users world-wide and the global population of 6 billion.[13] The use of ICT for communication between schools and other organisations in formal education needs to be seen in the wider context of the explosion of what is called social software,[14] the means by which many young people interact socially, build websites, make friends and share common interests. In other words, we can see here the protential for an emerging alignment between uses of ICT outside the school and within it.

The second is that virtual contact does indeed make a difference to pupils and teachers; Austin (2006)[15] refers to the evidence emerging from around the world, including the Dissolving Boundaries programme[16] which shows that alongside improved communication skills and improved self-esteem, digital contact is slowly breaking down barriers. Twenty-three per cent of project teachers overall (n=21) rated the impact of Dissolving Boundaries on North–South understanding in Ireland as very significant. Of this group, 21 per cent (n=8) came from Northern Ireland and 27 per cent (n=12) came from the Republic of Ireland. Forty-five per cent (n=39) of teachers considered that Dissolving Boundaries had a significant impact on 'North–South understanding'. Of this group, 52 per cent (n=21), came from Northern Ireland and 39 per cent (n=18) came from the Republic. There were some differences between teachers in the different types of school; 75 per cent of teachers in primary school said that the effect of the project was either very significant or significant in terms of 'north-south understanding', the figure for teachers in Special schools was 60 per cent while for those in post-primary schools it was 62 per cent.

These broad conclusions are supported by research in the Middle East (Hoter *et al.*, 2006)[17] and go some way to contradicting earlier worked quoted by Austin (2006) which was more ambivalent about whether ICT – enabled educational links changed participants' perceptions. There are a number of significant factors in the Dissolving Boundaries programme and in similar work elsewhere which deserve close scrutiny and may help to explain why the impact on young people has been effective.

Enabling conditions

We discuss here seven factors that we believe are both highly significant from the experience in Northern Ireland and which have wide-scale relevance.

Extended experience of ICT for inter-school links

The first is that Northern Ireland has a fairly long experience of using ICT to link schools for joint work; this goes back to 1986 and the European Studies (Ireland

and Great Britain) project[18] set up in the wake of the 1985 Anglo-Irish Agreement between Great Britain and Ireland and one of the first to use telecommunications to link schools in Northern Ireland, the Republic of Ireland and England to partner schools on the European mainland. During the same period, similar projects forged links between schools in Northern Ireland and Japan, the European Union and the USA.[19] These funded projects continued throughout the troubled decade of the 1990s and helped to shape the Dissolving Boundaries programme which was set up in 1999. To explain this substantial history of innovation, we need to recall the convergence between Northern Ireland's political need to address sectarianism and its geo-economic position on the periphery of the European land mass. It is one thing to say that ICT might have a role to play in addressing these interconnected educational, political and economic problems. But it requires sustained political will to take action.

Political will

In the 20 years between 1986 and 2006, Northern Ireland's educational and ICT policies were mainly guided by 'Direct Rule' Ministers,[20] generally Members of Parliament elected from outside Northern Ireland and appointed by the British government to help run the Northern Ireland Office. Nearly all were 'outsiders' who relied for guidance and advice on civil servants in the Department of Education, most of whom were from Northern Ireland and drawn predominantly from both Protestant and Catholic backgrounds. This combination of power, based on Ministers who were not answerable through elections to the local Northern Irish electorate and civil servants whose actions were judged in terms of financial accountability for policy implementation rather than the direction of policy itself, made it possible for political will to be exercised in a way that took a long term strategic view of what was needed. Austin (2007)[21] suggests that the engine driving policy in London, Dublin and Washington was first to 'normalise' the political situation in Northern Ireland by bringing sectarian violence to an end, second to recognise the potential role that Dublin could play in stabilising the situation and third, to require Northern Ireland to shoulder its share of public expenditure through improving the performance of the private sector in the economy. Educational policy, including the continued levels of funding for ICT, should be seen as contributing to these geo-political aspirations.

With Northern Ireland on the brink in 2007 of a possible return to devolved government and the election of local parties vying for electoral support, a new set of competing visions may contest the direction of policy followed in the final two decades of the twentieth century.

Theoretical models

A long history of ICT innovation and political will are necessary but not sufficient conditions to explain the sustained use of ICT for inter-school links. We turn now to consider a third and vital factor, the way that conceptual models of using ICT have moved inter-school work from small scale experiments to models that can be widely replicated. The influence of social psychology's 'contact hypothesis' has been significant in shaping the nature of the links that emerged. Allport's research (1954)[22] subsequently developed by others, including Tropp and Pettigrew (2005),[23] showed that contact was most likely to be effective when links between different groups were collaborative rather than competitive, involved groups of equal status, were sustained over a period of time and had institutional support.

From the mid-1990s researchers began examining the extent to which the contact hypothesis might be used to evaluate contact that was virtual rather than real. Meagher and Castaños (1996)[24] reported that in a computer mediated conferencing (CMC) link between high school students in Mexico and the USA, Mexican students' attitudes towards USA culture grew less positive though the students felt a greater commonality with the American students as individuals. Postmes *et al*. (1998)[25] and Postmes *et al*. (2002)[26] found that inter-group communication via the internet led to greater polarisation when the groups were 'depersonalised' as opposed to 'individuated'. These findings are important, touching as they do on the issue of how inter-school links can provide an experience that is 'personal' for each participant and also one that is mediated through group-to-group interaction. Group interaction allows pupils to have a better sense of the varied composition of the 'outgroup', refining any perceptions, positive or negative, that were based on purely individual contact.

Sundberg (2001)[27] reporting on links in the USA between five urban and rural schools in Illinois with students aged 10–11, 13–14 and 15–16 also noted that 'some students revealed an increased (supposedly more knowledgeable) negative perception towards the communities and individuals they had been in contact with'. However, he also pointed to the potential importance of the Common In-group Identity Model (Gaertner and Dovidio, 2000)[28] where students from different schools might develop a super-ordinate identity while not losing their positive original group identity.

Other researchers have reported positive outcomes from ICT enabled links; Mollov and Lavie (2001)[29] writing of virtual contact between Israeli and Palestinian university students who were studying Islam and Judaism through email exchanges, concluded that this one-to-one religious dialogue was a means for building Israeli–Palestinian understanding.

In terms of the relevance of this research for the expanding use of ICT between schools in Northern Ireland and elsewhere, two further points are significant. The first is that most of the contact described in the research to date has been either entirely or predominantly based on textual interaction. As the medium for interaction shifts to more multimedia (i.e. audio and video) transmission, such as the use of video-conferencing interaction which was built into the design of the European Studies and Dissolving Boundaries programmes from the start, we are already seeing a wider range of learners benefitting from virtual contact.

This theoretical framework has been particularly important in ensuring that when links have been established they have been based around both social interaction and smallish teams in each school working towards a common curricular goal, sometimes expressed through the development of a joint website. Alongside theoretical principles in social psychology, educationists were influential in the assertion that learning was 'a fundamentally social phenomenon' and that the key was social participation (Wenger, 1999).[30] This perspective guided the thinking of programme designers to develop the model for school interaction in two ways; the first was to accept that the apparently trivial messages exchanged by some of the students in computer conferences were a necessary part of the whole process of learning about different cultures, and adjusting to similarities and differences. The second was to provide the opportunity for all the teachers and some of the pupils to meet face to face for either planning and review conferences or to work and socialise together. As the most recent report on Dissolving Boundaries makes clear, the purpose of all this was to build a virtual 'community of practice'[31] in which teachers and pupils could construct an environment that cherished collaborative learning.

Finally, in this section on the influence of theoretical models, elements of constructivism have been at the centre of this work which starts from the premise that children should explore meaning and construct understanding through the curriculum by active investigation of agreed topics. In Dissolving Boundaries, teachers meet and plan a programme of joint work which could be on any area of the curriculum, provided that it offers opportunities for the exploration of similarity and difference and is based around a model of collaborative learning. In practice, topics chosen are often in science, languages, the environment, history or the creative arts. What matters is not the memorisation of known factual knowledge but the construction of meaning through interaction with pupils in not just one classroom but two. This happens because pupils are organised into small groups in their own classroom and then form a composite team by linking with a similar size group in their partner school. Teachers and pupils plan when to use synchronous communication through video-conferencing, when to use asynchronous software (such as the current use of 'Moodle' which is an open-source learning environment) and how best to present their joint findings in a digital form. The presence of a real audience for their work and the need to negotiate characterisation, the lay-out of web pages, or the design of a joint newsletter are all authentic learning experiences. Furthermore, this kind of collaborative enterprise helps build key citizenship skills of listening, clarifying meaning, working towards a common goal and resolving differences.

Professional development

The fourth significant factor in sustaining ICT is the nature of professional development for teachers provided through programmes like Dissolving Boundaries. In our judgment, there must be three core elements. The first is the obvious one that teachers need to learn a set of techniques to use video-conferencing, computer conferencing and the collaborative software that makes it possible for them to interact with their partner school. They have to be confident enough to introduce the technology to their pupils, knowing which digital tools are likely to work best in the classroom at any given time. The Dissolving Boundaries team has provided hands-on training at planning conferences and in local clusters of schools, ensuring that the training is delivered shortly before the teachers have to use it themselves with their classes. Evaluation evidence makes it clear that teacher motivation to master a new set of skills is influenced by the expectation that their partner school expects communication; the distant audience raises expectations for both pupils and teachers.

The second element is the management of communications technology within the context of a crowded curriculum and sometimes inhibited access to the hardware. Even when a teacher has learned how to operate video-conferencing resources, there are highly significant lessons to be learned about optimum classroom organisation (how many pupils at a time, what do others do when this is taking place and so on) and negotiating space to do this in ways that are seen to be consistent with the delivery of the curriculum and the achievement of worthwhile educational objectives. Every school is unique in its layout, ethos and staff culture but there are two approaches that the Dissolving Boundaries team have adopted to help build this 'professional knowledge'. The first is by requesting all teachers to attend the two face to face conferences which take place each year and making time for exactly this kind of professional discourse to take place. This is supplemented by an online forum where teachers are encouraged to post in their comments on the management of inter-school links. The second approach to building what we are calling 'professional knowledge' is to recognise that teachers cannot become proficient in a single school year; while schools receive close support in their first year of participation, they remain part of the extended family thereafter, invited to attend planning conferences and share their deepening experience.

The third element in professional development is also the most difficult to achieve. All teachers are invited to engage in critical reflection on practice as part of the process of reviewing their interaction and planning for the following academic year but the deep assimilation of lessons learned requires more time (and money) than most schools have so far been able to afford. While a minority used their experience in Dissolving Boundaries to enroll on Masters programmes where they have been able to set their professional development in the broader context of inter-cultural learning, most have not been able to travel far down this road. Yet the importance of doing so is vital.

Davis (2005, see note 8) argues that intercultural competence

> can be defined as transformation of learning and a growth process where an individual's existing, often implicit, knowledge is diversified to intercultural knowledge, attitude, and behavior. The learning and growth process allows individuals to incorporate intercultural knowledge into their high level cognitive schema.

She quotes Leeman and Ledoux (2003)[32] to make the case that such competency should not be an extra facet of teachers' professional development but an integral part. The General Teaching Council for Northern Ireland is refining a set of professional competences and values for teachers[33] to make explicit reference to the need for pupils to understand the diversity of pupils' diverse cultures, languages and faiths. To enable teachers and the guardians of professional standards to engage in discussion about this role in education, a second conceptual issue will need to be addressed.

This takes us back to one of the central messages in the book, the way that schools define themselves and their function in society; following the pioneering work of Istance[34] and McCluskey,[35] schools are being invited to imagine what 're-schooling' might look like, with schools as 'learning organisations' making extensive use of ICT to connect the school as an institution to the local and global community. This vision of what we call 'e-schooling' is a long way from the school as an organisation devoted solely to the transmission of knowledge and preparing young people to succeed in examinations. As we have argued elsewhere in the book, particularly in Chapter 3 on teacher professional development for ICT, a new phase of teacher development is needed for all teachers which enables them, amongst other things, to think through the values of using ICT for intercultural education.

External agencies

We close this analysis of enabling factors with three final organisational issues necessary for success in meaningful citizenship. The first is the role of external agencies in supporting curriculum innovation; the Dissolving Boundaries programme is managed by two University departments of Education, one in Northern Ireland at the University of Ulster and the other in the Republic of Ireland at Maynooth, a National University of Ireland. This partnership is important not only because of the way it models the creation of school partnerships and in sustaining them when things go wrong but because of the sound foundation of research and teacher training. Evaluation of the impact of the programme on teachers and pupils has been a feature of the work of the team, with externally validated publications connecting to the wider educational community.[36] But locating this kind of curriculum development in Higher Education also means that new cohorts of student teachers going through their initial training, as well as experienced teachers undertaking Masters or doctoral programmes, benefit from this research and development.

Working across all types of school

The second organisational issue, we might call strategic, was the decision to locate the work of Dissolving Boundaries in all kinds of schools, primary (pupils aged 4–12), secondary (12–18) and special (covering a wide age and ability range). This has been significant in two ways; first it demonstrated that communicative technologies worked in 'mainstream' education and could also break down further boundaries for learners in special schools. This has involved links from special school to special school and between special schools and those in mainstream education. One telling illustration of this has been the link between a school for deaf pupils in the Republic of Ireland working with a mainstream school in Northern Ireland. Joint work on issues of imperialism as a curriculum topic was initially pushed forward through text communication but the students wanted to 'see' each other; gradually, it was agreed that the deaf schools might 'teach' their partner school signing using the medium of video-conferencing. The teachers involved commented:

> … we had our first conferencing session with our partner school. It worked first time and both schools found it very interesting. It was good to see the girls we are currently working with and especially to understand and communicate with them. My students and I had learnt our names using the iris mantel alphabet and the Dublin girls were able to make them out, it was great. We are currently negotiating a face to face meeting and have agreed in principle that we will do one, probably in Dublin in February.

And, from the other teacher:

> I was delighted with today's conference. I must admit that I was apprehensive and worried that we wouldn't be able to understand each other. It was a huge relief and very exciting for us. I was very impressed at how well the girls communicated – I didn't have to intervene at any stage. Looking forward to the next conference.

This example shows us the power of real-time interaction by video-conference and it underlines the second reason why working with a wide range of different types of school is important. Breaking down stereotypes works at many levels, not just to do with whether you are on one side of a political border or another. As we shall see in the following chapter on the role of ICT in special needs education and inclusion, many teachers in mainstream schools are increasingly expected to help special needs children learn and they do not always have the depth of experience with such children as those working in special schools. So, to return to a point made earlier in this chapter, the community of practice in Dissolving Boundaries is an inclusive one with frequent opportunities for teachers in many different types of school to share good practice.

Affordable and sustainable technologies

It's a reflection of the very different histories of Northern Ireland and the Republic of Ireland since their separation in 1921 that not only do they have different school structures and curricula but they have taken strikingly divergent paths in terms of ICT in education. In contrast to the centralised approach in Northern Ireland, its southern neighbours have adopted a decentralised approach with schools given significant decision making in matters of hardware and software. At a strategic level, however, there is growing convergence between both sides of the border in regard to the roll out of broadband. This is installed in all schools in Northern Ireland and in a growing number in the Republic of Ireland; the different time scales for policy implementation have led to the adoption of a number of pragmatic solutions for Dissolving Boundaries.

For example, the decision to adopt computer conferencing software by the programme team was initially influenced by the presence and functionality in the mid-1990s of an early bulletin board system (Northern Ireland Network for Education) which was capable of admitting guest users from outside Northern Ireland. This was critical in terms of sharing good practice and helping to sustain an emerging community of practice. As C2K began to develop a new managed learning environment in 2005, the strict requirements for child protection and for firewall safeguards within a virtual private schools network initially limited the ability to accommodate external guest users. This led to a pilot of the use of an open-standards environment in 2005–7 which offers all the functionality needed for cross-border interaction.

Similarly, in regard to video-conferencing, the technology widely available from 1999 until 2006 involved direct connections through dialled access between school sites; while this provided acceptable levels of reliability, ease of use and quality of sound and vision it was expensive to use. As schools in Northern Ireland moved to broadband during this period, the programme team worked with C2K to make it possible for the C2K schools to use broadband to connect to schools south of the border which are still using dial-up. The next step in this process is the piloting due to take place in 2007 to secure all Internet-based connectivity across the border; this is a very big 'prize' in the sense that such links would have none of the costs previously incurred in direct dialled calls.

The piloting of Internet-based video-conferencing links between schools in Northern Ireland and those in Japan, as part of the long-running Japanese Studies project, has already delivered the schools a major reduction in project running costs.

What this story illustrates is the inter-connectedness of all the previous conditions which we have argued are necessary for success; cross-border connectivity would not happen unless there was the experience and the commitment to see that it is a necessary part both of citizenship and of the development of skills for a knowledge-based economy.

In concluding this section of the chapter, we should note that most of the work discussed so far has involved links between schools in Northern Ireland with those outside it. As we have seen, there are good reasons for explaining why this has been the case but readers might, at this stage, be asking how this work is being embedded in links between schools within Northern Ireland. We turn our attention to this pressing and puzzling issue.

ICT for local citizenship

We noted at the start of the book that the predominantly segregated character of Northern Ireland's schools has meant that 95 per cent of children attend schools with children from a similar religious background to themselves. Research by Niens and O'Connor (2005)[37] has also revealed the very limited extent of cross community contact between learners. The authors noted that 'large percentages of respondents claimed that none of their relatives (53 per cent), friends (53 per cent) and neighbours (38 per cent) was from the other religious community' (Niens and O'Connor, 2005: 23). But this clearly leaves us with a problem, of young people growing up with relatively little contact between their own community and the rest of society. It's a problem that affects not just education and young people.

We noted earlier that 'A Shared Future' (2005, see note 4) was an important lodestone in terms of policy direction for the whole of society in Northern Ireland; the report mentions that between 1995 and 2005 a number of educational strategies had been introduced to promote a 'more inclusive society'. Among these were the cross curricular themes of Education for Mutual Understanding and Cultural Heritage and the Schools Community Relations Programme which began in 1987 and provided funding for cross-community contact. However, a number of reports commissioned by the Department of Education between 1996 and 2002,[38] questioned the impact of such schemes and referred to other research which suggested that contact schemes were not reaching young people with sectarian attitudes (Cairns and Hewstone, 2001).[39] Perhaps most worryingly, the Chief Inspector's report for 2002–4[40] commented that only 21 per cent of primary school children had taken part in such schemes and that a mere 3 per cent of pupils in secondary schools had been involved.

By way of explanation, we can recall what Sundberg (2001, see note 27) wrote; he suggested that geographical distance lessens feelings of threat and anxiety and conversely that 'when groups are in historical or immediate geographical competition, increasing group members' perceptions of common in-group identity is the only realistic strategy for reducing bias'. In other words, it is far easier to work with partner schools across the border or in Europe and the USA than with schools from a different tradition in the same town. Furthermore, according to Sundberg, when links are being planned between local schools, they need to have a focus for interaction which will help them to develop a common 'in-group' identity. What does this mean in practice? Two schools might work together to develop a jointly-designed tourist trail or brochure for the town or area where they are located; others might mount a common front on an environmental issue or in commemorating a shared piece of history. Others could celebrate the diverse artistic, literary and creative aspects of their heritage. In short, diversity can be harnessed towards a common goal, when, as in the Dissolving Boundaries approach, joint teams work together towards an end product.

This vision is somewhat distant from the current practice of citizenship education in Northern Ireland or indeed from many of the previous attempts that were made to link schools through ICT. We consider each of these in turn.

ICT for citizenship within Northern Ireland

Austin (2007, see note 21) has reviewed three pilot projects that ran from 1998 until 2000 and which used ICT to enable pupils in Northern Ireland to interact. All three provided an online forum for pupils to engage in discussion about the emerging political situation after the Good Friday Peace Agreement. There was an air of confidence led by politicians that the time was ripe for a public debate about the controversial issues of releasing prisoners early for 'political' offences or the decommissioning of paramilitary weapons by Republican and Loyalist groups. Locally elected politicians, including Ministers, proactively engaged with young people from 14 to 18 in a moderated online exchange of views. While these were striking illustrations of what could be done, they were all seen as 'extra-curricular' activities, carried out on a small scale on the fringes of the curriculum. And the political will which had encouraged this pioneering work began to wane as the political climate deteriorated and ultimately led to the collapse of the devolved administration in 2002.

These tentative steps were not forgotten, however; in 2006, the Xchange conference in Belfast and the international conference on the role of ICT in bridge-building and social inclusion[41] heard about not only the work of Dissolving Boundaries but of two other examples where ICT was being used between schools within Northern Ireland. Significantly, in both cases the work could be described as education *for* citizenship rather than education *about* citizenship. In one, O'Neill and Morrow,[42] two student teachers, used ICT to link their schools together to study 'street history' and to enable the pupils to see the links between history and the political graffiti in their communities. Theirs was a very good example of how they moved the 14-year-olds in their classes from an exchange of social information to a discussion about relatively non-threatening elements of history into the decidedly contested history of the Home Rule crisis and the Easter Rising of 1916. In summary, this example suggests that valuable citizenship lessons can be learned through the appropriate use of ICT in subject teaching. We return to this point in the conclusion. But first, what exactly does the Citizenship curriculum in Northern Ireland entail?

The Citizenship Curriculum in Northern Ireland

As we saw in Chapter 5, the Northern Ireland Council for Curriculum, Examinations and Assessment put forward proposals for a reform of the curriculum[43] in 2003 which was designed to enable pupils to develop as individuals and as contributors to society, the economy and the environment. Local and Global Citizenship was introduced for the first time around the four key concepts of Diversity and Inclusion, Human Rights and Responsibility, Equality and Social Justice and Democracy and Active Participation. This revised curriculum will become compulsory for all post-primary schools from September 2007. It should be noted that this framework differs in some important respects from the Citizenship curriculum being followed in England where there is more focus on political literacy, the criminal justice system, the economy, the role of the media, etc.

At this juncture, we might recall the useful distinction drawn by Selwyn (2002, see note 1) at the start of the chapter; he claimed that ICT could be used in three ways to support citizenship. First, it might provide resources from the Internet that could be described as education *about* citizenship. Second, it could support education *through* citizenship which would involve pupils participating in citizenship activities in their communities or finally, it could support education *for* citizenship which encompasses both the 'about' and the 'through' by equipping students with a set of tools that enable them to make informed and responsible decisions. He notes that ICT is currently 'used to support only limited forms of citizenship education'. We wholeheartedly endorse the proposition that we should aim for education for citizenship but where we differ from Selwyn and to some extent the central thrust of the CCEA citizenship curriculum, is about the best means of achieving this.

The evidence of the Dissolving Boundaries programme and some of the more recent work using ICT for joint history projects underlines the power of ICT to work right across the curriculum in developing citizenship attributes. In other words, it is the process of working with others on neutral and contested issues that is as important as knowledge of human rights or any other body of knowledge in citizenship. The latter, on its own, is unlikely to lead to attitudinal change, an inference that can be drawn from Niens and O'Connor (op. cit.) whose evaluation of citizenship education noted that it was pupils in integrated schools who were more likely to learn about sectarianism and conflict than pupils in mono-cultural schools. In other words, it was where there was contact between learners from different backgrounds that the really challenging work could be done.

Global messages

- In this chapter we have presented evidence to show that a key element of e-schooling is the readiness of schools to use ICT for citizenship education and more broadly for the kind of connected learning that will help to deliver the range of academic and vocational courses that all young people need for a knowledge-based economy. We support the proposal made at the 2006 conference on ICT and Bridge-Building,[44] that every school should move towards having a local and a global e-partner. This will need to be taken into account in future professional development for all teachers.

- There is a need for an even closer alignment of ICT educational policy with wider social and political goals. In arguing this case, we are also saying that evaluation of the cost-effectiveness of ICT investment should look beyond the measurement of academic achievement to include the impact on social capital and particularly its contribution to the formation of informed and tolerant citizens.

- Although there are formidable challenges in local citizenship when 'territory' and 'space' are contested, we think the evidence shows that virtual contact, rather than being an optional element in schemes which value contact, should be an essential feature, allowing sustained, cost-effective relationships to develop.

- And finally, this chapter makes the case that e-schooling includes making the values associated with the use of ICT explicit.

Special and inclusive education 7

A key part of our definition of e-schooling is that the values embedded in ICT use in schools are made explicit. In Chapter 6, we argued that ICT has a central role to play in citizenship. In this chapter we assert that the benefits of ICT investment should be felt by all pupils and we examine the claims made about the role that ICT can play in special and inclusive education with an analysis of the impact of ICT on teachers and children working in this area in Northern Ireland. Evidence for this comes, in part, from published reports of the Education and Training Inspectorate (ETI) in 2003,[1] and surveys of both experienced teachers and trainee teachers in 2005.[2]

The education of children with special educational needs

Children in Northern Ireland who are assessed as having special educational needs (SEN) are educated either in mainstream schools or in one of the 45 special schools that provide support for those with moderate or severe learning difficulties. These special schools had 4,669 students in 2004–5 while there were 15,478 SEN pupils in post-primary education (10 per cent of the overall numbers in this sector) and 31,739 pupils in mainstream primary schools, 18 per cent of the primary school population. In line with governments in many countries, the Northern Ireland Department of Education's policy in regard to such children is to seek as far as possible to educate them in mainstream education. This will increase the probability that all teachers will, at some stage in their career, have the opportunity to work with children who have a statement of special educational need.

The value of ICT for SEN

There is considerable research evidence to point to the motivational role of ICT in general but also, specifically for children with SEN. This is a view echoed by staff at a special school in Londonderry, Northern Ireland, an award winning school for its successes in ICT.[3] A teacher comments:

> The amazing potential of ICT as a multi-sensory and motivating teaching tool for special needs pupils cannot be underestimated. It has been the magic key for so many of our pupils who have struggled in the past, unlocking the door to increased self-esteem, improved communication skills and more independent learning.

It is claimed that ICT can help facilitate inclusion by allowing access to the same programmes as other pupils resulting in 'greatly increased self-esteem, motivation and independence' (Becta 2000).[4] If ICT is so valuable, particularly for children with special educational needs, what are the reasons for this?

Phelan and Haughey (2000),[5] cited by Wynne (2004),[6] suggest that computers have one-to-one benefits; patience, privacy and practice. They also allow time intervals for pupils to respond which can be difficult within a traditional class lesson. A number of teachers in the 2005 Northern Ireland survey supported this saying that with ICT pupils can work at their own pace. Haughey also says that visual representation helps mathematical concepts become real. The value of visual (and auditory) stimuli was strongly supported in the 2005 NI survey where 18 per cent of the respondents suggested this was one of the reasons why ICT was beneficial in learning for pupils with SEN. Among the comments made were the following

> ... visually stimulating ... most of our children are visual learners and it motivates them ... the visual stimuli on the computer is good for keeping the children interested ... ICT makes learning fun and interactive to all pupils. Everyone enjoys looking at pictures and listening to music or songs or stories.

And in support of Phelan and Haughey above, 'In maths in key stage 1 adding on, subtraction etc. are brought alive with different characters.'

There seems to be little disagreement that ICT is motivating. The Northern Ireland Education and Training Inspection (ETI) report in 2002 stated that '... all pupils are motivated by the experience of ICT and keen to participate in activities which involve the use of ICT.' In our small scale survey of Northern Ireland teachers, 69 per cent said that they found ICT had a motivating effect on pupils. Reasons given included responses which mentioned the ease of editing and presenting work. Others suggested that children naturally liked the computer and saw it as a reward. Individual needs could be met and pupils could work at their own pace. Others mentioned multimedia – visual and auditory aspects helped.

Why do teachers so often report that use of computers is motivating? Is it that variety in itself is motivating? Or is it the nature of ICT itself which is motivating? It may be that ICT allows pupils to access the same programmes as their peers on equal terms. This was exactly the point made by staff at a Belfast Special School where the use of ICT packages in art, such as Adobe Photoshop, had enabled a group of learners to take the standard school examination, the General Certificate of Secondary Education (GCSE), at the age of 16 on equal terms with peers. Indeed, their work was of such high quality that it was selected by moderators for exhibition as exemplars of good practice.[7] According to Wynne (2004), whose research was based in the Republic of Ireland,

> a further motivating factor may be that the computer can move the locus of control to the learner, a rare experience for any child in the school environment but probably more so for the child with learning difficulties.

Some pupils, particularly those with language difficulties or delayed motor skills, may not often be in a position to take charge of a learning situation. The computer can give them a chance to be in control. Wynne's study asked teachers why they used ICT and found that 33 per cent reported a positive effect on self-esteem and motivation. They said that this was because of the pupils' enjoyment of ICT and as a result they spent more time on task.

A further factor in terms of the link between ICT and pupil motivation arises from the assertion that ICT increases pupils' sense of self-esteem. Blamires (1999)[8] suggests ICT is a high status activity and therefore pupils who can perform well with it have increased self-esteem because other pupils have a higher opinion of them. Students who have experienced regular failure in the past are likely to welcome a new medium in which they can experiment without feeling threatened. Wynne (2004) gives an example from her study where a child who had great difficulty remembering colours was able to use a multimedia package to write his own illustrated story. The need for him to select similar colours repeatedly helped him to internalise the names of the colours without experiencing the frustration caused by having to continually ask the teacher. A further example from the 2005 Northern Ireland teacher survey related to the experiences of a 17-year-old student:

> He was keen to use 'CreateaCard' to make greetings cards at a cost of 50p for teachers and pupils. He needed help to type the words correctly but wanted to do as much as possible himself. Sometimes he lost track of what he was doing and needed a prompt but when finished Ronan could take the card to the customer. He was very proud of himself and his self esteem was boosted enormously. Prior to this he had no way to prove himself to others.

One further point should be made about the reasons why ICT can motivate students; ICT use is valuable in promoting independence because the computer use can be individually tailored to meet the needs of the pupils by providing alternative and additional activities. This is supported by the 2005 survey of teachers in Northern Ireland, 71 per cent of whom believed that ICT helps make pupils more independent. Reasons given included the ability to differentiate for individual needs and because pupils could work at their own pace. ICT allowed them to navigate around their disabilities and keep up with the rest of the class. One of the teachers said:

> Pupils can learn individually and with differentiated content, on a much easier level for the classroom teacher. Pupils can work on tasks individually within their own time limit, and focus on outcomes relating to their own specific needs.

However, some teachers pointed out that independence may take time to develop and at the beginning much adult support is required. Where this support is provided on a consistent basis at school and home, particularly through the use of laptops, the learning impact is intensified (Stradling *et al.*, 1994).[9] The importance of SEN students becoming independent learners should not be underestimated; it is one of the key ways that they can feel included in mainstream education.

ICT and inclusion

Jordan (2000)[10] indicates that the provision of ICT had a very positive impact on the number of children with disabilities attending and remaining in mainstream schools. One of the main Irish teacher unions, the Irish National Teachers Organisation (INTO) has stated that technology can aid the integration of children into mainstream schools and hence into the wider community, a position which was endorsed by the Irish National Council for Curriculum and Assessment in 2002. For the teacher, ICT offers a different way of presenting material; for the learner, it offers a different way of interacting with the curriculum. The leading UK organisation on the role of ICT in teaching and learning, the widely respected British Educational and Communications Technology Agency (Becta) has summarised research in this area and concluded that children who previously could not communicate can, with the aid of technology, now make their needs known and can be included in ordinary classroom activities.

It is important, however, to be clear about the limitations of technology when talking about inclusion. To say ICT encourages inclusion is too simplistic. For example, Blamires (2000)[11] argues that 'some technology enables access to technology but in itself does not enable inclusion – in fact it may preclude this if it means that a child is sat by themselves on the adapted PC'. Blamires would also argue that it is possible for a child to be 'included' via technology even though he may not be in the same classroom, but because he is actively learning within a virtual learning community. There is impressive evidence of this taking place in a number of ICT projects, including the Dissolving Boundaries programme where, as we saw in the previous chapter, links have been formed between SEN children in different schools and between children in mainstream schools working with children in special schools. One further particularly impressive example of ICT being used between learners in two special schools in Northern Ireland was reported at the Xchange 2006 conference where pupils with severe learning difficulties had used Writing with Symbols software, digital cameras, recording equipment and video conferencing to work together on a presentation about their respective towns in Bangor and Magherafelt. Teachers reported that pupils discussed the progress of the project using LearningNI and noted a wide range of benefits, both academic and social.[12]

The role of the teacher

Most of the research suggests that technology itself cannot do much, that the role of the teacher is critical and it is his/her skill and understanding of how pupils learn which is the vital factor (Blamires, 1999). Wynne argues that 'the most crucial factor in the use of ICT in SEN is, that the needs of the individual are assessed first and the computer activity or application is then matched to that need'. This view is supported by NI teachers in the survey, several of whom said all ICT activities can be very successful if used thoughtfully.

> All [ICT activities] are capable of productive results in the right contexts and with sufficient support, 'Success or failure has more to do with relevance [to pupils' needs] and user competence/expertise than with the features of the resources per se. If staff or pupils understand fully how the resource works and see a link with the difficulty/need being addressed, then a successful outcome will be more likely. Resources which are not understood or left unsupported usually fail to make any impact.

Seventy-five per cent of the teachers in the Northern Ireland survey agreed that ICT helped to improve learning through better access to the curriculum and personal feedback. Pupils could reinforce their learning, work independently and at their own pace.

The survey also revealed that 50 per cent of the respondents agreed that ICT had changed the way they taught in the classroom although 25 per cent were not convinced. Those who said it had changed their practice said it was because ICT was being used to reinforce concepts or because it made learning less formal and more fun and it helped to make pupils more independent and raised self-esteem. A minority said ICT was changing their teaching because it was a different means of making resources. This restricted view was echoed by a teacher in a specialist SEN unit in a mainstream school who said that ICT 'can be used in ways that don't impinge too much'. This honest appraisal is worth noting in the context of debate about the optimistic claims made for ICT. Malouf (2001)[13] suggests a lot of the beliefs about the value of ICT in SEN are based on teacher opinion rather than statistical data. However, McFarlane (1997)[14] says that teachers should not necessarily rely too much on the above and should be convinced when they see the change in attitude and behaviour as a result of ICT.

> When that excitement, wonder and empowerment of children is harnessed and focused by informed practitioners, the intellectual development it facilitates is worth the initial angst.

But some researchers such as Crook (1994)[15] suggest that there is a real need for teachers to understand learning theories and how the different types of computer software reflect theory. Lack of understanding can lead to misuse of software and blunt the potential of ICT for SEN children. This goes to the very heart of what is involved in professional development for teachers and the interface between theory and practice.

Theoretical learning models, SEN and practice

Much of what has been written about ICT and SEN refers to four broad theoretical models; these models are based around constructivism, social constructivism, behaviourism and the work of Vygotsky on Zones of Proximal Development (ZPD). We argue here that knowledge of these theories is a crucial dimension to the use of ICT in teaching and learning, not least because some of these models are built into the design of software and can also shape the ways that hardware is managed in the classroom.

Briefly, the constructivist model assumes that learning is an individualised process and the learner needs to be active since it is through actively engaging with the material that he or she develops thinking and constructs meaning. In the social constructivist model, the innate abilities of memory, perception and attention are developed through interaction with people and tools, e.g. language, counting, art, computers. Learning takes place within a situation and context.

The behaviourist approach takes the view that a subject or learner responds to a stimulus. The correct response is reinforced and therefore the desired behaviour/learning is developed. The value and use of these models has been sharply contested by researchers and have exposed fundamental questions about the nature of learning. For example, there is much debate over the use of drill and practice and arguments about whether they fit into the constructivist or behaviourist view of learning and therefore about their value in teaching and learning. Ofsted (2001),[16] the educational inspection service in England, showed that ICT could assist those with reading difficulties but other research, as above, has found that these areas are dominated by spelling and word recognition programs.

Many teachers, including those in the 2005 Northern Ireland survey would argue that drill and practice activities allow valuable opportunities for over-learning which pupils with SEN usually need. Drill and practice do provide self-paced programmes which are a motivating factor for SEN. They also include other motivating factors such as immediate feedback and response and early correction which may help eliminate the reinforcement of errors. They are effective with students in specific reading areas such as mastery of sight vocabulary and basic mathematical facts which pupils need before they can make progress in higher order number concepts. This may be why teachers remain positive about their use. (Bonnet, 1997;[17] Lick and Little, 1987[18]). The reasons given by Wynne's sample of teachers for the use of this type of ICT with SEN children included the ability to give plenty of practice in basic skills, the facilitation of individualised training programmes, the non-judgmental response of the software and immediate feedback. However, Underwood and Underwood (1994)[19] points back to the importance of supplementary teacher instruction and the need to use drill and practice in conjunction with other activities which use the same skills. So there are circumstances where drill and practice may have a part to play but these activities offer few opportunities for understanding any material read nor do they help recall detail, sequence or critical thinking. If ICT is concerned with changing the nature of how children learn, unthinking use of behaviourist approaches has limited value. Even programmes such as Integrated Learning Systems (ILS) which have replaced computer assisted learning packages rely heavily on the management style of the teachers for their success. Ravitz *et al.* (1999)[20] however note that strong constructivists do not necessarily reject drill and practice software outright but they do make use of it, not just for pupils with SEN, but use it across all ability levels.

So, in summary, behaviourist ideas of learning have been widely used in the application of ICT to children with SEN but there are some underlying assumptions about learning which teachers need to consider carefully.

Constructivism, social constructivism and Vygotsky

The influence of psychological theories

Constructivist approaches change the very nature of the learning process by altering the balance between transfer of knowledge to the learner and the production of knowledge by the learner. Mulkeen (2004)[21] believes that the teacher should become a 'facilitator' in order to make it possible for pupils to learn using ICT.

However, there are others, like Cox (1997),[22] who argues that the role of facilitator only is not ideal for children with SEN as they often need explicit instruction. Cox suggests that facilitation can have a negative effect on children with SEN because they need structure, scaffolding and cannot cope with too much open-ended independent decision making.

We believe that there is emerging evidence that teachers in Northern Ireland and in the Republic of Ireland are starting to consider social constructivist ideas in their use of ICT and SEN; sometimes they may be doing this without consciously recognising it. This is happening partly because of a belief that the use of computers in teaching and learning is encouraging collaboration and assisted learning. This belief has drawn upon Vygotsky's idea of peer tutoring to enable progress in the ZPD.

The ZPD is the difference between what the child can achieve on his own and that which could be achieved with the help of an adult or more capable peer. The purpose of a teacher is to help the child through the ZPD. Interaction is therefore essential for learning. This supports the idea of peer tutoring and is supportive of the common method of computer use in schools, i.e. pupils working in pairs. In the 2005 Northern Ireland survey of teacher trainees, paired computer use was the most common method in classrooms where computer suites were not used.

Wynne also suggests that the curriculum in the Republic of Ireland is heavily influenced by Vygotskyian philosophy but large classes make it impractical and there are still elements of behaviourism particularly where low level basic skills are being taught. She claims that this approach is more common with children of low ability or those having special educational needs.

Pachler (1999)[23] believes that the multimedia approach is applicable to constructivist theory as it has potential to create 'near to life' microworlds.

> The multiple formats enable the learner to access the material using their preferred learning style and may be more in keeping with their most developed area of intelligence. Presentation of material in multiple formats has been shown to improve retention and the development of memory skills.

Software: practical applications

Here, we can see how the multimedia character of ICT (Perzylo, 1993)[24] connects both to constructivist learning theories and the concept of multiple intelligences. Howard Gardner's work (1999)[25] has underlined the complexity of intelligence and the need for learning strategies that address the requirements of different types of learners. He has made us aware of the need to stimulate the auditory or tactile senses in those with visual impairments and this acknowledgement of different learner needs opens up powerful opportunities for the use of ICT with all children, but especially with SEN pupils.

There is some research to suggest that the computer can actually act as a peer tutor providing scaffolding. In Wynne's study 80 per cent of teachers felt that collaborative learning was aided by working with ICT and that it helped to develop cooperation and collaborative skills. This compares to only 59 per cent of NI teachers in the survey who agreed that ICT encouraged collaboration. However, it was pointed out by many teachers in Northern Ireland that a large number of their pupils were working to individual education plans and therefore collaboration was not realistic in many cases. When experienced teachers were asked about managing ICT 93 per cent said that classroom assistants worked with individual pupils in ICT. The most common way of working was that the teacher introduced the task to the pupil(s) then the classroom assistant supported the pupil as he/she worked through it.

They did cite a number of ways though in which collaboration within ICT was very successful. These included sharing of skills between pupils and, in particular, the use of the interactive whiteboard or data projector where data could be discussed, shared and enjoyed together(see note 26). Having pupils working in pairs can be used with pupils who have Emotional and Behavioural Difficulties (EBD):

> Many learners with EBD find it hard to establish relationships and have little ability or perceived need to relate to others. Using a computer can avoid this problem and can often offer an entry point for another person to join in alongside, in a non-threatening manner.

Although it is very important not to use ICT as a way of excluding pupils with SEN there are times when it may be in the pupils' best interests, e.g. pupils with EBD do not respond well to group work when there is an authoritative figure and turn-taking and waiting for attention are required.

> The use of ICT therefore renders the relationship less confrontational, and teaching becomes more individualised with emphasis on discussion and problem-solving rather than passive listening.[26]

Many pupils with special educational needs are used to individual attention and find it difficult to interact and share with others. This may be particularly true for children with behavioural difficulties or those on the autistic spectrum. They may not feel the need to communicate and may therefore be excluded from some learning experiences.

> Using a computer can avoid this problem, and can often offer an entry point for another person to join in alongside, in a non-threatening manner.

In schools there seems to be a mixed view of using ICT collaboratively. Where ICT is used widely and innovatively there would appear to be a positive view of this. One student teacher quotes this as an aspect that worked particularly well in the special school where she was on placement;

> I used the whiteboard in the classroom and asked pupils to join in as a class to play educational games. The class can work together on different activities using the whiteboard.

Interactive boards seem to be a good way of teaching larger groups in an involved and engaging way. Collaborative writing and maths games are very popular. Several experienced teachers mentioned the use of digital cameras and personal photographs as being particularly useful in learning.

> The children enjoyed sharing class photographs on the overhead after a trip and talking about where we went.

However, the student teacher survey does not uniformly support this positive view of collaborative learning; one commented,

> I have not witnessed ICT being used for collaborative learning. These children would not work well in pairs or groups on the computer as they fight easily.

In concluding this section on social constructivism and children's learning, we would wish to argue that the range of conditions which qualify a child to be described as having special learning needs means that it is unwise to be dogmatic about which learning model is most appropriate. What is vital, however, is that teacher training in ICT and SEN needs to expose the underlying values and beliefs behind learning models; knowledge of this type is critical, particularly when classroom practice has to relate to the needs of the curriculum and decisions about which software to use.

Learning and the curriculum

One of the central tensions in regard to SEN children is the extent to which they should be expected to 'cover' a nationally agreed curriculum and, in the context of this chapter, the extent to which centrally delivered software and hardware can offer educational provision that is genuinely inclusive.

The Northern Ireland curriculum is still very heavily influenced by the examination and assessment structure and schools are under increasing pressure to produce evidence of results. The need for evidence encourages individualism and teachers of SEN children in mainstream classes may find it tempting to use ICT in a 'behaviourist' way to improve assessable skills. The NI teacher survey suggests that ICT is still for many an extension rather than an integral part of teaching, being used often for reinforcement or production of resources rather than teaching of new concepts. The total immersion of ICT into all curriculum areas is rare but is happening on occasion. One teacher commented:

> It doesn't really change what I do, it is incorporated in what I do in order to make my day as interesting and stimulating for all abilities. It is part of most lessons and not used as an extension; it is for all the pupils to explore.

A special school in Northern Ireland attributes much of its success to the embedding of ICT and it is able to do this through relatively high staff–student ratios, good access to hardware and software and high levels of staff professional development in ICT. A further factor here is the role of assessment where a framework has been developed to record the capabilities of the pupils across the various strands of ICT competence in the Northern Ireland Curriculum. Progress is noted and portfolios are kept so that monitoring and evaluation are effective. This approach to assessment seems to be more frequent in special schools than for SEN pupils in mainstream schools.

The findings of the 2005 student teacher survey would suggest that newcomers to the teaching profession felt it was most important to be able to teach ICT skills to pupils. However, they also rated the need to relate ICT to curriculum topics as of high importance too; in the following section we examine the role of software in this complex equation.

Software

Software effectiveness

There has been a phenomenal growth in the amount of educational software available and in particular, for the SEN market. Blamires (1999, see note 8) suggests that until recently most software has only impacted at basic knowledge level and has been confined to a fairly narrow range of learning activity. Given the capacity for the computer to be able to retrieve information quickly and exactly when it is needed, there is less interest in software that is simply based on the recall of information.

Pachler (2000)[27] asks what we know about the designers of software for special educational needs? What are their assumptions about learning?

There are many different types of software available to schools including open-ended software where pupils are provided with tools to create their own work, and content-rich software which includes games, talking books, etc. where the activities are already defined to achieve certain learning objectives. The whole area of software games for education is diverse and these can range from basic 'drill and practice' activities such as learning number tables to adventure-type games where pupils have to solve problems and make decisions.

One baseline for examining the use of software in Northern Ireland comes from the Education and Training Inspectorate report on ICT and special educational needs in 2002. This report said that while the majority of teachers were using ICT effectively 13 per cent of lessons were poorly planned and not challenging to pupils. These consisted of dull, routine, decontextualised activities with inappropriate software. So how do teachers decide whether a piece of software is effective? The teachers in Wynne's study in the Republic of Ireland listed four important factors; 38 per cent said the ability to hold attention of a child and allow it to interact, 18.5 per cent said good software provided successful and enjoyable learning experiences, 28 per cent said it allowed the transfer of skills to other contexts or successful achieved targets and others (percentage unknown) said an important factor was the ease with which the programme could be used independently and its ability to provide scaffolding.

Provision for pupils with special educational needs

In Northern Ireland where software provision for ICT is now centrally managed through C2K, each school has a basic, yet fairly extensive set of software designed to meet curriculum needs. Special schools also receive the most extensive collection, including software from both the primary and the secondary builds, reflecting the wider age range of pupils in many special schools. In addition a number of pieces of software designed specifically for SEN have been supplied for the needs of pupils with learning difficulties. While the managed service has the advantage of providing a common platform, it has been noted that having a managed service can be restrictive (Becta, 2000, see note 25) because it will not accept commercial software packages other than those originally chosen for the network. In the C2K system, this issue was originally addressed by enabling the computers to operate in a complementary 'local school-managed' mode which enables any choice of locally selected software to be used on any managed computer without compromising the managed service reliability. With the continued development of the C2K system, and in response to the wishes of users, special and secondary schools are now able to add their own titles to the managed service side of the networks.

In the 2005 survey of teachers on an SEN course, a question was asked about the value of C2K. Reflecting inspection evidence and the findings of user satisfaction surveys, the majority of the teachers agreed that it had a beneficial effect. One commented that it was 'Fantastic to have on hand a computer and all the software for pupils to use and also for teacher and classroom assistant after 3.30 (pm)'. There were also comments regarding the wide variety of software provided and the fact that a common platform meant that pupils could be sure that they would know how to work any computer station they were using.

Although the sample numbers are too small to make definite statements it would seem that staff in special schools are more likely to be positive about C2K. The reason why teachers in mainstream schools, whether primary or secondary, disagreed was lack of time available and access to get to know the facilities available on C2K better.

Further evidence regarding teacher use of SEN software in mainstream primary schools comes from the student teacher survey where only 16 per cent of students reported seeing the SEN software on teaching practice. Only two students observed a teacher using the SEN toolbox, one using the management tool IEP writer and the other using Talking Clocks, Spider and Friends and Face Paint. This is supported by the teacher survey as very few of these packages were mentioned as being used regularly. Penfriend and Read and Write were specifically mentioned as being useful to aid word processing, while others mentioned SEN programs in general as being used frequently and 'short sessions with SEN programmes' as working particularly well.

'Special' should not be too special

It is important though, to remember that one of the overwhelming reasons to use ICT with pupils who have special educational needs is to give them access to the same curriculum as everyone else, therefore dependence should not be upon using 'special' software. Often simple adaptations to the everyday software will be much more effective. Becta (2000, see note 25) considers that where possible, generic software used by mainstream pupils should also be used by children with learning difficulties but it notes the problems for teachers in advocating this position;

> There are two main difficulties that education staff seem to have when it comes to creating resources for ICT: time and confidence.
>
> The first of these is a real issue. I think that school management should realise that a lot of time needs to be set aside for the creation of ICT resources, especially in an inclusion situation.

It would seem that this is the approach taken by most experienced teachers, as word processing is still the most common activity used in Northern Ireland schools according to the teacher survey. This was described by 72 per cent of the teachers as the most frequently used application. This response was common to all sectors of compulsory education.

Word processing

Despite not being designed particularly for pupils with special needs, Microsoft Word was also mentioned by a number of student teachers. This may be because the students themselves were more familiar with this program. Wynne found that word processing was used more often by inexperienced teachers whose general ICT use was limited.

Moreover, as a number of commentators, including those at Becta have noted, there are very many useful features within Word that make it very adaptable,

> Planning can be carried out using Outline in Word. … Start in 'Outline' and write the headings. Expand these in the 'Notes' area, which can also be used by the teacher to create a writing frame.

Pupils can use a thesaurus to check a word, substitute synonyms and see how the meaning and tone change. Above all, encourage them to use a spellchecker. Although many people are critical of spellcheckers and believe they encourage laziness, students do learn to spell by having their work 'marked' by the machine and seeing the correct alternative suggested. It makes them aware of their errors and helps them to focus on common words that they are getting wrong. The fact that they find their mistakes while they are composing, or as soon as they have finished a piece of work, makes it more meaningful than red pen corrections a few days later.

It is important to remember though that we should not assume that word processing is easier for pupils who have special educational needs. Brown-Chidsey and Boscardin (2001)[28] report a student's view:

> ... when I wrote that report ... it just took forever. And just using it [the computer] took hours and hours and hours and just using it was very boring and I wasn't, I just, I had trouble focusing on it and stuff like that ...

The 2005 Northern Ireland survey showed that while word processing was one of the most commonly used tasks in ICT for SEN; it was also one of the ones which caused most problems.

> Some lower ability pupils struggle greatly with general word processing using Word, using spell checker proves to be difficult.

Recent versions of Word have built in text to speech and this can be very helpful in encouraging independence. Even where pupils have a classroom assistant to help, best practice suggests that they should be using specifically designed talking word processors which are adapted especially with the needs of special need users in mind, rather than a standard corporate word processor, as using a classroom assistant keeps the pupil dependent. If there is a talking word processor, there is more support for tackling tasks and worksheets as difficult words can be read out so there is no need to keep asking for help and work can be completed more independently. Not having a classroom assistant at home is one of the common excuses for not doing homework. If pupils are taught to use a word processor and have access to hardware at home, this can alleviate learning problems related to poor memory, difficulty with spelling, lack of organisation or poor handwriting.

One of the findings from the Northern Ireland survey of experienced teachers of SEN was the continued belief in the value of neat copies of work, and work that was well presented. We surmise that the value attached to this type of work may lend weight to the extensive use of certain types of software which places a premium on 'appearance' more than any other feature of learning. Any moves to change this would require a high level of critical reflection through teacher professional development.

In summarising this section on the very extensive use of word processing with SEN pupils, we can see that the key issues are an appreciation of the potential of this application for some students, the challenge of ensuring that tasks have the right degree of scaffolding and that teachers need to beware of the risks of allowing narrow definitions of 'literacy' to dominate their use of word processing.

Literacy tools

From our evidence, one particular piece of software stands out as being very extensively used; Clicker is an extremely popular program with the student teachers and those that were more experienced. Support for use of Clicker with SEN was also obvious in Wynne's study in the Republic of Ireland. It was described by 33 per cent of teachers as being an excellent tool because of its ability to link writing and reading and because it could be used as a teaching and a learning tool. It is a program which is set up with two areas, one a notepad area where writing is input and an area of cells which contain pictures or words. A pupil can select the words/graphics he or she wants for their writing and the selected text or graphics will appear on the notepad area. It also has the option of sound which allows the pupil to hear the word/sentence he has chosen. Clicker comes very highly recommended, particularly for pupils with Down's Syndrome because, according to a website on inclusive education:[29]

> It can very effectively integrate words, sound, speech, pictures, animations and video to produce the very best types of learning materials to capture a child's interest.

Student teachers also said they had used it more broadly;

> KS1 child with ADHD used Clicker4 to create own sentences.

> Used Clicker4 with very weak pupil for story writing to help with spellings so that her writing could be read by teacher.

It is the versatility of Clicker that attracts teachers, both those about to start in the profession and those with experience.

What is particularly striking about the student teacher data is the predominance of software that is aimed at either literacy or numeracy.

Further evidence for the predominance of this type of software can be found in the use of Talking Books (both those supplied by C2K and others on CD ROM), considered to be 'excellent learning resources' because of their interactive character. Wynne found in her 2004 study that Talking Books were also very popular with teachers working with SEN in the Republic of Ireland, particularly with teachers in their first five years of teaching when they were making infrequent use of ICT.

Talking Books also make use of multimedia, e.g. graphics, text and animation. Phelan and Haughey (2000)[30] say

> they provide a valuable experience allowing the child to move between the written and spoken text, providing the necessary scaffolding which allows the reader to engage with the text.

Other research from Becta points to a range of learning benefits for SEN pupils:

> Many teachers report that [pupils] seem to have increased attention span whilst working on a computer. Interactive talking books are one example of efficient use of ICT for children who have short attention spans.

McKeown (2000)[31] summarises these as follows:

> Most of the talking books have lots of repetition that children can join in with, so that they are learning and practising different spoken language structures. Wellington Square … provides a very structured approach. … The pupil is in control and can read and listen to the text, either word-by-word or sentence-by-sentence. There are also matching and sequencing activities which can be used to check and extend comprehension skills.'

Although research shows that talking books do result in improvement in word accuracy and also in helping children understanding the meaning of the story, Medwell (1998)[32] points out that they are most useful as an additional experience together with teacher interaction since they do not lead to improvements in all aspects of reading. It is also important that the use of interactive books is chosen by the teacher as Collins *et al.* (1997)[33] point out that if the content of the book chosen is pitched too low it will not hold the attention of the reader nor encourage them to use the support available.

Mention should be made of one other piece of software that is designed to promote literacy; as we noted earlier in this chapter, Writing with Symbols 2000 is beginning to be used by teachers, particularly for 'visual' learners such as those with dyslexic type difficulties. The symbol support is built in for text and spell-checking. This allows a pupil to prepare an essay or report with symbols which can then be removed when a pupil is happy that he/she has correctly written what is desired. It can also aid those who have difficulty remembering and/or understanding written or oral instructions. Knowledge of this software in Northern Ireland seems to be confined to special schools. As with all software, this one comes with a health warning; it is important not to rely on any one piece of software as overdependence can actually disable a pupil from making further progress. ICT should be seen as a tool to be used to provide links to further learning, not as the solution.

Alongside the extensive use of software to develop literacy, there is evidence that classroom use of ICT in SEN involves considerable drill and practice type activity intended to reinforce basic concepts in numeracy. This can be seen in the use of the 'Talking Clocks' software and 'Number Box'. One of the student teachers commented:

> Number Box allowed SEN pupils to experience success in creating graphs, something they would normally find difficult to do by hand.

The student data suggests that these are widely supported and found useful by teachers and students alike. This is similar to the findings of Wynne (2004, see note 6) whose research in the Republic of Ireland found that drill and practice type software was used by all the teachers in her survey and as the only software used by 20 per cent of the teachers.

Going beyond literacy and numeracy

While few would deny the importance of developing the key skills of literacy and numeracy for children with SEN, the potential dangers of an overemphasis on this type of learning were noted by the European Agency (2003).[34] They argued that it is vital that SEN children get access to more stimulating programmes to limit the dangers of creating a digital divide between SEN pupils and others.

Our research has provided only limited evidence of the use of ICT in more creative ways in schools with SEN learners in Northern Ireland; but it is happening. Under the banner of 'Being Creative,' an art teacher at a special school has been using ICT to enable her learners to imagine, generate ideas, invent and take risks in the creation of a digitally-filmed clay animation which addressed the issues of discrimination and inclusion for young people with physical disabilities head-on. Her presentation to the Xchange conference in 2006[35] included the following approach to the use of ICT in art with her students:

- Seek out questions to explore and problems to solve
- Experiment with ideas and questions
- Make new connections between ideas/information
- Learn from and value other people's ideas
- Make ideas real by experimenting with different designs, actions, outcomes
- Challenge the routine method
- Value the unexpected or surprising
- See opportunities in mistakes and failures
- Take risks for learning.

Other examples spring from the use of the Internet.

Use of the Internet

The European Agency 2003 found that up to 75 per cent of children in special schools in the Republic of Ireland have access to computers at least once a week and 50 per cent made use of the Internet for research purposes. While we don't have directly comparable data for Northern Ireland, there is some evidence related to the use of the Internet in mainstream primary schools from the student teacher survey. None of the student teachers mentioned the use of the Internet in relation to pupils with SEN but the response to the use of the Internet in the classroom generally showed that around half used it at least once a week with some pupils. This is similar to Internet use in the Republic of Ireland found in Wynne's study. Use of the Internet did not appear frequently in the Northern Ireland survey of experienced teachers although there were several non-specific references to searching for information and data manipulation. A very successful use of the Internet is described by a special school when they used the 2003 Special Olympics website as a focus for whole class discussion. They then used it as the basis of a project to develop their own website on the theme of Special Olympics where they created their own images, used cameras and scanners together with word processing. According to the school's web site:[36]

> The children and parents are extremely proud of this work and aware of the potential of the Internet to provide a worldwide showcase for the pupils' work.

Computer-based games

Some research suggests that computer games can be used to develop problem-solving skills such as making inferences, predicting, testing, making hypotheses and decisions. In the traditional classroom these opportunities are restricted and 'practical experiences are inherently time consuming and subject to frequent disappointments' (Wynne, 2004, see note 6). Using computer adventure games can allow a child to practise these skills without detrimental consequences. Despite the tendency for many to think of these games as 'playing' on the computer, 'the element of play is an important factor since play is so important in a child's development' (Wynne, 2004, see note 6). But it is necessary for the teacher to identify the skills within the game and to plan tasks on and off the computer to promote these skills. According to the Republic of Ireland's National Council for Curriculum and Assessment (NCCA), it is important not to dismiss these for use with SEN as they can help to promote problem-solving skills for all children even though the challenge may be greater (Phelan and Haughey, 2000, see note 5).

Wynne's 2004 study showed that the use of these types of programmes seemed to increase with the experience of the teacher. Experienced teachers used ICT more frequently and used a wider variety of software including adventure-type games two or three times a week. They can provide a particularly valuable environment for cooperative and collaborative learning.

In summarising the section on software, we need to underline two key points; there appears to be a strong use of ICT with SEN children for the development of literacy and numeracy in Northern Ireland and this is similar at least to findings from the Republic of Ireland. The extensive range of software provided by C2K, which has the potential to broaden learning well beyond drill and practice has not yet been fully deployed and this probably reflects the relatively recent arrival of this in schools and teacher training institutions. What this underlines is the critical role of training at both pre-service level and during professional development.

At all times it is vital to remember that a piece of software alone will not solve all the problems; Fennema-Jansen (2001)[37] made the point as follows:

> Simply providing a student with a piece of software, even if it is effective for that [pupil], is generally not sufficient! Strategy instruction should be combined with instruction in the use of technology to better meet the needs of [pupils].

Training

In this final section of the chapter we consider the question of training for both experienced teachers and those undertaking initial training. One key issue to be clear about is that systematic training for all teachers in SEN and the use of ICT in SEN is comparatively new. None of the primary teachers in the survey had been using ICT in SEN for five or more years. Furthermore, the full impact of the inclusion agenda is taking time to be fully embedded in all mainstream schools. One illustration of this is that when teachers in Northern Ireland of SEN from both special and mainstream schools were asked about the place of ICT in the development of pupils' Individual Learning Plans (ILP) there was a marked difference between the two sets of responses; in special schools teachers are required to use ILPs and made it clear in their responses that ICT was planned as part of an individualised programme. This was not the case for SEN teachers in mainstream schools.

When asked about the training received, all respondents identified the need for further training. A number of experienced teachers in the survey were still unfamiliar with the programs available for special needs and complained that lack of time to familiarise themselves with the software was one of the reasons for under-use of ICT.

Despite the apparent lack of training, the majority (56 per cent) considered themselves as competent or better in the use of ICT and 62 per cent considered themselves competent or better in SEN. This apparent paradox might be explained as showing that teachers have general confidence in their ability to work with SEN children and general confidence in their use of ICT, but that they needed development in the specific use of ICT to promote learning with SEN pupils.

There are some impressive examples of how things are changing, however; teachers and advisors of SEN have recently completed an online programme of professional development set up by the Regional Training Unit where the focus was on how 'employability', a key target in the revised Northern Ireland curriculum, could be supported with SEN children.[38]

Student teachers' initial training

In Chapter 4, we analysed the nature of ICT provision for students in their initial phase of training through a case study of one particular institution; data from that 2005 survey also throws light on the extent to which student teachers feel ready to use ICT to support their work with SEN children in mainstream schools. These students were all given specific training in the use of the C2K software for SEN, encouraged to use this on their teaching practice and to take part in online discussions about their experience of working with SEN children, including the use of ICT with such children.

In the survey of their experiences on this one-year training programme, data was gathered at the end of their year; students were asked how useful they found the SEN session on ICT. The percentage of students who reported finding it useful or very useful was 88 and, more generally, in terms of the importance attached to the use of ICT in SEN, 35 of the 67 students considered this to be one of the five top priorities to be taught. In relation to other topics, it ranked 7/13 in order of priority.

One particularly interesting finding from this survey relates to the value of online discussions about SEN and the effect of such reflection on improving professional practice. In answer to a question about this, 84 per cent of student teachers believed the discussion had helped to improve what they did with SEN pupils.

The other key findings from the student teacher survey was that those with the highest levels of personal ICT competence were the ones who were most likely to make the greatest use of the SEN software. As levels of expertise in ICT steadily improve through the greater use of ICT in schools, we can anticipate that student teachers will bring with them a far deeper experience of ICT and will be able in their professional training to focus more thoroughly on the pedagogical use of ICT.

Global messages

What are the main messages from this chapter about the place of ICT in supporting inclusive and special education in Northern Ireland which may have significance? We list four which we believe are important.

- A managed learning environment, in this case provided through C2K, offers the potential for significant improvement in the learning experience of such children. At present, this is more likely to be found in special schools than for pupils with special needs in mainstream schools and this presents a formidable challenge in terms of training at all stages of professional development for mainstream teachers. This is not in any sense a criticism of the excellent work done by many teachers of SEN in mainstream schools; the differences arise more from issues to do with professional development and awareness, access to appropriate hardware and staff–pupil ratios. It is significant that, in recognition of the major gains for special school learners, the ratio of core provision centrally resourced to pupils in special schools is 1:5. In other words, sustainability requires on-going opportunities for professional development and good levels of access to resources.

- Learners with special needs can benefit from the application of ICT in all areas of their curriculum, not just in improving literacy and numeracy, although these are clearly important.

- Third, we maintain that professional development of teachers around the use of ICT for SEN needs to enable teachers to think through the underlying learning theories that underpin the design and use of software and the assumptions about what types of learning are regarded as important.

- And finally, e-schooling requires an explicit recognition about values associated with the use of ICT, in this case, that every child, irrespective of need, should be able to reap the benefits of digital technology.

8 Enterprising education

In the Introduction to this book, we said that one of the key features of the e-schooling process was that there should be a clear alignment between broad policy objectives and the types of ICT activities in schools. In Chapter 2 we noted how the needs of a more knowledge-based economy were highlighted in government thinking about the justification for a systemic approach to the funding of the ICT infrastructure for schools. In this chapter we investigate the roles that ICT plays in preparing young people in Northern Ireland for the world of work. This is a particularly acute question to pose given the high levels of investment in the educational ICT infrastructure and the frequent justification of such costs as a necessary investment in the economic future. We do not wish to imply that the only justification for ICT use is its capacity to meet economic needs; other chapters have underlined the significance of ICT for social cohesion, for promoting inclusive education and overall, for improving the quality of learning. However, we argue that the needs of a global economy, increasingly based on creativity and information, require some hard thinking about the matches between ICT experiences and enterprise.

The Empowering Schools strategy gives a clear steer to the relationship which needs to exist between the type of ICT activity that takes place in school, to ensure that young people have the skills needed to be economically active in the global knowledge community, and how well these skills and activities match what employers want.

Young people need to be prepared for work in a knowledge economy, developing high-level cognitive skills for:

- Working safely in teams (whose members may be in different locations);
- self-reliance and self-management;
- collaborative problem-solving;
- creativity and innovation;
- high-level reasoning, analysing, conceptualising;
- communicating and understanding within multi-cultural environments;
- autonomous learning.[1]

But what is actually happening in classrooms in Northern Ireland? The chapter begins with an analysis of evidence of the use of ICT in schools for enterprise. This is followed by discussion of data which throws light on the relationship between employers' needs and what the education and training sector are providing through ICT. The chapter concludes with two case studies of projects which have explored new models of training and learning in the development of creative and multi-media skills. We justify the inclusion of this data on the basis that a definition of enterprise has to include the notions of innovation, risk-taking and creativity.

School ICT skills and the work place

We noted in Chapter 5 how the curriculum in schools has become more skills based, more closely orientated towards employability and the central role that ICT plays across the curriculum. Relatively little work has been done, however, on the relationship between the types of ICT activity that takes place in school and the links to enterprise education.

In Northern Ireland evidence related to this question was collected in June 2005[2] when a small representative cross-section of learners taking Business Studies as one of their GCSE examinations was questioned about their use of ICT. These learners were aged 15 at the time of this study. Such learners have to study English, maths and science but are then free to choose a range of other subjects for study.

Learner experiences of ICT

Learners were asked to place in rank order the subjects making most use of ICT. Business Studies was the subject using ICT most often (38.8 per cent), followed by English (14.9 per cent), Information Technology (10.4 per cent), Maths (10.4 per cent) and Technology (9 per cent). Two findings should be noted here; the first is the significant amount of use of ICT in Business Studies and the second is the near absence of ICT use in modern languages.

Learners were also asked to indicate the frequency of their ICT use in their subjects studied. The subjects using ICT most frequently '2–3 times per week' in this small sample were business studies (23.9 per cent), information communication technology (11.9 per cent), construction and mathematics (7.5 per cent).

Types of ICT use

Learners were asked about the uses of ICT in the compulsory subjects they had to take; here, subjects making the most use of ICT were English 47.8 per cent, followed by mathematics 25.4 per cent, and science 11.9 per cent. Learner perception of compulsory subjects' use of ICT was dominated by presenting information (86.5 per cent), followed by searching for information (68.7 per cent). Almost half of the learners agreed that ICT was used in their chosen compulsory subject in a range of ways; to solve problems creatively, using spreadsheets and working as part of a team.

Usage of ICT in optional subjects was also dominated in this sample by presenting information (86.6 per cent), closely followed by searching for information (74.6 per cent) and creativity (74.6 per cent). Such a high return for the creative use of ICT is perhaps explained by the subjects selected by learners as the ones making most use of ICT, i.e. technology 19.4 per cent and ICT 14.9 per cent. Learners studying technology and construction all agreed that ICT was used creatively. There was also clear agreement among music and art and design students of the creative use of ICT. In the optional subjects, 32.8 per cent of learners (primarily studying ICT and technology) indicated they used ICT for simulations/role plays and designing web pages.

Three conclusions are worth noting here; the first concerns the variations in the *amount* of use of ICT in teaching and learning. Two years after the introduction of C2K the data shows learners have a perception of a high level of use of ICT in business studies but a low use of ICT in science, one of the core subjects.

The second conclusion relates to the type of use of ICT. The predominance of information retrieval and presentation of information are striking; while not denying the relevance of this type of ICT application which is expected in the teaching of these subjects and its value in learning, it is not at all clear that these skills are the only ones that are most valued by employers. We wonder if it is the availability of software like PowerPoint and relatively easy access to the Internet that are the drivers of these types of ICT use.

We leave this section of the chapter with questions for further investigation; are learners acquiring the breadth of skills they need to be enterprising when they leave school or college? In the following sections, we offer an analysis of data that throws light on these issues.

The role of the Further and Higher Education sector

Thus far in the book, we have focused attention on the school sector's ICT infrastructure and its impact on teachers and learners; but in examining the relationship between education, ICT and employability, we also need to take account of the influential Costello (2004) and Bain reports (2006) which recommended that one way to ensure that all learners receive the right balance of general (academic) and vocational skills is to strengthen the links between secondary schools and the

Further and Higher Education sector. Northern Ireland has at present 16 colleges of Further and Higher Education, providing vocational training for learners, predominantly in the 16–19 age group. From 2007, the 16 further education colleges will be merged into six 'super' colleges. These FHE colleges have been autonomous since 1998 and have evolved their own ICT framework, quite distinct from what has happened in schools. The FHE colleges are the responsibility of the Department for Employment and Learning (DEL). DEL clearly sees the FHE sector as having a key role to play in providing a skills base for employers. Their 2005 publication 'FE means Business' underlined the importance of links between the colleges and employers and the need to develop entrepreneurial attitudes among lecturers and learners. It has sponsored a 'Lecturers into Industry' scheme since 2001 which has been popular with staff and found to have been a powerful form of professional and personal development.

ICT connectivity

The FHE colleges have been linked together through the UK wide Joint Academic Network (JANET) which provides connectivity for all Higher Education institutions in the United Kingdom. Until 2005, the FHE colleges' ICT infrastructure was outside C2K, making it difficult for learners to use ICT easily if they were based in school and 'released' to work in their local FHE college for part of the week. However, the links that have been established since August 2005 between the C2K and the JANET networks make connectivity between schools and the FHE colleges feasible.

ICT and FHE lecturers

Given everything that has been said about the role of ICT in education, the extent to which college lecturers are able to use ICT in their work with learners is critical. Most of the learners in the FHE sector are aged 16–19 and have transferred from either non-selective secondary schools or in a few cases from selective 'grammar' schools.

To examine the place of ICT in the FHE sector, evidence was gathered in June 2005 from 91 lecturers who were completing their mandatory one-year training course, the Post Graduate Certificate of Further and Higher Education.[3] It is a measure of the differences in culture and organisation between the FHE sector and the school sector that whereas schools routinely talk about ICT (information communications technology), the FHE sector refer to ILT (information and learning technology). In the following section we have used ILT when referring to teaching and learning since that is the language of the FHE sector.

How ILT is used

The percentage of staff who used ILT for planning and preparation every day numbered 59.3, 89 per cent using ILT at least once a week. Staff using ILT in teaching classes every day constituted 42.9 per cent, rising to 74 per cent at least once a week and 44 per cent of staff indicated that learners use ILT everyday, rising to 86 per cent using it at least once a week. Staff use ILT mainly to communicate/present information and for information retrieval.

Staff were also asked about learner use of ILT; replies showed a predominance of information retrieval, followed by developing literacy and communicating/presenting information, with creative uses of ILT a much lower priority.

Regarding the use of ILT to communicate and to present information, staff commented that 'students complain about "death by PowerPoint" and don't like using it', while others said they 'would use [ILT] more if facilities were available' and that 'some classes [are] delivered by PowerPoint but not enough areas set up for delivery', and 'I don't have computer access in my classroom'.

The most striking conclusions about staff use of ILT are the high percentages (89 per cent) who claim to use it so often it would seem to be fairly embedded in the normal pattern of teaching and learning. Second, we can see further evidence of the predominance of two types of use, communicating and retrieving information. The risks of boring learners with over-use of presentation software are starting to emerge. However, there are some signs of ILT also being used to develop learner literacy and to use it in courses which demand creativity. There was no correlation between the number of years teaching and staff use of ILT in teaching classes. This is an interesting finding and contradicts the easy assumption that it is the younger members of staff who are more likely to use ILT.

Extent of use of ILT

There was an extremely close correlation between staff who use ILT every day and learners using ILT every day. The majority of staff using ILT in teaching every day appear to have learners using ILT either every day or twice a week. The exception to this was construction where the majority of staff claimed to be using ILT often but this was not matched by learner use of ILT. Few staff agreed (14.3 per cent) that most of their learners' learning was online; one of these staff was an 'e-learning manager teaching a majority of students online'. Staff commented that 'a severe lack of ILT resources has a strong impact on teaching and delivery strategies', while another said 'online learning takes place in the classroom, but not distance learning'. Further comments were that 'this is the way forward but facilities as yet are not in place', 'not quite yet, but moving towards that area. However, a balance should be maintained so that students do turn up for classes, as both are very needed', and online learning 'will be more apparent through VLE-Blackboard when the system is supported more through team members'.

Subjects making the most frequent use of ILT tended to be in subjects with a strong basis in technology: ICT, construction, engineering and administration.

What role does knowledge of employer needs play?

All subjects have some kind of link with employers and 71.4 per cent of FE staff said they were clear about the ILT needs of employers in their sector. This was particularly notable among staff teaching ICT. A majority (58.2 per cent) of staff used this knowledge to shape learners' learning experience and 44 per cent of staff responded that their learners were clear what ICT skills employers needed, with 40.7 per cent suggesting that learners use the knowledge to shape their ILT experiences.

The research indicated a correlation between high levels of learner use of ILT and staff understanding of employer needs, although the extent of learners' use of ILT was also influenced by factors such as timetabling and access to resources. The importance of staff awareness of employer needs was highlighted through staff comments 'must be aware of market place and how skills fit in', and that you 'never know what employers need'. Staff commented that 'employers fail to see the need of computer training' and that 'skills [are] always changing so continuous updated courses [are] needed' in developing awareness.

There was strong agreement from staff who expect an acceleration in ILT becoming more central to their teaching and learning; one commented that it 'has started to creep in slowly. Not getting enough time to develop'. There was however strong disagreement among ICT specialist staff, perhaps an indication that ILT has already become so central to their work. One said that while it was 'difficult to keep up with changes from major computing companies' nevertheless they expected little change and increase in the use of ILT.

Where lecturing staff agreed that their use of ILT over the past 12 months had become more central to their work there was a close match in their opinion that it had also become more central to the work of their learners. Equally, those staff who agreed that they expect to see an acceleration in their use of ILT over the next 12 months, assumed this would be true for learners. In nine subject areas all staff expected to see a greater increase in their students' use of ILT than in their own. The main exceptions to this rule appear in 'electrical/electronic engineering' and 'construction, built environment and civil engineering', where there was a sharp divergence between staff expecting to use ILT more but with no corresponding increase expected in use by learners.

What general conclusions can be drawn from the data? We can point to the growing use of ILT, to the lecturers' belief that it will become more central and to the lecturers' claim that they are aware of employers' ILT needs. The connectivity between the FHE colleges' ICT infrastructure and that of C2K presents a basis for significant opportunities to develop vocational education for all young people aged 14–19.

Creativity and innovation

In this section of the chapter we consider two case studies that reflect our view that enterprise education is predominantly about creativity, innovation and risk-taking. The first case study examines a project called Dreamlab which set out in 2002 to

> develop and test ways in which young people (15–18) could further their skills in art, design, music and technology through programmes of production-based training that are led by industry professionals.[4]

The project responded to concerns that the speed of advances in the ICT sector means that there is a widening gap between the ICT skills of teachers and those that are required in employment. While schools and FHE colleges provide generic skills training in ICT for all learners, and more specialised learning at GCSE, A level and through vocational ICT qualifications, advances in software widely used in industry are taking place at such a rapid pace that there is danger that learners will emerge from education unable to capitalise on the new opportunities that global markets are creating.

Education and industry links

To address this problem, specialist learning centres with a strong focus on the role of ICT in the creative and media arena have been set up; the first such centre, the Nerve Centre,[5] has been operational since 1990 and has been followed by three other centres, each initially supported by an Education and Library Board. The most recent resource is a mobile unit, designed to bring maximum accessibility to all the schools in the North Eastern Education and Library Board and in the Monaghan region of the Republic of Ireland. These centres are all in one form or another, a response to the government initiative called 'Unlocking Creativity' which was launched in 2000 and brought together complementary goals of four government departments, coordinated by the Department of Culture, Arts and Leisure (DCAL). Its website[6] explains the key purpose of this initiative; to develop the capacities of all people for creativity and innovation, and so promote and sustain the social, cultural and economic well-being of Northern Ireland. Since the inception of the Unlocking Creativity initiative, the concept of creativity and the development of creative industries have been seen as central to Northern Ireland's ability to respond to the challenges of the global economy.

As we shall see in the following section, the type of learning model that can link education to industry was central to a programme that has sought to bridge the gap between the creative industry's ICT needs and the experience of learners in schools.

Setting up the Dreamlab model

Dreamlab Generation was set up in 2002, funded by NESTA (the National Endowment for Science Technology and the Arts),[7] the Southern and South Eastern Education and Library Boards (who provided finance through their Dissemination of Innovation and Good Practice programme) as well as one year of funding from DCAL. Dreamlab worked with the advisers for creative and expressive learning in the Education and Library Boards to identify 10 secondary schools that were interested in applying innovative approaches to the use of ICT in art, design, music and technology. At the same time, Dreamlab identified appropriate trainers from industry skilled in industry standard software, particularly Photoshop, Dreamweaver, Flash, Cubase, Sibelius and Hypersonic software for music, 3D Studio Max, and Solid Works. This project is particularly interesting because of the model of teaching and learning it developed; interviews for an external evaluation carried out in 2005 with staff and learners in almost half of the schools that took part revealed how the industry professionals carried out their training.

The learning model that Dreamlab developed was distinctive, unusual and highly innovative; quite simply young industry trainers, described by one teacher as 'freelance web designers, multi-media designers, digital artists … young and trendy!', arrived at the school to provide ICT training … for both older learners and teachers. While the training which took place after school was challenging, it had the advantage of being an intensive preparation which was immediately put into practice. It also meant teachers and learners learning together, as one of the teachers remarked.

> I sat at a desk between a sixth former here and a sixth former there and to all intents and purposes I was part of it all … a couple of the ICT staff were involved , we had a couple of A level Art teachers … we all sat in the room together.

Learners as mentors

The partnership that emerged between the teachers and the trainers created a new set of learning dynamics; one teacher, who was commenting on how quickly his pupils had become mentors said:

> … we don't actually need to know everything, there is a threshold of knowledge I think the teacher needs about the software and about how that is delivered but you

don't need to know all the software, you need to know where to direct the pupils and how to shape their learning.

This was clearly an arrangement that had benefits on all sides; one of the A level pupils who had been in this role said:

> to be honest we're kind of teaching the teachers now how to use these programs and they're getting a lot out of it and a wee bit of confidence is great for me.

The awareness of new models of teaching and learning also made some staff realise the limitations of more traditional approaches; a teacher in one of the rural schools was very clear that the Dreamlab training resulted in her setting higher targets arising from task-based work. There are important messages here about the nature of training and learning to which we will return in the conclusion.

Access problems
To turn the training into real learning experiences presented the teachers with a set of challenges in many ICT projects in school; in one of the schools the teacher had to 'use a lot of sweet talking' to get access to the computer room, found that the school policy disallowed long term bookings and that the technicians were already under pressure to sort out other ICT problems in the school. This teacher managed to get four PCs in her own teaching room and while this worked well with small groups of sixth formers and even GCSE students, it was impossible to teach a whole class of Key Stage 3 learners. However access to hardware was not a problem in the other three schools.

Matters of capacity
During the period of the Dreamlab project the Northern Ireland managed ICT service for schools, Classroom 2000 (C2K) was implemented in most primary and secondary schools. As described in Chapter 2, schools are provided with a common hardware and software base and broadband connectivity to the Internet.

Here and in other schools, and in respect of the unusually large data files created by multimedia assets being used in applications, the basic amount of memory allocated to individual learners on the C2K network presented a problem: one of the schools resolved the problem by using the school's flexibility within the managed service to allocate extra memory space to selected learners while another encouraged the GCSE and A level students to use their own memory pens for storage. At times, the system firewall, which prevents learners from coming upon pornographic and other undesirable web sites, prevented access to some sites for legitimate research by the learners.

When these difficulties had been addressed, there was the pleasure of enthusiastic learners, fully engaged with the realities of high quality software and doing exactly what Dreamlab had hoped; here's just one of the learners explaining how a piece of software helped him to design a bicycle frame:

> Basically what it is, it's when you make the components, they're not made out of a certain material but just a component and what you can do is render them is, you can change the material they're made out of so you can see what it would look like if it was made out of that material, you can change the scene they're sitting in, you can change where the light is coming from and you can see pretty much every single angle and you can move them while rendered, you can see the shadows and the light shining on them and it's all different materials that I've used and they're coming up in different colours.

Impact on the learners

All the learners interviewed in every school were very positive about their experiences with Dreamlab and their comments were often reinforced by teachers. In one school the overall effect was a marked increase in the number of learners choosing to do A level in IT and improved grades attained. The teacher believed that the experience was helping them both in terms of higher education and employability, a view supported by teachers in other schools. Another learner made it clear that his experience with Dreamlab had changed his career plans:

> Whenever I finished the first year I was really enthusiastic about it and during the summer we won the chance to go and work and make a music video from DreamLab, and after doing that I really changed my career prospects. I already had decided what choices I made for university but after that I changed them all and they're all now multi-media based or something like that ...

This student, commenting on what he saw as an emerging growth sector in multimedia in Northern Ireland, saw the potential of setting up his own business. In another school, the teacher talked about the authenticity of the work the learners were doing:

> They can identify with it, it's so real, they're looking at their CD covers, their game covers, videos, DVDs and they can make theirs look so much like what they're buying in the shop.

These learners had designed a logo which had been adopted by their local council, a recognition that was not missed by the senior management in the school. Another teacher described a project in which four GCSE students had to design a web site as a 'very real-world experience':

> There was an outside audience and they had a valid target and they had deadlines that had to be met because the prize was to go to Jamaica over Easter with the project so they had four weeks to do it, they were pushed for time, they had other work going

on, they had to budget their time, and they had to be prepared to put in the extra time after school, all of which they did, and they had the pressure that it wasn't going to be ready in time.

At its best, it meant that the learners had to work out solutions to design problems as a team:

> They worked as a team, in other words instead of four kids sitting in a classroom environment and all of them learning the same skills because there was a time frame for this to be done in, a couple of them worked on the video aspect of the thing, somebody else worked on the time and they all learned different skills and came together to complete the task ... it was one of the first times that I was able to give them a real live situation and they worked and learned different things and helped each other.

In another school this led to learners making more effort, partly because, as the teacher recognised, they were exploring new areas of creativity where the weakness in traditional skills in drawing were not holding them back and where achievement by learners with lower ability had a significant effect on their sense of self-worth.

> They got a lot of advantage out of working with the Industry professionals, I think it gave a lot of meaning to what they were doing and put it in a context of the real world and what lay ahead, it opened their eyes a lot, even down at the Odyssey at the presentations last year. There were people from TV and the Film Industry and they were talking to them, I think they saw a lot of opportunities there as well.

> One little boy I had is a lower ability and he's a very quiet child anyway and unsure of himself and he just thought he was wonderful when he created this piece of work, he was so pleased with it; very important for his self-esteem.

Learner achievement was also highlighted by a music teacher who first explained one of the tasks the learners had done as part of their GCSE coursework:

> ... they have a 'commission competency' where they have to compose music for set briefs, one of which is film music and structured as you would in music industry if you were writing music for a film ... there's a certain action and the music represents that action. The musical ideas that the children were bringing themselves were quite basic but the enhancement of Dream [Lab] was in showing how to use modulation and other special effects to make those basic ideas more professional.

Overall, these comments are a convincing testimony to the power of multimedia to motivate learners; the links with industry through Dreamlab had clearly raised learner achievement, enhanced their employability and broadened their choices in further and higher education.

Sustainable learning
What conclusions can be drawn about the learning model used by Dreamlab? Without exception, teachers said that they had really appreciated the professional development from the trainers, and there was evidence that their growing confidence had enabled them to try other ICT applications. The experience had also whetted their appetite for more training, not least because the arrival of additional hardware through C2K was helping them see new possibilities for implementing creative work in their normal timetables. The particular learning model that Dreamlab used worked well in the first year when older examination students and teachers could acquire new skills together but this approach was less successful when efforts were made to use this with larger numbers of younger learners. In the long term, up-skilling teachers is the only way that creative and innovative work can be widely disseminated. Such training is likely to be most effective when the teachers have an immediate need to introduce new software into their teaching and have regular access to sufficient hardware to be able to implement this in a whole-class setting. The learners who have been part of this project have had their eyes opened to a new world and have benefited enormously from a unique partnership between their teachers and industry trainers. They have acquired not only new technical skills but have, in many cases, become more confident as a result of the quality of work they have produced. In a few cases, this confidence enabled them to mentor both their peers and their teachers.

Creative Learning in the Digital Age (CLDA)

Setting up CLDA
The final illuminative case study is of a project which also began in 2002 and focuses on ways in which the digital moving image could be used to transform the study of history. A group of ten secondary schools were selected to examine how digitised archive film, much of it capturing the rich experiences of life in Northern Ireland during the twentieth century, could be embedded in the teaching and learning of history. The schools were given an iMac, a digital video camera and access to an archive of film which had been selected for its relevance to the Northern Ireland curriculum. The project was managed by the Northern Ireland Film and Television Commission and the Nerve Centre, one of the specialist multi-media centres. This project adopted a model of training that was in certain key respects different to the approach taken by Dreamlab. This case study is also important in examining how the notion of creativity finds expression in an area of the curriculum which has not been noted for creative approaches.

External evaluation of this project, based on classroom observation and extensive interview data with teachers and learners at three different times between January

2004 and June 2005, has provided an evidence base[8] which throws light on four key issues. These are the impact of the project on the learners, how staff embedded the project in their teaching, the impact of the training on their professional development and how the technical challenges in working with multimedia were addressed.

The context in which this project took place is important both in a curricular sense and in the wider framework of ICT structures within Northern Ireland. Between September 2002 and August 2004, extensive discussions were taking place about the nature of the curriculum, particularly at Key Stage 3 for learners aged 11–14. The main thrust of the proposed changes, as described in Chapter 5, has been to reduce the amount of prescribed content and the specification of broad learning outcomes, a move which is seen as offering teachers more flexibility over the amount of time they can spend on topics and choice of methods for how they are taught. Guidance from the Northern Ireland Council for Curriculum, Examinations and Assessment (CCEA) indicates that there should be greater connectedness between discrete subjects. The newly emerging curricular framework was significant for the Creative Learning in a Digital Age project in offering teachers the opportunity to set historical work in a more creative context. In particular, the learning outcomes for history now state that learners should be able to 'communicate effectively in oral, written, visual, numerical and ICT formats, showing clear awareness of purpose, for example through ... video/digital documentation'. A further learning outcome makes specific reference to the learners' ability 'to work within teams' and to demonstrate 'creativity, initiative and perseverance in carrying out tasks and developing own ideas'. In this case study we explore how creativity in history can mean drawing upon multimedia opportunities to present a narrative that can be 'creative' by, for example, the use of music, moving image, voice-overs and other digital assets. In other words, learner narrative of the past explored and presented using these resources has the potential to carry a much richer meaning than an essay relying purely on text.

First steps

In the first year of the project, teachers learned how to embed moving images on the Home Rule Crisis and the First World War in their teaching, particularly through the use of PowerPoint. When it came to putting these tools in the hands of an entire class, they ran up against a series of difficulties; to access the moving images required access to a computer laboratory which had both the 'raw' moving image material and digital editing software. Of the ten schools involved, only one was able to negotiate sufficient time on the timetable to do this. In all the other schools, teachers had to treat this work as an after-school activity for a small group of volunteers. These smaller groups were able to make faster progress and were taught by their class teacher how to use the digital video camera and the editing software on the iMac they had been given. While this arrangement led to a small number of impressive DVDs being made on a range of historical topics, it led the project team to reconsider how they might enable whole classes to experience this type of work. The solution came in two forms, both based on significant additional hardware being provided by a specialist multimedia centre. The Nerve Centre had both Macintosh laptops and experienced staff to support the CLDA project and in the course of the second year all the schools either spent two days in the Nerve Centre or had the staff and their hardware as guests in their schools for two days. The normal timetable was 'collapsed' and whole classes were able to work in pairs to produce their own short films in DVD format. The success of these arrangements was extended in the school year 2004–5 to include support from 'Studio On', another digital learning centre which has some similar facilities as the Nerve Centre.

Impact on learners

One teacher described what happened when two staff from the Nerve Centre arrived in her school for a two-day intensive training programme during which the normal school timetable was suspended:

> they brought with them 12 laptops into a classroom not a computer suite, loaded with WW1 archives photographs, footage, pictures, propaganda, posters; the boys played around with the computers for the first day learning what the clips were about then eventually each pair made their own film; a lot of them worked on different stances. Some told a story but they all focused on different areas…how the men felt about going to war, life in the trenches, why the government brought out propaganda posters …

Focus and motivation

What this did was to unleash a wave of creativity among a class of 30 adolescent boys; their teacher explained that each team

> was able to use word text and put in whatever they wanted the viewer to see … even the music was amazing, some of them found very emotional music, some were upbeat and some had bands playing 'in the military way'.

The digital camera was also brought into play, not for the curriculum work but 'to film what they were doing, the idea of working in groups because they are going to do an assembly on it in school to the whole of the year 10 group'.

And the effect of this on the learners? Their teacher said:

> they are grabbed, for two days they are focused on what they are doing and want to take part and of course they are learning in different ways.

In the case of a small group of potentially disruptive learners she said, they really got into it and they were so proud and they must have showed me at least 4 times, 'come here to see this, look what we have done now'. ... I saw a real sense of team work with them and they probably achieved more in those two days than what they would have achieved in a month in class.

Evaluation of this project identified a number of key outcomes for both learners and teachers; for learners the first of these was in terms of a far stronger motivation to learn and pride in what was achieved. One teacher reported that

> ... they are outside that door well before the bell in the mornings trying to get in ... they don't normally like to be praised, they get embarrassed, but with this project they were praising themselves. They all wanted to take part in assembly, from boys who haven't even talked in front of the class they were happy to stand up and say 'this is my project'.

These comments were echoed in all schools and were valid for both boys and girls from selective and non-selective schools. One of them said 'It was a good way to learn history because the pictures and music made it interesting and hard to forget' while another, describing how she had watched all the movies her class had made said 'It was an easy and fun way to learn history ... because we saw more views of the World War'.

Key factors in this are the combination of actually making something, working in compact teams with clear learning targets and working in a medium that is multisensory.

The effect of studying powerful visual material from the early part of the twentieth century had evidently affected learners' sense of broader ethical issues to do with conflict. One teacher commented that they had an increased awareness of the brutality of conflict and were asking questions about 'man's inhumanity to man'. In her view, the learners were readier to consider what she called the 'big questions' and far more able to make connections to other areas of history and ethics such as, for example, the Holocaust. This is potentially significant in the context of the relationship between history and citizenship and the far more explicit reference to values in the Curriculum Council's guidance for Key Stage 3.[9]

Thinking skills

The process of identifying suitable images to give a certain effect was also leading in at least one selective school to improved thinking skills; one teacher reported that:

> the level of understanding increased significantly and that's what I was most delighted about, I thought their higher order thinking skills of questioning sources improved because they recognised the idea of there being some interpretation, to slant things in a certain way.

One of the learners in this school, asked about the nature of the clips he had been using in one of the films the class had made said:

> It did show a lot of interesting aspects of what was happening but it could be very biased only showing one side, there was none from the German side.

In one school where a small team had built up substantial experience of making films, the experience of working in this way was also spilling over into the way they were watching television; one learner said that he now watched TV more perceptively, recognising techniques that he himself was using for his film. His teacher later confirmed this:

> the pupils told me that they were going home and watching television programmes and looking for all the little tricks of the trade that had been shown to them in class and they were looking for narration, background music, different shots from camera men and were much more critical and able to evaluate beyond history.

Several teachers believed that as they became more confident with this multimedia approach to the teaching of history they would be in a stronger position to move their learners from a mainly narrative approach in the use of film to one that featured more interpretation. In other words, we can predict that experience and confidence with the technical aspects of this work will lead to learning that includes the development of higher order thinking.

ICT and multi-media skills

The project has extended learners' ICT skills and raised expectations about what can be accomplished. One of the teachers said 'the pupils have come back and taken a lot of film footage and acted in the same way as a TV programme editor'; looking back on the early stages of the project when the use of PowerPoint with embedded moving images would have been seen as ambitious, was he felt 'division three' compared to the sophisticated ways they now had for delivering the archive and programme making. One of the learners reflected on what had been learned about the process and accepted that we could have had more scene separations which would fade in and then fade out into the next scene or used the Ken Burns effect which pans into the shot or pans out of it.

Team work, autonomy and collaborative learning

The nature of the resources available to the teachers made many develop work based around groups and it is clear that this strategy brought real benefits; one teacher, commenting on the way that work had been carried out with staff from the Nerve Centre, said:

> they were working as teams and they were very competitive…some boys were quicker at editing and focusing on the clips but the boys that needed a bit of help or were

struggling they just went and helped them; they were very good with each other and it was the first time you really saw them working as a class and trying to get something achieved.

One of the consequences of this emerging team coherence was that the learners gradually developed a degree of autonomy from their teacher in the planning and execution of the work; one of the learners said 'after the first of the videos we were completely confident I think of making one ourselves'. This is impressive evidence of how teamwork can have both a competitive edge and a collaborative dimension.

Teachers and professional development
The impact of this work on learners was significant but of at least equal importance is the effect of this work on the teachers who took part. A number of educational researchers have commented on the dynamics of change in schools and of the key role that teachers play in this process. A distinction has been made between superficial change, sometimes involving teachers using different resources or content being taught, and deeper change which affects they way those teachers see their role. Fullan (1990)[10] has argued that:

> The ultimate goal is changing the culture of learning for both adults and students so that engagement and betterment is a way of life in schools.

There is also a substantial body of literature on the ways that curriculum innovation can lead to professional development when the innovation is mainly driven by teachers. Crockett (1998)[11] suggests that:

> Effective planning is a shared process of evolution within which accumulated experience coalesces into shared visions and goals, the most effective change taking place in the hinterland between stability and instability where it is impossible to be sure what is going to happen next, where change arises from multiple actions and where plans emerge rather than are imposed from the outset.

The teachers who took part in the CLDA project were all experienced teachers of history, and just under half had positions of responsibility in their schools, generally as Head of Department. While some had considerable prior experience of using ICT in history, others had done relatively little and none had used iMacs, digital video cameras or edited moving image material. For several of the teachers, therefore, this project offered an opportunity to do something new. When questioned about the impact of the project, one teacher said:

> I really have learned to see a lot of these [history] topics in a new light. I think that I had become moribund; my thinking was governed by making sure year 10 had all the knowledge they needed for their exams. Creating these short productions allows the

basic facts to come to the fore, rather than being buried in detail. It is really good to be involved with other teachers.

Apart from the clear value of having a mid-career stimulus to regenerate interest and motivation for teaching one's subject, what other benefits were there for the teachers involved in the project? Teachers' interview comments indicate that they saw professional development in three related ways.

Links with other subjects
Teachers may have a somewhat ambivalent attitude to working with other subjects in their school which may spring from the need to 'protect' the numbers of learners taking their subject (and ultimately therefore the viability of their department). When project teachers have invested in their own professional development by learning new skills such as those in the CLDA project, there may be some reluctance to share this expertise outside their own department, particularly if they see that the effect of this type of work at Key Stage 3 leads to high learner motivation and larger numbers wanting to continue with their subject at GCSE. However, both the limited amount of time on the timetable given to history and the encouragement from CCEA to promote stronger skills-based dimensions to the curriculum at Key Stage 3, have led some teachers to explore possible 'alliances' with other subjects. One teacher put it like this:

> Our longest time with any history class in Key Stage 3 would be a maximum of an hour but that would only be once a week and if we were linking up with another subject much of the work that we're actually doing in history, the skills are transferable, they go across all subjects and you could link up the computer department with the English department.

He underlined the importance of language and of wider definitions of literacy that embrace the visual and multi-media. It would seem that the potential for subject cooperation and connectedness is more likely to happen between history and subjects that are not seen as direct competitors for learners at GCSE. Given that English at GCSE is compulsory, it is easy to see why cooperation with this subject may be seen as less threatening to teachers of history.

ICT and media skills
All the teachers involved in this project learned new skills around the use of the iMac. They have also learned about the use of moving image and its incorporation into whole-class teaching using PowerPoint. All project teachers have also developed a level of confidence in the use of a digital video camera and have also been able to gain experience of editing moving images. Some have been able to extend this to teach whole classes but this has been mainly at the level of studying moving image

rather than editing; in effect, this key part of the project has only been possible for whole class teaching through the Nerve Centre.

One of the teachers who was building on what the project had provided in an innovative way said: 'I've experimented with TV capture cards as well as bringing in new film so not just relying on the archive'. He believed that he was avoiding any difficult copyright issues by using 'very small snippets of film incorporated in with material taken from the internet and used only for educational purposes'.

Another teacher drew on the expertise of the art department in his school to include '16 seconds of material from the Michael Collins movie' when he was creating a short film about the 1916 Rising with his 14-year-old learners. This teacher was also interested in converting the substantial number of VHS tape videos used in his department into DVD format so that they could be used in a more selective and focused way.

When C2K made digitised historical material like the Pathe News archive more accessible to more learners in manageable portions, learners could more readily analyse the nature of moving image material. One project teacher was keen to use this to help learners 'think about the packaging of the past' and the powerful way that, for example, wall murals and TV images shape perception of what happened.

Relationships with learners

Teacher interviews confirm that, in a number of schools, the effect of working together for the defined purpose of creating a short film had changed the nature of the relationship between teacher and learner. One of the project teachers said, 'it made the relation between me and the boys stronger, they see me as a bit more approachable'. Another talked of 'a learning exercise for all of us, teacher and pupil'.

But this changed relationship was not without its side effects; this teacher said that the more relaxed atmosphere with learners moving around and working as teams took some adjusting to both by her learners and herself.

In concluding this section on the impact of the project on teachers we might recall the views of Leonard (1996)[12] who was discussing problems faced in schools 'where key features of teacher life, isolation, hierarchy, territorialism … shortage of time for reflection, lack of support and opportunity for collegiality and lack of resourcing' all discourage professional development. It is a striking feature of the CLDA project that none of the barriers described above apply; quite the reverse. This project has provided time, resources and training to make it possible for critical reflection on practice to be carried into new ways of thinking about learning and teaching and a greater confidence with technology. From the outset, teachers developed a sense of ownership of the change process and this involved the key characteristics of 'participation, initiative taking and empowerment' (Fullan and Stiegelbaur, 1991).[13] Pring (1995)[14] also reminds us that 'if we want autonomous thinking pupils we have to have autonomous thinking teachers'.

Part of this process has involved responding to a number of challenges during the course of the project.

> If we shift school culture to support adult learning, professional development is experienced as a personal journey of growth and discovery which engages the learner on a daily basis and perhaps hourly basis. In the best cases, staff professional development includes an emphasis on self-direction, transformation and experience. One learns by doing and exploring, by trying, failing, by changing and adapting strategies and by overcoming that by many trials.
>
> (Fullan, 1990)[15]

Conclusions
In concluding the analysis of this project, what are the most important lessons to be learned? The first is that we need to have an understanding that creativity can be unleashed through ICT in subject areas far outside those normally thought of as providing learners with this vital part of their experience in school. The second is that where such work is supported through adequate resources and training, the impact can be extremely powerful for both learners and teachers. Third, expansion of this type of work to all children even in a relatively well-supported environment such as exists in Northern Ireland is difficult for some schools. It may be that some schools will develop particular expertise in this kind of work and, seeing the value of the investment in terms of learning outcomes and higher attainments, will devote their own resources, or attract additional funding, to increase access to digital video cameras, editing software and enhanced memory capacity on the network. Fourth, it is difficult to imagine how valuable work of this kind can be sustained within the current arrangements for timetabling in most secondary schools where the school day is split into short units of time, typically 30–40 minutes, for discrete subject study. There are schools elsewhere in the United Kingdom and around the globe where forward-looking headteachers have started to collapse the traditional timetable. These initial positive experiences of doing so here, may initiate more creative organisational arrangements in Northern Ireland with the implementation of the revised curriculum.

Global messages

Drawing together all of the different strands in this chapter, three particularly important messages come through.

- The first is about alignment between key strategic goals for education and the actual practice of ICT in schools; while there is clear evidence of increased usage of ICT by learners in schools and colleges, the type of learning that goes on is often dominated narrowly by the use of technology to support information retrieval and presentation. It is unusual to find many applications of what we have called creative uses of ICT, except in small scale-projects. We believe that there needs to be far greater reflection on the links between ICT uses in education and what is needed in the work place, and greater dissemination of the examples of convincing evidence for teachers of what might be achieved in schools in relation to those needs; at present we would say that there is a wide, and potentially widening, gap.

- The second message is also about alignment, in this case, the alignment of the daily timetable of schools and the kind of creative learning that has been analysed in this chapter. At present there are too many constraints imposed by a timetable that continues to place primacy on discrete subject 'space'.

- Finally, we believe this chapter has highlighted key questions around the theme of sustainability and, in particular, about the efficacy of models of training teachers in the use of ICT; while this has been raised in other chapters, we would wish to underline the significance of links between teachers learning new ICT skills, the setting of the development of these new skills in purposeful and demonstrably worthwhile educational contexts, the wider spread of pedagogic practices which emphasise practical and active learning and the necessity for rapid use of these skills with learners. Even with the investment in C2K, there remain many technical and knowledge obstacles to the embedding of some of the most innovative work. The evidence is that these can be addressed and resolved, which demonstrates further the value and importance of ground-breaking pilot work.

Leadership for quality in an e-school

Leadership qualities

Research[1] into educational effectiveness points to the magnetic north of change in schools – the school principal. However, while the principal may well be the keeper of the lodestone, the journey of discovery and change cannot be effected by the leadership qualities of the principal, without both leadership and followership being exercised by teachers, school staff and the wider community of governors, parents and learners. In such a complex environment, where multiple factors promote and inhibit innovation,[2] the effectiveness of the school leader is the closest we have to a 'silver bullet'. Leadership is, as we declare in the Introduction, a key element in the principle of sustaining the transformation of a school into an e-school. For, as we demonstrated in Chapter 5, outstanding practice in embedding ICT in learning in Northern Ireland e-schools is found only where there is excellent leadership to inspire and instil the curriculum changes which makes the most effective use of technology as a powerful resource. Where that practice is not found, the vision too is lacking.

In this chapter we also examine briefly the nature of the e-school environment, which will be essential if enhancement of today's practice with ICT is to shift gear into transtormational change. What needs to be done to ensure that schools' environments are aligned with the vision of an e-school as a 'learning community'?

Leadership for change

In Northern Ireland, headteachers (we commonly use the term 'principal') have a demanding job which ranges across strategic, curricular, pedagogic, budgetary, management and administrative roles. All principals are responsible for the delivery of the curriculum; some 40 per cent, in our smaller primary schools, in predominantly rural communities, are 'teaching principals' teaching for four days a week.

Fertile ground for transformational change requires good school leadership together with effective ICT leadership. Change requires vision, willingness and commitment as well as a strategic deployment of ICT. All must be underpinned by good ICT resource planning and management as well as adequate staff competence in ICT skills and in embedding ICT in practice. Collectively, this results in the institutional capability to implement ICT in ways that make a difference.

Hargreaves, quoting Collins,[3] describes leaders who focus on their organisation, not themselves; they ensure that the right senior people are in place and then collectively agree the direction for organisational transformation by focusing on sustained outcomes (Collins calls them 'Level 5' leaders):

> The headteacher's attitude to the new technologies is crucial. Level Five leaders invest in ICTs; but they do not use them as the primary means of igniting a transformation. They do not incorporate all the latest gadgets and follow the various fads and fashions of the ICT market. Rather, they select their ICTs very carefully to fit and advance the core mission of the company. As Collins explains, they use ICTs to accelerate, not to create, the momentum of transformation. In the case of schools, this would be to improve administration and assessment as well as teaching and learning.[4]

While this is wise counsel, there are some important differences between companies and schools. In school, the learner's experience of ICT and the competence which is acquired through using ICT are also important educational goals. Belfast principal, Adeline Dinsmore, OBE, a Teaching Awards winner and a Becta ICT Practice champion, is a Level 5 leader who sees ICT as the accelerator rather than the starter motor, gear shift or steering wheel:

> ICT, and embedding ICT in learning is a lever in its own right, but not on its own. It's when you combine it with a flexible approach to learning that you begin to see real transformation.[5]

The Department of Education's strategy acknowledges the centrality of the principal's role in strategic leadership.

> School principals and senior management teams need to be able to lead change to transform their school into an 'empowering' school. Principals and senior teams ... should be highly personally visible in their use of ICT for a variety of purposes, including for their own professional development. Planning, resource deployment, staff development and the management of change across the school needs to be coordinated by senior and middle management teams who can ensure that organisational change occurs by design rather than by drift.[6]

Preparing the leader for an e-school

Given that the principal has such a central responsibility for ICT decisions within the school, how are they supported in that role?

While there are no mandatory requirements for the appointment of a school principal, other than that aspirant principals are qualified and recognised teachers and have sufficient experience and expertise to be able to compete for their appointment, in practice there are increasing expectations that they will have completed a Professional Qualification for Headship (PQH (NI)) to national standards.

The role and aim of the Regional Training Unit in Northern Ireland (RTU)[7] is to provide leaders at different stages in their careers (aspirant, new and serving) with the best development opportunities possible,

> ... secure in the knowledge that with leadership development the core purpose of schools is demonstrably enhanced.[8]

The RTU interprets the concept of 'school leader' in the distributed manner referred to by Senge,[9] recognising that many staff within a school can add immeasurably to the leadership agenda.

The PQH (NI) was introduced in 1999 and there was unanimous support for the model of a qualification to prepare teachers for the role of principal, which is a licensed adaptation of the National Qualification for Headship in England. It is underpinned by a version of the National Standards for Headteachers which defines the knowledge, understanding, skills and attributes required for headship. The PQH (NI) reflects Northern Ireland's circumstances which include the differences in scale (both in the larger proportion of small primary schools, and close working relationships between the various education bodies, providing opportunities to pool expertise and resources); the curricular differences; and the systems differences such as the computer-based school management information systems which provide management tools. That 900 candidates (from a registered workforce of 27,000) engage in the Professional Qualification for Headship (PQH (NI)) programme (for which the RTU is the designated Lead and Awarding Body) at any time is a graphic illustration of the dynamic accompanying leadership development for schools.

The PQH (NI) is rooted in school improvement, draws on the best leadership and management practice, signals readiness for headship without replacing the selection process and provides a baseline from which newly-appointed principals can continue to develop their leadership and management abilities. Most significantly, compulsory elements of the PQH (NI) modules can only be undertaken and completed online, and this online working by aspiring principals is a seminal experience which leads them to understand the value of communicating with their peers to address, discuss and resolve issues of shared concern and importance. There is great value for principals in being seen by their staff as a prime user of communications technology as a means for engaging in a collegial approach to problem solving and in personal and professional development more generally. The tutors on the programme observed that the compulsory nature of the online experience makes all the difference to the quality of the candidates' engagement in debate.

Teachers may also choose, and many do, one of the Masters in Education programmes offered by the five local providers of higher education; some delivered face to face, some online, some making use of videoconferencing. What the programmes share, whether they focus on education management, ICT, library management or teaching and learning, is a three-year course of part-time study based on critical reflection of practice and a hard look at how research evidence from around the world can improve the quality of learning.

As a consequence of their personal experience of online professional learning, today's newly qualified school principals bring to their role an integrationalist's perspective of ICTs. They bring personal facility, an expectation that they have a role to play, an ability to identify the right tool for the job; and they plan and act accordingly. It is as big an advantage as being able to speak the local language when travelling abroad. It's not, *pace* Collins, that they think about technology as the way of starting the engine of transformation, but rather that their thinking of their school as an e-school has already been transformed. Transformation of the entire cohort of school leaders will take time, of course; with respect to the primary sector, the inspectorate note that

> in just over one third of the schools, there is a lack of any coherent vision or understanding at a senior level about the potential of ICT to enhance the children's learning experiences.[10]

While in the secondary sector, there are clear weaknesses in the quality of management and leadership of ICT in almost one half of the schools.[11]

School empowerment through ICT

When faced with complex change – and e-schooling is a complex change – it is only human nature to try to manage by breaking it all down into small, separate, rationally manageable components and handle these in isolation, delegating, in a larger organisation, wherever possible. Unfortunately, this is not the right approach. No part of a system can be changed without reference to the effect on the remainder.

An aspiring e-school can invest in all the technology it desires, but without staff development, nothing changes. It can concentrate on cultural change, but without change in the curriculum, nothing much will happen. They can, within limits, adjust the curriculum offer, but without changes in approaches to teaching and learning, again nothing. And, if assessment and examination targets and methods are not re-engineered, then everything stays the same. Complex, counter-intuitive and messy it may be, but complex change has to be handled holistically and in an integrated way.

And in schools, where these problems are limitless in scope, and endlessly demanding in time and resources, and where there is little consensus about what the solutions might be and how they might be achieved, then a range of different solutions have to be tried out and tested, and failure learnt from – with a consequent risk to the progress of the learners. Many tasks, apparently not connected, have to be tackled in a coordinated way and at the same time because, in the round, they are connected. Small, incremental changes in behaviours and procedures and processes add up to a change in the tone and the environment of the school – all the aspects which comprise its 'culture'. The aggregation of small, incremental changes makes it easier to encourage the deep changes in behaviours of teaching and learning which are required for transformation. This is a key principle in the concept of e-schooling. How should we address these steps holistically?

Following from the New Opportunities Fund (NOF) teacher education programme evaluated in Chapter 3, the Regional Training Unit led, with the equally active engagement of the ICT advisory staff from the Education and Library Boards, an institutional development pilot programme for school empowerment through ICT in 2005–6. School development planning became compulsory for Northern Ireland schools from September 2005 and, recognising that ICT competence was integral to improvement, requiring capacity building beyond the NOF programme, it was based upon a multi-faceted institutional development model.

A vitally integral part of the programme was a tailored element for the school leader. Targeted at the principal, with substitution not permitted, their commitment is seen as a measure of the extent to which change leadership is perceived as a personal responsibility. Many recognised at once the dynamic relationships between ICT, teaching, learning and leadership, and appreciated that cultural change requires them to be seen by teachers and learners in their school to be modelling new behaviours; other principals remained to be persuaded that responsibility for ICT should not be delegated away. Such fragmentation runs the risk of conveying a view of ICT as of incidental value to school administration and classroom practice.

The design of the programme demonstrated the effectiveness of an approach where schools agreed to a common project for embedding ICT and worked collectively on it, sharing innovations and testing both online and face to face. The model of 'institutional development' proved to be a very workable methodology for the support of whole school improvement, accelerated through ICT.[12]

How does a principal manage change in practice?

The importance of leadership

According to a survey conducted by European Schoolnet in 2005, this specific central role of school principal in embedding ICT in British schools (indeed this entire conceptualisation of school leadership) does not find a ready analogue in many European countries.

> The lack of specific leadership training…seems to suggest that 'intuitive leading' prevails in the majority of countries.[13]

Alan McCluskey, observing Northern Ireland in a policy review,[14] commented on the perceived importance accorded to school leadership.

> Liberating teachers to be creative and to think beyond subject boundaries is part of the leadership agenda in Northern Ireland that seeks to cultivate the idea that the head is the 'lead learner'. Many heads show the capacity to lead the debate within their schools about what is meant by quality learning. Despite constraints due to examinations, summative assessment regimes and subject parochialism, the leadership of heads is contributing to moving away from learning in a shallow sense to something that is much more profound and to an appreciation of the contribution that technology can make in shifting the focus away from teaching and more to learning. A learning-centred environment would be a key objective of any leadership.

Clarity of vision

So what does the management of complex change look like in practice?

A Catholic grammar school in east Belfast is described, in the EMINENT portraits[15] written by the Northern Ireland Inspectorate for European Schoolnet, as an ICT-rich school where the development of ICT is effectively and enthusiastically led and coordinated. The principal provides that all-important clarity of vision about how ICT supports learning and teaching across the school. The professional development of staff is strongly valued, continuous and central to the work of the school. The principal facilitates a core team, the result of whose dynamism, hard work and effectiveness enables the staff to value their competence, understand its role as a learning tool, and embrace its use with evident enthusiasm and commitment. The school management team places a strong emphasis on self-reflection and especially on the evaluation of the quality of the pupils' learning experiences, enhanced by ICT.

The former principal, Michael McClean, identified the accelerating impact on change and how ICT integration emerged from and enhanced the school's culture.

> The big things that happened here were intuitive. There was an opportunity which fitted in with the vision and culture of the school.

Echoing Hargreaves, McClean welcomed the introduction of the government-provided resources. The timely arrival of C2K technology supported and boosted the changes in practice in the classroom which were already emerging.

> There is fantastic potential with C2k. The developments here happened the right way around, Aquinas had ICT in subject classrooms before C2k was installed.

The school quickly invested their own budget as part of a new school build programme, extending the core C2K resources which had been centrally funded, thus making the best of government's investments to create a single, comprehensive network, with broadband Internet connectivity and interactive whiteboards, connected to ceiling-mounted data projectors in each of the 44 teaching spaces and a ratio of 3:1 learners to computers. Aligned with considerable staff development in the technology and its associated pedagogy, the school reported a very significant beneficial effect on the use of ICT in learning and teaching.

Following Hargreaves' maxim, the principal had identified teaching as the 'core business' of the school and 'selected their ICTs very carefully to fit and advance the core mission'. The school portrait details excellent use being made of the interactive whiteboards across the full range of subjects. In addition to centralised suites, computers are distributed to good effect throughout the school, including the school library, giving pupils good access to computers before, during and after school for research and presentation work. Staff collectively garnered from a variety of sources, including the Internet, interactive teaching resources and learning objects which they shared on the school server, creating not only a valuable pool of resources for exposition, but a collection for learners to use for their own projects and study.

Not only is this an award-winning school, with several national award-winning teachers, but other principals regularly visit as a key part of the RTU's ICT leadership programme and report being inspired by the opportunity to see, at first hand, the kind of enhancements of education which add up collectively to transformational change.

Easing the transformation

E-schooling does not come without effort, especially for those who are already competent practitioners and who worry about the dip in their effectiveness as they take time to master new approaches. The leader can ease the transition in the pedagogy of the teachers as they integrate ICT. The EMINENT portraits[16] of schools point to some specific steps:

- the provision of laptops, and memory sticks for all staff to facilitate easy transfer of files between different computer systems;
- good quality staff development in the pedagogy of the range of ICTs in use in the school, based on a realistic audit of their training needs;
- good technical support and good pedagogic support;
- the encouragement of staff to share learning resources, techniques and expertise, to explore innovative ideas, experiment and to tell each other about their successes and failures;
- the excellent development of the learners' ICT skills, building upon rather than repeating the capabilities already developed by the learners in primary school and at home, and taking account of their views on how they would like to learn.

Resourcing the vision

In a non-selective girls' school in north Belfast, also highlighted in a school portrait, the school committed to producing high quality, interactive, curricular and extra-curricular materials through a Learning Resource Unit within the school library with highly skilled ICT support staff. The unit is used extensively by teachers, management and learners including for the following: managing attendance records; maintaining a computerised reward system; preparing learning materials; facilitating the borrowing of laptops, digital cameras and other equipment by pupils and staff; designing and producing school publicity materials; supporting staff with computerised reports and helping pupils involved in competitions and project-work. The unit's manager has an information management role, is well connected at management levels and sits on several committees which provide insight into the needs of the curriculum and the need for management information. An e-school will require just such changes in the deployment of staff, which transform the roles of resource assistant, clerical assistant, technician and librarian found in more traditional schools.

E-schooling calls for excellent levels of provision and access. And because government funds the core ICT service, the school can often afford the additional investment needed to reach the ratios of 3:1 or 4:1 which are typical of the excellent practice in these portraits.

An international dimension for leadership development

A key goal for e-schooling is to build the capacity of school principals to lead and manage change. One of the successful methods adopted by the RTU is international study, and for this the agency pairs with education authorities in Europe and the USA. Over the past years, RTU's international programme has included assignments undertaken by Northern Ireland principals on placement in schools in Montgomery County Public Schools, Maryland, peer policy review visits by principals to schools in, for example, Finland, France and the Netherlands, and the attendance by small groups of educators at the Aligning Technology Summer Institutes in Boston.[17]

Alan November, a consultant familiar with developments in Northern Ireland, puts his finger on the importance of leadership development for sustainability.

> Northern Ireland is at the forefront of asking critical questions about the role of ICT and building capacity for implementation. In the world of ICT it is essential to know when the technologies have fundamentally changed and to let go of the current plan and move on. Northern Ireland has a global radar of incoming ideas around ICT. Further, the country is building capacity for school leaders (who are at the center of adopting any innovation) to develop the skills for managing change. As an American who has had the privilege of watching these NI developments during the past four/five years, I am embarrassed for my country's inability to do the three critical things: scan for global developments, move on, and build leadership capacity for managing change. We need to send more Americans to Northern Ireland.[18]

Alastair Mackay, OBE, principal of a primary school outside Belfast, describes how the exposure to the international dimension changed his world view in a way that then transformed his school. 'Having been a student with Alan November ... I am conscious of the present and future global implications of ICT in education and in life'. Alastair Mackay explains[19] that when his school moved to a brand-new building their dream was to install an interactive whiteboard and multi-media system in each classroom. With private sector partners and C2K, they achieved their goal. The technology was fully integrated into the fabric of the building and every one of the 17 classrooms, enabling them to exploit the technology and transform how teachers and learners behave in the classroom. The traditional teacher's desk disappeared. Teacher and children share hi-tech, flat panel workstations linked to a C2K system, scanner, and television/video/DVD with amplified audio and through a whiteboard to Internet access.

He describes the changes:

> ... the teaching and learning implications are enormous. After only one month the teachers gave written feedback: every one was a complete convert. They say they feel invigorated, challenged and immensely rewarded. Now, all are certified interactive whiteboard users and many are keen for advanced training. Whole-class teaching is taking on entirely new dimensions: lessons are more imaginative, stimulating, appealing and thought-provoking.

The teachers see the children, from as young as four years of age, engage in information searches, research, and use interactive learning techniques. Older children make technically challenging presentations to their peers and engage in complex problem-solving projects using the technology. Teachers use memory sticks and public folders online to share ideas, links, work and presentations they have prepared and to complete administrative tasks. As the principal comments,

> Our school is transformed into a 'community campus', used by our community partners for adult education. It's an integral part of our strategic vision. One of our aims is to become a 'centre of excellence' in the use of interactive teaching, enabling us to stay at the cutting edge and inspire others within and beyond our own community.

Technology itself did not realise the vision, rather its use boosted the achievement.

Management information systems and organisational improvement

The importance of school leaders being seen to model practice in the use of ICT in their leadership role ought to be one of the most approachable for a school, so rich is it in opportunity. Yet evaluations find repeatedly that while administrative applications are commonplace, especially where workload can be eased through data gathering and collation, data transfer and data analysis to inform planning, the use of management information to inform decision-making is much less common.[20]

Project evidence[21] elsewhere indicates that, after an initial learning curve, ICT use can lighten teacher workload through more efficient management, storage and maintenance of administration and preparation for three-quarters of principals and for two-thirds of teachers. Teachers frequently invest the time saved back into preparing to teach, which improves practice.

Gains can be achieved through streamlined administration, integration of curriculum and administration (such as tracking pupil performance, individual education plans, and online assessment and test results) and easier sharing of information and resources through school intranets.

Just as classrooms are closed and teachers are described as isolated professionals, so it is for principals in the school office. The appeal of an online environment is the benchmarking of a school's performance on a range of measures and of sharing insights and solutions to similar problems through online professional communities and bulletin boards. For principals, using management information systems and online communities of leadership practice is their way of learning how to learn online; they no longer need to be the lonely, long-distance decision-maker.

One small, incremental enhancement shows how. As part of a plan to maximise the impact of teaching on the pupils' experiences, one Belfast school monitored disruption to lessons. The management team created an online diary facility, updated by teachers, to monitor the disruption potential of events and activities. The online diary was accessed at home by the teachers and successfully provided the team with an effective management tool to track, and through the identification of patterns, to understand how to minimise disruption in lessons.

An e-school would make use of many such tactics to strengthen the principal's task in working closely with parents to support learning. C2K has provided a service of administration and management information system tools to schools since 1991. For example, a Parental Gateway provides online access for parents to information about their child's performance. The introduction of a learning platform should make possible a more sophisticated level of integration between the management information system and the curriculum and assessment systems to allow reports to be generated about pupils' progress and attainment.

However, when it comes to integrating data, the challenge is a large one, as most of our computer-based education information systems which need to be brought together were designed for different purposes by different agencies and organisations and grew up over a long period of time. They represent significant investments not easily abandoned or modified, and are effectively closed to each other.

Nevertheless, the integration of curriculum, assessment and management systems is a high priority. For the benefit of the learner, progress should be tracked individually and use needs to be made of online testing to develop computer-managed learning applications. Individual needs can be illuminated by feedback from diagnostics, and learning supported on a personalised basis. Learners should benefit from teaching which is informed by a growing understanding of multiple intelligences, of thinking skills, of how learners learn, and of neurological research. Progress by learners should be recognised and credited by recording, through an e-portfolio, their improvement over time. An e-portfolio can be carried by all learners to support accreditation needs.

Technology can enable access to dynamic, live information without schools devoting significant administrative effort to produce it and this will improve on the dated annual snapshots upon which policy-making depends. While reducing the administrative burden on schools it will produce better management information for the broader service. At this level of data analysis, the school principal will begin to see the advantages in evidence-based decision-making as an alternative to 'intuitive leadership'. Leaders, as well as learners, parents, and teachers, should be able to use assessment information to review the real costs of teaching and the value added by the school.

Both improvements could also support a broader life-long learning agenda, stimulate a culture of continuing education and retraining and strengthen the local economy.

To move these ideas beyond the aspirational, two linked steps are required, the technological and the cultural. The technological 'next step' is to create a data-warehousing facility, allowing information that sits in administrative silos to be gathered in a repository, available for use within regional administrative networks.

The cultural requires a recognition that information about learning progress and achievement belongs primarily to the learner, and that testing and assessment are tools for learning, rather than experiences to be suffered.

e-School as an extended school

The potentials for improving management through better information flow takes the e-school concept in the direction of the community and community accountability. In this sense, we can see that ICT-led improvements give momentum to a larger movement of schools becoming 'extended' or 'full-service' schools[22] and closer to Istance's definition of re-schooling in which schools become 'core social centres' – the social and community hub with substantial and inclusive community activity taking place within the school.

The whole service school aims to provide higher specification multi-functional facilities such as sport, ICT and catering and aims to achieve greater community use of these facilities. Changes in teaching practice are anticipated to respond to closer family involvement in learning and the inclusion of pupils with a wider range of special needs. Such an extended school contributes to community regeneration by servicing the needs of the whole person – for their health, their social and economic well-being, and also for their lifelong learning.[23]

Hargreaves (quoted by McCluskey 2004)[24] describes schools as being on a continuum with regard to the provision of services for young people, their families and communities. These services include not only education, but also youth, parenting, health and social and careers guidance. Hargreaves argues that schools should be involved in the provision of all of these services for a range of reasons:

> ... the need to address barriers to learning and teaching due to outside factors; the requirement to enrich the learning experiences of young people outside the curriculum; the realisation that parents are co-educators and that the school is a resource to community, and that by forming part of a neighbourhood renewal can assist in raising social capital. However, schools cannot provide these alone – it requires partnerships and collaboration with other professionals and organisations. When these services are co-ordinated and integrated within the culture and ethos of the school they become far more beneficial to all stakeholders.

It is believed that integration of services can help improve the attendance, behaviour and attainment of young people, promoting early intervention and minimising the need for belated, more costly and less effective statutory interventions.

The challenge for the new Extended Schools Initiative[25] will be whether such developments will enhance the role of the school in the community, without making much fundamental change of its role, or whether they will, in practice, re-engineer the school as the integrative hub for a range of lifelong social and community services.

Networked digital technologies are the one element which has the potential to accelerate integrative movement, for they have something to offer in all of these areas, but physical school buildings will have to change significantly to enable the vision to be achieved.

Building an e-school

There is a popular programme on British television called 'Changing Rooms', in which house-owners let experts, and sometimes even neighbours, remodel and redecorate their homes to their resulting shock or delight; there are many look-alike programmes in other countries. In the USA, however, there is an 'extreme' version (no surprise there), in which the entire house is knocked down and building starts from the foundations. It would be a service to education if broadcasters were to take on schools as well.

The largely rural community in Northern Ireland, with a higher proportion of smaller schools than elsewhere in the UK, together with community divisions, leads to school resources being thinly spread. Taken together with falling school rolls (there are 50,000 empty seats in schools) and a need to tackle the backlog of repairs to schools across Northern Ireland and to improve the school estate by 2010, the opportunity to refurbish and build schools which will accommodate flexible styles of technology-based learning is ripe. Such refurbishment needs to be seen in the light of the demographic downturn mentioned above as well as the impact of the new curriculum on the use of space within schools and the changing role of schools in the local community.

> The diversity of school type, the selective system of education, the existence of single sex schools, and the substantially rural nature of Northern Ireland largely explain both the relatively large number of schools that exist and the sizeable proportion of small schools. Although the range of provision is explained, and indeed justified, by the principle of parental choice, the inefficiencies manifest in the system need to be addressed as a matter of urgency.[26]

Yet, McCluskey's review of ICT policy in Northern Ireland[27] observes,

> Higher priority is being given to capital investment in education. A handbook for school estate sets out guidelines for investment. This handbook is currently being revised, but such a handbook has very serious limitations. The difficulties of long-term planning that capital investment requires are revealing. The flexibility being introduced by the new curriculum and the intensified relationships with outside organizations due to post-primary reform, amongst other things, are making planning the longer-term needs very difficult. Rapid changes in technology also complicate planning; think of expenditure on cabling that has been rendered partly unnecessary by wireless Internet.

It is almost impossible to ensure that thinking about school design is kept in step with thinking of curriculum and learning. To reward the creative thinking of designers, a more imaginative approach would give credit to flexible designs which can be changed readily over time. Cultural change of the kind we have discussed throughout this book is slow, complex and incremental in the way it continues to build towards transformation. Buildings have a concrete finality about them. Built to accommodate today's technologies and behaviours they could still be imprisoning innovation into the next century. For example, today's plan contains an allowance for an audio-visual (AV) room, specified when such resources were large and expensive enough to be locked away, rather than found in everyone's pocket. Search in vain however for the school's 'video-conferencing suite', which, although if built now, would quickly become redundant as the quality of video on portable devices improves over time.

Yet, without any loss of financial control over costs, planning guidelines need not be as prescriptive about how much space is devoted to certain types of accommodation. The old-fashioned division between *general* and *specialist* accommodation no longer reflects the variety of approaches to teaching and learning which are emerging in an extended e-school. Corridors, for instance, essential for transport between lessons, are a waste of space at other times. They allow the mass migration of learners every 35 minutes from one room to another, but moving rooms at frequent short intervals disrupts directed learning and dissipates learning energy.[28] Increasingly now in Northern Ireland schools you will find pupils in small groups, crouched in a corridor – sometimes on the floor – both during and between lessons, able to work productively because they are using a wireless laptop – no longer just a transport system, the corridor is now a learning space, needy for a more appropriate design. Social, eating and circulation spaces need to be used by groups working and learning; digital performance of pupil learning calls for large-screen display technology. Access to these kinds of resources and communication tools will be more easily enabled by wireless technology as the C2K system is refreshed.

There needs to be a wider range of different sized rooms and multi-functional spaces which will require effective partitions, screens and sound-damping – generally a 'looser fit' between purpose and function than found in today's buildings.

More than this, the concept of extended schools will need buildings which are capable of multiple education and community service uses, and consequently, with higher capital and running costs, unless a more economic approach is characterised by better environmental sustainability and energy-saving designs.

e-Schooling will not mean much without a design challenge. That challenge will be to balance the needs of different users, by creating inspiring buildings with functional spaces, which are appropriate for new thinking about social learning and innovative technologies, and be adaptable enough to cater for changing needs.

Some schools are now being designed to be the first in Northern Ireland containing many of the physical characteristics necessary for an e-school. The visionary principal of one, writing her personal prospectus for a school of the future, 'Millennium High', cites a quotation from a pupil in the Newsom Report[29] – a report which, nearly 45 years ago, recommended that the curriculum should be made more relevant to the needs of pupils of differing abilities.

> ... when, on being shown the 'improvements' in his former school said, 'It could be made of marble, sir, but it would still be a bloody school'.

'Millennium High' seems to me to come close to the realisation of Ivan Illych's vision of the transformation of schools from 'repressive institutions to convivial institutions'.[30]

We'll see you there.

Global messages

Effective leadership is strongly allied to the principle of sustainability in our concept of an e-school. Good leadership is essential to ensure that the incremental enhancements which technology may bring to teaching can 'tip over', collectively changing the culture and creating the learning community of an e-school. We identify some transferable lessons which are contingent on effective leadership.

- Good quality, sustained school leadership and co-ordination of ICT provides learners with ICT experiences which are not only worthwhile but challenging.
- A coherent approach aligns staff development, curriculum development and improvements in the ICT infrastructure as parts of the big picture.
- Sound baseline technology-based and focused training is initially required (such as the NOF ICT training evaluated in Chapter 3), but further professional learning is essential.

- Such an approach could be well-supported by a resourced and representative core ICT group in each school with a clear remit which is able to debate the potential of ICT to improve learning; share that understanding by demonstrating good practice; enthuse and motivate; provide opportunities for innovation; gain the confidence of the staff and develop their professional expertise; and monitor the incorporation of ICT in learning, teaching and management.

- Leaders need to encourage staff to 'try things out', to innovate and experiment; to learn from both the successful and the not-so-successful pedagogy and expect, as the norm, to tell others.

- There needs to be an open and frank approach to critical reflection and self-evaluation: for instance, it is essential to be able and willing to recognise when interactive whiteboards are used skilfully and effectively – that is to say, when their use facilitates the embedding of ICT into learning; provides better opportunities for pupils to participate and engage in discussion and collaborative work; encourages the sharing of resources, ideas and learning and teaching strategies among teachers; assists the teachers to reflect on and modify their pedagogy; and improves learning through increased levels of motivation, concentration and enjoyment by learners – and when they are not, when their use merely automates approaches to whole class teaching which would be more easily achieved without the bother and investment.

- Learning resources and other ancillary staff can play a significant role in developing the use of ICT across the curriculum to support learning. All the support staff need to be well-informed about their role in supporting learners, have a good understanding of the curriculum on offer and have taken part in appropriate training to enhance their own skills.

- Management information systems have the potential to significantly improve the efficiency and effectiveness of school administration and management; be used to benchmark and analyse the performance of pupils in assessments and public examinations and give learners and parents/guardians continuing personalised feedback on progress and attainment.

Global messaging

In this book, we set out to explore the extent to which, when thinking anew about schools, e-schooling is a useful concept which has intellectual leverage when it comes to understanding and assessing how the education service is changing. It is changing in response to the social, demographic, industrial, business and economic conditions of the twenty-first century, so as to prepare young people appropriately for life and work.

In the Introduction we said that e-schooling, in essence, has learners at the heart of the system, supported by autonomous teachers, behaving collegially, teaching a relevant curriculum, with assessment for learning, and an ICT infrastructure that nourishes a knowledge-rich, constructivist approach to learning. Schools are community hubs, sustaining learning communities, which enhance the life-chances of learners by collective social, education, health and welfare action. There is a norm of collaboration within the learning community and between schools, businesses and the education community both for the purpose of professional learning for teachers and for the development of the global ease of young citizens. Crucially, there should not only be alignment between all these parts of the picture, but also at all levels in the systems between policy, strategy, resourcing and practice. Community structures need to be in place for curriculum provision and for professional development and the technology renewal needs to be sustainable to support enhanced learning as it builds towards transformation.

In fact, we went further to claim that reform of schooling in the twenty-first century cannot occur without the effective embedding of technology to enable educational change at all levels in the system.

Here in this final chapter on our journey *from the school of today to the e-school of the learning community*, we seek to explore some global messages from a small island in terms of three essential principles of our construct:

- Alignment
- Sustainability
- Leadership

while at the same time looking at some pointers to further progress, which may be of value to those elsewhere, as well as being short, salutatory messages to ourselves.

Alignment

The messages which come from our experience find echoes in those described by Tom Cassidy,[1] who has identified a number of common misalignments in technology which inhibit transformational change.

He believes that better alignments are needed where:

- curriculum and assessment is out of alignment with economic needs in a global market-place;
- teachers have no experience of learning and teaching through technology-enhanced programmes;
- students do not have the global perspective and the knowledge, skills and attitudes needed for employability and citizenship;
- there is a lack of coherence at all levels through the education system – from classrooms through to government offices;
- management information systems and communication systems are out of date.

The alignment of all parts of the educational system (curriculum, assessment, professional development and ICT infrastructure) in a clear and coherent way at all levels in this system is essential. But alone, this is not enough; a coordinated approach within education also needs to be aligned to wider policy goals in regard to the economy and broad social goals. What have we learnt about alignment? In the preface, we argued that in e-schooling, the effective embedding of ICT in teaching and learning, was dependent on alignment in three key variables – alignment of the actors in a common purpose; the internal alignment of curriculum and pedagogy, and finally, alignment of technology provision with educational goals.

Alignment of the actors

On the first part of this question, the Reform of Public Administration in Northern Ireland, due to start in 2008, will merge the bodies responsible for the curriculum, assessment and examinations, leadership development and C2K with the employers' organisations for Catholic schools, Irish medium schools and integrated schools and with the five education and library boards, whose role is also to support schools and teachers. The newly established organisation, which will also have responsibility for the school estate will for the first time, bring together these key stakeholders as a single agency – ten administrative agencies merged into one. This is a very significant potential step in terms of alignment. For any government desiring progressive change, coordination of all of the partners, sometimes with overlapping roles, is a major challenge.

But what we can also see clearly here is that we are analysing a moving picture; key decisions were taken about ICT infrastructure as early as 1999, reform of the curriculum was planned in the early 2000s ready to start roll-out in 2007, with a five year timescale, and fundamental changes to the administration of education were announced in 2006 for implementation from 2008. In other words, alignment, even within a relatively compact education system rarely happens all at once; there are time lags and disconnects; and this underlines one of our central conclusions. Stakeholders in the different parts of the educational system need to have the broad shared vision to see their responsibilities in the context of the big picture and be ready to adapt the part they are responsible for to ensure it fits the overall strategic goals. Broadly speaking, strategic leadership effort for ICT has been about ensuring that a vision is created and shared, and collective responsibility for the whole has been marshalled into a coherent force for change – or to put it more bluntly, that all of the arrows of change (in some 20 organisations in total), are pointing pretty much in the same direction.

In his evaluation of the ICT strategy in Northern Ireland, Alan McCluskey identified the relevant global message[2] about coordinating complex change across multiple partners to create just this coherence.

> ... an integrated approach implies that a number of semi-autonomous institutional actors, each with its own agenda and objectives, work together on a common strategy. As a result, coordination is required. The response of most actors to the need for coordination is consultation. Consultation makes sense. It shows a willingness to listen to others. It also allows actors to ascertain needs and possibly integrate them into their own strategies.

McCluskey goes on to identify the role of any government, which is where accountability for overarching issues rests:

> First, the department has to modify the remits of agencies and service organisations to make the actors collectively responsible for the crosscutting issues and the formulation of an integrated policy for the whole system and its relationship to wider issues (e-government for example). Secondly there is a need to set up a suitable structure to organise that collective responsibility.

Internal alignment of curriculum, pedagogy and assessment

Second, on the issue of alignment between ICT and the curriculum, we should note two key points. The first is that the revised curriculum, due to be introduced from September 2007, provides for a more skills-based curriculum and includes provision for Personal Development, including Health Education, Citizenship, Employability and ICT. The curriculum content will be slimmer, while ensuring that the fundamentals are well covered. It places greater emphasis on the education of learners as citizens, as future contributors to the economy and as individuals, through the development of key skills, and with a stress on learning for life and work. With reduced prescription of content, there will be greater flexibility for schools to tailor their curriculum to meet the needs of the learners. In terms of achieving these goals, we might expect ICT to play a central role. The revised curriculum is a good culture for what we define as knowledge-rich, constructivist approaches to teaching and learning, rather than being a peripheral element; but whether it does so depends on how learning is assessed and attainment is measured. Planning to introduce a pupil profile in primary school as a basis for a stronger emphasis on formative assessment outcomes, together with the intended revision of the curriculum offers a strong potential degree of alignment between the role of ICT and learning outcomes. Innovative developments of this sort are more likely, we believe, to take root in the arena of assessment for learning, but only much more slowly when it comes to high-stakes external examinations, which typically have low expectations and make very few explicit demands in terms of ICT competence. Since teachers tend to teach towards external assessment and the use of ICT remains optional, then the risk of misalignment is always present.

For McCluskey the issue is a challenge to schools,

> … many schools do not grasp the underpinning nature of ICT in the current [curriculum] changes, for example, the importance of ICT in assessment. This could be seen as failure to develop a holistic vision of what is happening at a school level.

For Wood,[3] however, the misalignment of assessment and ICT embedding points clearly to the need for systemic action on regulatory issues. For Wood, the regulatory context 'includes curricula, assessment, examination, accreditation and accountability'. He recognised that we were convinced that 'radically new approaches to assessment are needed to exploit and establish the benefit of curriculum changes and the impact of ICT'.

Wood argues that having designed and started curricular reform, started to prepare teachers for their new roles and initiated training for school principals, it is clear what our remaining regulatory challenge is.

> NI policy makers now face the challenge of developing educational assessments to meet the demands of
>
> ■ Formative assessment to support and guide the learner;
> ■ Summative assessment to provide reliable and valid bases for vocational guidance, selection and indexes of readiness for further learning or training;

- Communicative assessment designed to assure paymasters and citizens at large that the system is healthy and making a cost-effective contribution to society.

Our global message is that regulatory changes are needed on all of the fronts identified by Wood, and that change in curriculum is in itself not sufficient to create e-schooling if matching changes in assessment, examinations, accreditation and accountability are not put in hand in a coordinated fashion. Without regulatory reform in these areas the best we can expect, as Alan November indicated, is 'automation' of current practice.

What we can say is that bringing together computer-based curriculum and administration and management onto the same computer network is only the beginning of the integration of ICT services which can support e-learning and the computer-assisted management of learning. However, there is much more to be done to ensure that assessment information can be used by pupils, their teachers and educational managers to manage learning, to provide progress reporting and to support self-auditing and review processes. This is especially true given the immaturity of the market place for learning platforms products (such as for virtual and managed learning environments – VLEs and MLEs) and a major lack of experience in how to make effective use of them. There's a commonly heard wisecrack that VLEs and MLEs are a solution to a problem which most teachers don't know that they have! Planning needs to take a longer term perspective as such products will continue to come and go over time, requiring the provision of a central data repository to ensure the continuity of access to the data about learning of the sort required for e-portfolios and e-assessment. The development of just such a data-repository – a data-warehouse for all schools – is under development in Northern Ireland.

In a private paper, Martin Ripley[4] identifies the technology trends that ought to shape the uptake of e-assessment for an e-school:

- handheld and personal technologies changing assessment for learning in the classroom;
- virtual worlds in which to assess higher order skills as part of the examination process;
- computer-delivered tests assessing research skills in real time;
- e-porfolios to help learners track patterns of progress and to aid progression and transfer.

Alignment of technology provision with education policy goals

We noted above that alignment is also concerned with the relationship between educational policy, including the use of ICT, and wider social and economic goals.

We think that Northern Ireland, in common with many governments justifying their investment in technology, has demonstrated a strong link with economic values in terms of that investment. However, the relationship between ICT and wider social goals is not so well understood, nor often articulated in many education systems. To be fair, there is a conscious effort to make values in education more explicit in Northern Ireland.[5]

McCluskey quotes the GTCNI Registrar as saying in the context of values:

> The notions found in the new curriculum – creativity, independent learning, team working – fit well with what the GTCNI consider the general teaching activity is – collegial, de-privatised practice and shared learning, involving the development and changing of knowledge through the application of it.

And McCluskey's assessment is that 'this alignment of values amongst institutional players is certainly a positive factor contributing to the success of the Empowering Schools strategy'.

We are less sanguine however. For example, Northern Ireland's 'Shared Future' policy document (2005)[6] is a radical forward-looking plan, issued by the Office of the First Minister and Deputy First Minister, calling for a concerted attempt across all government departments to address the divisive issues of sectarianism and for action towards a 'Shared Society'. However, in a section on 'Shared Education' one seeks in vain for a reference to the contribution that ICT plays in enabling learners in schools from different religious denominations to work together. Yet, as we reported in Chapter 6, a growing number of schools in Northern Ireland are using ICT for cross-border links with considerable success but, as yet, this remains underdeveloped in terms of links between schools from different backgrounds within Northern Ireland.

To take another example, of relevance in many education systems: in Chapter 5, we described the innovative development for distance access to some courses to be provided in a blended way, with elements of online learning and tutorial interaction through various forms of conferencing – text, video and audio. Given that all schools share a common ICT platform and communications capacity over broadband, there are no technical reasons why some learners could not experience part of their curriculum, at least between the ages of 14 and 19 years, as e-learners within an e-schooling environment. We have identified what course design and development, and online teaching skills are required to provide successful learning. There are explorations taking place at a local level within Northern Ireland, with leading edge schools creating partnerships to share teaching resources and teaching online. We believe that local arrangements for sharing resources can make sense but they more often put an emphasis on the physical transportation of learners from one neighbouring school to an adjoining one. It is only by looking across the whole system and identifying where there are shortage of subjects which lend themselves to forms of distance learning, that the real benefits of online/blended learning will emerge. It is worth adding that such an approach would also leave a significantly smaller carbon footprint than bussing learners from classroom to classroom!

In Chapter 5 we also looked briefly at government's plans for 'extended schools'. For governments seeking to strengthen community regeneration by servicing the needs of the whole person (for their health, their social and economic well-being, and also for their lifelong learning) as well as making the most efficient use of the investment of public money in education, health, welfare and other social services, an extended schools initiative has the potential to deliver Istance's notion of schools as 'core social centres' with ICT facilities as a resource for economic regeneration and for schools as learning communities, open to all. It has much to commend it. In practice, there are few examples perhaps because there are insufficient incentives for schools to move in this direction. At present, not even a quarter of schools facilitate access by the local community to the centrally provided ICT resources.[7]

In these few examples, perhaps the message is that there is, as yet, insufficient confidence that innovative online arrangements can deliver the goods for a significant proportion of learners, highlighting the task of sharing and 'selling' understanding and confidence at all levels in the school service. The other clear message would be the need for professional developments for the teaching force, a message we have identified strongly throughout this book, but this is also true for the health and social welfare professional, so that they understand how to dovetail their professional roles and responsibilities.

Sustainability

In our definition of e-schooling, we argued that in addition to ensuring that all parts of policy are pulling in the same direction that sustainability in the infrastructure and sustainability in innovative teaching is necessary.

The paper *Technology in Schools: what the research says* identifies four miscalculations made by educators relating to benefit realisation.

> The reality is that advocates have over-promised the ability of education to extract a learning return on technology investments in schools. The research studies now suggest that their error was not in citing the potential of technology to augment learning — for research now clearly indicates that the effective use of technology can result in higher levels of learning. This review of the past decade suggests four miscalculations on the part of educators.[8]

These are, in essence:

- [innovative teaching*]
  Being overly confident that they could easily accomplish the depth of school change required;
  The lack of effort in documenting the effect on learning, teaching practices and system efficiencies;
- [infrastructure]
  Overestimating the time it would take to reach a sufficiency point for technology access;
  Underestimating the rate of change in technology and its impact.

We will consider the second set of points first, before returning to the first set.

Sustainability of infrastructure

While these dimensions have their own demands, the lessons from Northern Ireland on the two infrastructure points are that technology access is an essential precursor for changes in classroom practice and that negotiating contractual technology arrangements to enable an entire school service to step forward can take longer than anticipated, as both supply and demand sides come to understand the nature and the implications of the contractual partnership.

One of the most distinctive features of what we have learned in Northern Ireland in terms of e-schooling is that, unlike many other innovative educational systems, the hardware and software solutions in our case study have been planned and designed to be sustainable. When we use the term sustainable we mean that the infrastructure is being provided to every school at an affordable cost to government (not to the school) and, crucially, that the contract for this service is built on short cycles of renewal (every three to five years for different components) until 2010. So what are the most significant messages emerging from here, some six years after its introduction?

Appropriate, industry-standard education technology solutions cannot be delivered in classrooms by the private sector or the public sector alone. However, a partnership, which safeguards public spending through stringent service delivery, financial, legal and economic measures, and which harnesses specialist knowledge and skills from the technology industry with educational insight and pedagogic understanding from the education sector can be established.

Ensuring sustainability requires ensuring its reliability, value for money and affordability as well, all the better for being secured centrally than separately by 1,200+ smaller customers. The continuing 99 per cent availability of the C2K service in classrooms results directly from the demanding penalty-based performance

---

* We have inserted into the quotation the grouping of these four issues into two distinct groups so as to deal with them in two sub-sections.

measures and is a major boost to user confidence, which we have seen is central to wide-scale adoption.

Taking a managed service approach not only moves the challenge of software and network integration, but also the risks of technological redundancy to the computer companies best able to carry them, freeing up teachers, principals and schools to concentrate on using ICT effectively to provide high quality education.

Comparing the position in Northern Ireland before the introduction of C2K with the position in 2007, recent inspection evidence[9] makes it clear that many more pupils are using ICT now than they were. As confidence grows so too does usage and 91 per cent of secondary schools reported that they were either 'very satisfied or 'satisfied' with C2K. Our case study examples, throughout the book, demonstrate that getting the best from a centrally managed core service requires schools to extend and enhance the core service. The core service was never designed to meet every possible ICT need in schools; it was created to supply a *core* to help ensure that every child had some equitable level of access to ICT, to give schools the best start by meeting what Fadel and Lemke call the 'sufficiency test'.

Our case studies also show that when they extend and enhance the service through their own devolved budget, the evidence is that they obtain good value for money for that investment.

Addressing Fadel and Lemke's second point concerning infrastructure, the service needs to be sustained not only economically, but through innovation and technological change. The early adopters and innovative practitioners will always be pushing the boundaries of what it is possible to do within a managed service. They may find the pace of change frustrating at times – for example, the growth of creative use of multimedia authoring produces demandingly large video, audio and graphical files, which outstrip online storage capacity leaving users reliant in the short-term on portable drives and large capacity memory sticks, until improved capacity can be provided through change control (a process of enabling upgrades to take place on a shorter timescale than refreshment). However, for the vast majority the pace will be adequate.

A strength of a managed service is that the risk of the rate of technology change can be factored into the business plan so that the service can be upgraded to take advantage of new opportunities and demands, and a close relationship with the technology provider helps to ensure that the user is well-informed about technology change and might anticipate it.

The regular refreshment of the ICT service and upgrades through change control will enable more pupils to make more effective use of ICT. As increased use occurs, and as the case studies show, schools move steadily towards improved computer: pupil ratios and if ICT activity is to be genuinely embedded in the teaching and learning of all pupils in a way that transforms learning, the hardware will need to be personal, ubiquitous and mobile, and not just deployed in fixed locations in classrooms and computer suites. And, as e-schooling is a process, rather than a completed journey, such mobility requires access to networks through wireless connectivity throughout the school. In these circumstances, as Hargreaves indicates when discussing the growth of 'communities of practice', it is government's role to ensure that a regulated networking service is in place in schools – just as they have a responsibility to ensure that the services of water, electricity and gas are provided and regulated . Given the way in which mobile web-surfing devices are becoming almost disposable commodities, government is unlikely to be resourcing the devices themselves.

This notion of resourcing the learner with technology (and therefore ensuring that the network service is in place – in the way that drivers buy and drive cars on the assumption that there is a serviceable road network to use), rather than resourcing the school (and therefore being concerned about the affordability by government of computer ratios), is counter-intuitive at this moment in time at all levels throughout the system.

For Professor Wood, when comparing the ICT strategy for Northern Ireland with that for Finland and France, such a move requires embedding the costs of 'network services' fully and permanently into base-line budgets and creating permanent partnerships to deliver a sustainable service. While he recognised that Northern Ireland had moved further, his conclusion was that:

> Moving funding from such 'special' status into base-line budgeting and creating permanent partnerships to replace bridging arrangements is proving a source of challenges for all three partners [NI, Finland, France]. None has yet completed a strategy that appears to *guarantee* sustainability. (Our emphasis)

Sustainability of innovative teaching and learning

We now turn to address the first two issues identified by Fadel and Lemke, that is to say, securing the depth of school change and documenting the impact on learning, teaching and school efficiency. We discuss this under two headings, the scale of professional development required and second, the nature and focus of that development.

The inspection evidence we have cited from surveys in 2005 and 2006 on ICT make it clear that in just over half of the secondary schools inspected, the weaknesses in the quality of provision for ICT outweighed the strength; in primary classes, the quality of the learning and teaching with ICT was good or excellent in nearly half of the primary lessons for the older primary learners, but in under half of the lessons for the younger learners. For us, this points to a very clear conclusion. While satisfaction with resourcing is high, and user confidence is evidently improving, Northern Ireland needs a further wide-scale effort of professional development, with suitable incentives for teachers. We have described in Chapters 3 and 4, that this might be achieved in the context of an institutional development approach to whole school improvement and pointed to the evidence of success with just such an approach. However, the trends in evaluation and inspection evidence point to how much more readily teachers adopt ICT to support teaching methods, and how much less readily they are comfortable with applying technology to develop and support approaches to learning. Based on our research we therefore suggest that the focus of that professional development should be in three key areas we highlighted earlier in the book.

It is relatively unusual to find much *creative* use of ICT, beyond the small scale projects we have described in Chapter 8. We believe that there needs to be far greater reflection on the links between ICT use in education and what is needed in the work place in order to overcome a wide and potentially widening gap. While creative work throws up some technical challenges, a major constraint to the embedding of some of the best work is imposed by a classroom timetable that places primacy on discrete subject 'spaces'. The work being done by the Northern Ireland Film and Television Commission, the Creative Learning Centres and Dreamlab on moving image technology which has led to the 'collapse' of the normal timetable for a whole day or even two offers a valuable model that is worth disseminating.

The use of ICT for *Citizenship* is also relatively undeveloped in spite of the evidence emerging from Chapter 6 about the ways that schools are using new technologies to work across the border between Northern Ireland and the Republic of Ireland in the Dissolving Boundaries programme. The evaluation of that approach suggests that *every* school in Northern Ireland, and elsewhere, could be expected to have at least one e-partner school, locally and globally.

Improvements in the learning experience of children with special educational needs are more often seen in special schools than in mainstream schools, and the potentials are even greater in these contexts. Much of the current use of ICT in special education is focused on the need to improve literacy and numeracy; while this is clearly important in terms of inclusion and offering life opportunities for all young people, we have provided evidence of impressive use of ICT which is both creative and connects to citizenship.

In all three of these examples, teachers need time to see and practise with software but they also need to understand the learning theories behind the design of software and the often-hidden values in the use of ICT. Understanding the affordances which digital and interactive educational resources bring to the classroom, and how teachers and learners should respond in the face of those facilities, is a gap in pedagogic understanding.[10]

Leadership

The examples of innovative teaching offered above, in creativity, citizenship and inclusive education, which have the effect of developing active opportunities for engagement by the learner are all central to an e-curriculum, but helping the educational community to use ICT to move towards transformed learning in these areas requires a particular visionary leadership. Our term for this vision is the creation of the 'e-school as a learning community'; which is where the process of e-schooling ought to be going, we believe.

We claimed in the Introduction that the reader would come to understand the distinction we make between enhancing learning and teaching (which is itself just one step beyond automating teaching) and transformed learning in the e-school. We hope that has become clear throughout our story. However, what is it that *makes the difference* between the minority of schools which demonstrate transformation across the life and work of the whole school – perhaps no more that one in five – and those which do not?

We argued in Chapter 9 that the answer lies in the quality of the leadership in the school. We think that it is the communicated insight and vision of the leader which allows small-scale, isolated enhancements which take place across the school to 'tip over' into transformation, because leadership sees the whole picture and can create the coherence needed to *make the difference.*

In Chapter 9, we quoted McCluskey as saying that,

Liberating teachers to be creative and think beyond subject boundaries is part of the leadership agenda in Northern Ireland that seeks to cultivate the idea that the head is the 'lead learner'. Many heads show the capacity to lead the debate within their schools about what is meant by quality learning.

Despite constraints due to examinations, summative assessment regimes and subject parochialism, the leadership of heads is contributing to moving away from learning in a shallow sense to something that is much more profound and to begin to appreciate the contribution that technology can make shifting the focus away from teaching and more to learning.

A learning-centred environment would be a key objective of any leadership.[11]

Leadership of an e-school seeks a means of bringing about change in a clear and coordinated way. Even in a schooling system that is marked with very strong ties to the past, e-schooling can support the broader economic and social change agenda, provided that there is strong alignment between curriculum, teacher education and continued professional development, the infrastructure, the political will and clarity about the function of schooling in society.

That message can be conveyed to schools generally by the way in which reforms are identified and shaped from the centre. If technology is embedded in the goals of reform, then it can also be afforded within those budgets, and the result will be an acceleration of that change. We argued earlier that reform itself is not deliverable without the implementation of technology to enhance and eventually to transform learning.

Where direction from the centre is muffled or missing, the evidence is that it can be successfully substituted by the leadership in individual institutions. This may go a long way to explaining the common finding both in NI and elsewhere in the UK, that only, at best, one in five schools can be seen to have embraced technological enhancements substantially, and with demonstrably effective and worthwhile outcome. Presumably, the leaders of the remainder of schools sense nothing at all hurrying at their backs that might make them consider picking up the pace.

Can technology help with e-school reform?

Before concluding, we wanted to put our thoughts about e-school to a test. Professor James Bosco[12] confronts what he calls four common, yet false, mantras about ICT and education reform. We have much sympathy with Bosco's tests and note the way in which our concept and evidence of e-schooling helps to add weight to his swing at arguments which miss the point.

- 'Curriculum integration is the key to effective use of ICT in school.'
  The issue of whether ICT improves learner achievement and attainments is beside the point if that curriculum fails to meet the needs of the learner in the twenty-first century. And, if curriculum takes precedence over pedagogy, then e-schooling reform is still-born.

- 'From the sage on the stage to the guide by the side.'
  Learning is not value-free. Using technology simply to improve learning is no guarantee that the values inherent in what is learnt are worthwhile; or that what is taught and tested for in school is the sum of all valuable learning in the world. The 'learning community' foundation of our concept of an e-school is the first step to looking more broadly at schooling in the wider world. Communications technologies accelerate the connection and ensure that our learners, no longer so sheltered, come face to face with different value-laden challenges to their ethical judgment much earlier than we have comfortably come to expect.

- 'Increasing and improving professional development is the key to effective use of ICT in schools.'

The astute reader will not have failed to notice that professional development comes high on our shortlist of priority actions, but it is not itself sufficient to ensure transformation. Bosco argues that it is the particular nature of schools as organisations that provide the challenge to school reform, and we agree with him. A teacher, even a cohort of teachers in a school can become highly ICT-enabled educators, but if they are teaching against the flow of the prevailing culture of the school, they will not make a difference.

- 'It's only a tool.'
  If the power-tool is not to hand, then one can revert to hammer and chisel, if not available, then hit stone on stone – it's not that vital. Yet ICT tools will continue to lead to completely new ways to experience and create human culture. As they become ubiquitous they will become invisible, and free us from our obsession with the tool and the skills needed to use it, free to concentrate on the cultures we are creating for our world.

A local message

In a book about global messages from a small island, it might be wise to end on a short note to ourselves. Complacency can be a terrible fate. As ships move forward in the fog of change, it is useful to hear some warning bells to guide them forward.

Roger Blamire[13] puts his finger on the foghorn,

> Over the past seven years much has changed in Northern Ireland's schools and people will be watching what happens now the 'tipping point' or critical mass adoption has been reached in many parts of the system and schools. What is the vision for exploiting the potential of next generation technologies and the more radical changes they make possible in schooling? How to innovate both from the top and from the grassroots – and empower those involved, whether learners, teachers, school leaders or policy-makers? Crucially: where will the new ideas come from? One possible threat in Northern Ireland (and the rest of the UK) is insularity, and from that, complacency.

It is evident from our study of tomorrow's classroom in Chapter 5 that the development and spread of e-schooling is complex and multi-faceted and that many enabling conditions will need careful strategic leadership, coordination and management. As the Department of Education reports:

> It (also) leaves little doubt that there are considerable challenges ahead for policy makers and implementers in securing the necessary willingness and enthusiasm of teachers, affording them the time and training to reach the levels of competence and confidence needed and supporting school managers in the well-planned integration of VLE-type technology in their schools.[14]

One might easily conclude that the growth of e-learning will be uncertain and spasmodic unless government is proactive.

It is salutary to note the rapid growth and popularity in the UK and USA of online tutorial services aimed at the British and American school curricula, outsourced from highly-educated teachers – located in India. According to Thomas Friedman, 'in the new flat world, you can outsource any knowledge work anywhere'[15] – and education is unarguably the prime *knowledge–work* industry.

The commitment and determination evident in developing countries, those which are recipient nations dependent on overseas aid, to reform their education systems as part of a larger plan to become developed and leading nations, is awe-inspiring, and ought to give education leaders in the western world pause for thought. Many of these countries do not carry the burdensome legacy of a perception of how education ought to be conducted, shaped largely by gazing fondly in the rear-view mirror of history. They have a very perceptive grasp of the power of technologies to enable change in business, industry and public services, and are usually starting their reform agenda with a relatively clean sheet.

Education in the west can still be passably well conducted, delivering the goods, without any real sense of urgency driven by the need for change; it would be a complacent and insular error, however, to believe that such a view is common across the globe.

Notes

Introduction

1. ORT Wingate Seminar 2003, quoted in Giladi. M. (2005) 'Windows of culture: an analysis of Israeli ORT school websites', M.Ed., University of Pretoria, South Africa.
2. Hargreaves, D.H. (2003) *Education Epidemic: Transforming Secondary Schools Through Innovation Networks*, London: Demos. Available online at http://www.demos.co.uk/catalogue/educationepidemic/.
3. McCluskey, A., with Hofer, M. and Wood, D. (2004) 'Schooling: a sustainable learning organisation? Perceptions and forces at play in institutional change in education in the light of the up-take of ICT', ERNIST Organisational Change Study. CTIE, Hunibach.
4. November, A. (1998) 'Creating a new culture of teaching and learning', Asilomar Symposium on Standards, Students, and Success. Available online at http://www.anovember.com/Default.aspx?tabid=159&type=art&site=18&parentid=18.
5. Austin, R. (2004) 'History, ICT and values: a case study of Northern Ireland', in M. Munoz and D. Perez (eds) *Formacion de la Ciudadania: Las TICs y los nuevos problemas* (translated as *Citizenship Training: ICTs and New Problems*), Alicante: Asociacón Universitaria del Profesorado de Didáctica de las Ciencias Sociales, pp. 45–57.
6. Illich, I. (1973) *Deschooling Society*, Harmondsworth: Penguin Books.
7. 'What Schools for the Future? OECD, Paris (2001) and 'Networks of Innovation: towards new models for managing schools and systems', OECD, Paris (2003). OECD/CERI (2000), Knowledge Management in the Learning Society, Paris and OECD/CERI (2004), Innovation in the Knowledge Economy: implications for education and learning systems, Paris. 'The OECD Schooling Scenarios' (2003), chapter 62 in Brent Davies and John West-Burnham (eds) *The Handbook of Educational Leadership and Management*, London: Pearson.
8. Heppell, S. (2005) Keynote Speech at XChange conference Birmingham. Available online at www.xchange2005.com.
9. Collins, K., McAleavy, G. and Adamson, G. (2002) 'Bullying in schools: a Northern Ireland study', Research Report Series, No. 30, Department of Education, Northern Ireland.
10. Cuban, L. (2001) *Oversold and Underused: Computers in the Classroom*, Cambridge, MA: Harvard University Press.
11. Conlon, T. and Simpson, M. (2003) 'Silicon Valley versus Silicon Glen: how do the outcomes compare?', *British Journal of Educational Technology*, 34(2): 137–50.
12. Department of Education School Census 2006. Available online at http://tinyurl.com/y5dgs5.
13. Private email with authors.

1 The state of e-schooling in Northern Ireland and its capacity to change

1. Austin, R. and Anderson, J. (2006) 'Re-schooling and ICT; a case study of Northern Ireland', in Leo Tan Wee Hin and R. Subramaniam (eds) *Literacy in Technology at the K-12 Level: Issues and Challenges*, London: Idea Group Reference, pp. 176–94.
2. 'Schools and pupils in Northern Ireland 1990/1 to 2005/6'. Available online at http://tinyurl.com/y5dgs5.
3. 'School for the future: funding, strategy, sharing', *Report of the Independent Strategic Review of Education*, December 2006.
4. Nick Mathiason, *The Observer*, 31 July 2005.
5. *IT Insights: Trends and UK Skills Implications*. E-skills UK/Gartner Inc, November 2004.
6. Eskills Bulletin Q3, 2006.
7. Annual Report of the Global Digital Divide Initiative (2001–2) World Economic Forum. Available online at http://www.weforum.org/pdf/Initiatives/Digital_Divide_Report_2001_2002.pdf (accessed 14 January 2007).
8. Barber, M. (2001) 'Teaching for tomorrow', in OECD Observer. Available online at http://www.oecdobserver.org/news/printpage.php/aid/420/Teaching_for-tomorrow.html.
9. http://www.detini.gov.uk/cgi-bin/get_builder_page?page=381&site=10.
10. Uhomoibhi, J.O. (2005) 'Implementing e-learning in Northern Ireland: prospects and challenges', *CWIS International Journal of Information and Learning Technology*, 23(1): 4–14.
11. Department for Employment and Learning, FE Means Business Policy. Available online at http://www.delni.gov.uk/index/publications/pubs-further-education/fe-means-business-policies-paper-12.htm (accessed 16 January 2007).
12. Future post-primary arrangements in Northern Ireland, the Costello Report. Available online at http://www.deni.gov.uk/pprb/costello_report.htm.
13. http://www.ccea.org.uk/.
14. 'The Independent Strategic Review of Education', Professor Sir George Bain, December 2006 (the Bain Report).
15. Hagan, M. and McGlynn, C. (2004) 'Moving barriers: promoting learning for diversity in initial teacher education', *Journal of Inter-cultural Education*, 15(4): 243–52.
16. McGlynn, C. (2004) 'Integrated education in Northern Ireland in the context of critical multi-culturalism', *Irish Educational Studies*, 22(3): 11–28.
17. 'A shared future. Policy and strategic framework for good relations in Northern Ireland', Office of the First Minister and Deputy First Minister, March 2005

2 An integrated strategy for ICT in schools

1. The Stevenson Report 1997. Available online at http://rubble.ultralab.anglia.ac.uk/stevenson/summary.html.
2. Department for Education and Skills (DfES) (2005) *Harnessing Technology: Transforming Learning and Children's Services*, London: DfES.
3. Email correspondence with the authors.
4. http://oldcomputers.net/pet2001.html.
5. McMahon, H.F. and Anderson. J. (1980) 'Building a springboard: regionalization within the microelectronics in Schools and Colleges Development Programme', *British Journal of Educational Technology*, October.

6. Anderson, J. (1977) 'Educational Evaluation in CAMOL at the University of Ulster', *Report to National Development Programme for Computer Assisted Learning*, London: Council for Education Technology.
7. Fothergill, R. and Anderson, J. (1981) 'Strategy for the Microelectronics Education Programme (MEP)', *Journal of Programmed Learning and Educational Technology*, 18(3), August.
8. Information Technology in Northern Ireland Education. NIRPC (MEP) and NICED. Belfast 1986.
9. *Information Technology*. Northern Ireland Economic Council. Report 74, March 1989.
10. Access Guaranteed. *TES* Online. 26 April 2002.
11. *Leapfrog to the Information Age: Strategic Framework and Action Plan*, Belfast: Department of Trade and Investment, 2000.
12. *The Software Skills Initiative: The Way Forward. The IT Skills Action Team*, The Software Industry Federation, 1998.
13. *The Foresight eBusiness Report: The Future Impact of eCommerce on Business in Northern Ireland*. The Henley Centre, 2000.
14. *Report on the Educational Themes: Primary Inspections 1998–99*, Department of Education. Education and Training Inspectorate, Rathgael House, Bangor, 1999.
15. *The Foresight eBusiness Report*, Foresight Northern Ireland and the Henley Centre, Belfast, 2000.
16. *Survey of Education Technology in Schools*, KPMG, Belfast, 1997.
17. *A Strategy for Education Technology in Northern Ireland*, Department of Education for Northern Ireland, 1998.
18. *Connecting the Learning Society*, National Grid for Learning Consultation paper, London: DfEE, 1998.
19. *Education Technology Strategy for Northern Ireland*, Department of Education for Northern Ireland, Rathgael House, Bangor, 1998. Available online at www.deni.gov.uk.
20. McMullan, T. (2001) 'Classroom 2000', in J. Gardner and R. Leitch (eds) *Education 2020. A Millenium Vision: Issues and Ideas for the Future of Education in Northern Ireland*, Belfast: The Blackstaff Press, pp. 45–53.
21. *C2K Primary Customer Satisfaction Survey*, PricewaterhouseCoopers, Belfast, April 2004. Available online at http://www.c2kni.org.uk/news/pwcpp.htm. *C2k Post-Primary Customer Satisfaction Survey*, PricewaterhouseCoopers, Belfast, September 2005. Available online at http://www.c2kni.org.uk/news/publications.htm.
22. Current details of the C2k service are available on www.c2kni.org.uk.
23. http://www.c2kni.org.uk/learningninews/lnihome.html.
24. *ET Strategy Review*, Department of Education, 2002. Available online at www.c2kni.org/ET_Review.
25. *The Paperless Examination Project Reports*, CCEA, Belfast, 2004.
26. http://www.empoweringschools.com.
27. McCluskey, A. (2005) 'Policy Peer Reviews: ICT in Schools. Northern Ireland', *Insight Observatory for New Technologies in Education*, European Schoolnet, Brussels. December. Available online at http://insight.eun.org/ww/en/pub/insight/policy/peer_reviews/p2preports_ni_finland.htm.
28. McCluskey, A. op. cit.
29. *Empowering Schools Progress Report*, 2005. Available online at http://tinyurl.com/yc9y85.

3 Teacher development for e-schooling

1. Adams, D. (2002) *The Salmon of Doubt: Hitchhiking the Galaxy One Last Time*, New York: Harmony Books.
2. *Empowering Schools Consultation Report*, Ballymena: ET Strategy Management Group, October 2004. Available online at www.empoweringschools.com.
3. Ministerial Endorsement of the emPowering Schools Strategy, December 2004. Available online at www.empoweringschools.com.
4. *Impact of ICT in Schools: A Landscape Review*, Coventry: Becta, 2007. Available online at http://publications.becta.org.uk/display.cfm?resID=28221.
5. *An Evaluation of Information and Communication Technology in Post-Primary Schools*, Bangor: Department of Education, 2007. Available online at www.etini.gov.uk.
6. *A Strategy for Education Technology in Northern Ireland*, Bangor: Department of Education, Northern Ireland (DENI), 1998.
7. *Empowering Schools Strategy*. DE, 2005. Available online at www.empoweringschools.com.
8. Fadel, C. and Lemke, C. (2006) *Technology in Schools: What the Research Says*, San Jose, CA: Cisco Systems and Culver City, CA: the Metiri Group.
9. *Teacher Workload Survey*, PricewaterhouseCoopers, 2002.
10. *ICT in Schools: The Impact of Government Initiatives*, Ref: HMI 264, London: OFSTED Publications Centre, 2001.
11. *Final Report on the NOF Programme in Northern Ireland (1999–2003)*. Available online at www.elearningfutures.com.
12. *ICT in Primary, Post-Primary and Special Schools, 2001–2002*, Bangor: ETI, 2003. Available online at http://tinyurl.com/y8bqrb.
13. *The Teacher Education Partnership Handbook*, Bangor: Department of Education for Northern Ireland, September 1998.
14. *GTCNI Reviews of Teacher Competence*, 2006. Available online at http://www.gtcni.org.uk//index.cfm/area/information/page/ProfStandard.
15. Hargreaves, D.H. (2003) *Education Epidemic: Transforming Secondary Schools Through Innovation Networks*, London: Demos. Available online at http://www.demos.co.uk/catalogue/educationepidemic/.
16. Schon, D.A. (1971) *Beyond the Stable State*, Harmondsworth: Penguin.
17. Fullan, M. (2004) *Leadership and Sustainability*, Toronto: Ontario Institute for Studies in Education, University of Toronto. Available online at http://home.oise.utoronto.ca/~changeforces/pdf/UKpre-reading.pdf.
18. McCluskey, A., with Hofer, M. and Wood, D.A. (2004) *Schooling: A Sustainable Learning Organisation? ERNIST Organisational Change Study*, Berne: CTIE, Swiss Agency for ICT in Education.
19. *Empowering Schools Strategy*, DE 2005. Available online at www.empoweringschools.com.
20. www.elearningfutures.com.
21. Thompson, H. and Kelly, V. (2002) *Effective and E-learning Online*, Northern Ireland e-Learning Partnership Newsletter, November.
22. Price, N.P. (2005) *Online EPD for Special Education Teachers*, Termtalk. GTCNI, June: 7.
23. Synnott, F. (2005) *Learning How to Teach Online*, P22–3 Connected, No. 13, Summer. LT Scotland. Available online at www.LTScotland.org.uk.
24. Hargreaves: op. cit.

4 Transforming learning within early teacher education

1. General Teaching Council for Northern Ireland. Available online at http://www.gtcni.org.uk//publications/uploads/document/Teacher%20Education%20Report.pdf.
2. Selinger, M. and Austin, R. (2003) 'A comparison of the influence of government policy on information and communications technology for teacher training in England and Northern Ireland', *Technology, Pedagogy and Education*, 12(1): 19–38.
3. The revised competences are contained in draft form in 'Teaching: the Reflective Profession', General Teaching Council, Northern Ireland, December 2006.
4. McNair, V. and Galanouli, D. (2002) 'Information and communications technology in teacher education: can a reflective portfolio enhance reflective practice?', *Technology Pedagogy and Education* (formerly *Journal of Information Technology for Teacher Education*), 11 (2): 181–96.
   McNair, V. and Marshall, K. (2006) 'How ePortfolios support development in early teacher education', in A. Jafari and C. Kaufman (eds) *Handbook of Research on ePortfolios*, Hershey, PA: Idea Group Reference, pp. 474–85.
5. http://www.crossborder.ie/events/scotenshome.php (accessed 28 December 2006).
6. The Post Graduate Certificate in Further and Higher Education (PGCFHE) is a one year part time course run by the University of Ulster. Available online at http://prospectus.ulster.ac.uk/course/?id=3238 (accessed 28 December 2006).
7. http://www.elearningfutures.com/templates/template3.asp?id=1 (accessed 28 December 2006).
8. Austin, R. (2003) 'Getting results: a report on laptops and wireless technology', *Educational Computing and Technology*, March: 74–5.
   Abbott, L., Clarke, L. and Austin, R. (2005) 'Student teachers' use of laptops in Schools', *Irish Educational Studies*, 24(1): 103–16.
9. Sime, D. and Priestly, M. (2005) 'Student teachers' first reflections on information and communications technology and classroom learning: implications for initial teacher education', *Journal of Computer Assisted Learning*, 21(2): 130–42.
10. *Empowering Schools Strategy Progress Report*, Bangor: DENI, 2005. Available online at http://www.deni.gov.uk/index/85-schools/15_ict_in_schools_classroom2000_pg.htm.
11. I am grateful to my colleagues Dolores Loughrey, Deirdre Graffin and Clodagh Kelly for access to this data.
12. Simpson, M., Payne,F., Munro, R. and Lynch,E. (1998) 'Using information and communications technology as a pedagogical tool: a survey of initial teacher education in Scotland', *Technology, Pedagogy and Education*, 7(3): 431–46.
13. Taylor, L. (2004) 'How trainee teachers develop their understanding of teaching using ICT', *Journal of Education for Teaching*, 30(1): 43–56.
14. Clarke, L. (2002) 'Putting the "C" in ICT: using computer conferencing to foster a community of practice among student teachers', *Journal of Information Technology in Teacher Education*, 11(2): 157–73.
    Lambe, J. and Clarke, L. (2003) 'Initial teacher education online: factors influencing the use of computer conferencing by student teachers', *European Journal of Teacher Education*, 26(3): 351–63.
15. *ImpaCT2: The Impact of Information and Communications Technology on Pupil Learning and Attainment*, Coventry: Becta, 2004.
16. Interview with Dr Jude Collins, December 2004.

17 Education and Training Inspectorate report, 'The Induction and Early Professional Development of Beginning Teachers', 2005.

5 An e-curriculum for an e-school?

1   Chief Inspector's Report for 2002–2004, Education and Training Inspectorate, 2005.
2   Report of the IT Cross Curricular Theme Working Group, June 1989. Department of Education for Northern Ireland.
3   See the web site of the Council for Curriculum, Examinations and Assessment (CCEA). Available online at http://www.rewardinglearning.com/development/index.html.
4   Anderson J. (1991) 'Information Technology – a cross-curricular competence for all pupils', *Computers in Education*, 16(1): 23–7.
5   CCEA website op. cit. Available online at http://www.rewardinglearning.com/development/index.html.
6   ICT Accreditation Scheme at KS3, Principal Moderator's Report. June 2005, CCEA, Belfast.
7   CCEA website op. cit.
    'Education for the 21st Century', the Burns Report. Available online at http://www.deni.gov.uk/review_body/index.htm.
8   Gallagher, C. (2005) *Think Piece for QCA Futures Project – Designing a Curriculum for the 21st Century* (A How-To Guide to Curriculum design based on a case study of Northern Ireland's Curriculum Review process), London: QCA.
9   Gallagher, ibid.
10 Gallagher, C. (2003) 'Curriculum, assessment and e-learning futures', Becta Online Forum, CCEA.
11 White, J. *et al.* (2003) Unpublished Report on the CCEA Pathways Proposals, London: Institute of Education.
12 Wood, D. (2006) *Policy, Peers and Practice. Peer Review as a Tool for Policy Development*, Brussels: ICT EUN Schoolnet.
13 www.empoweringschools.com.
14 ET Excellence Awards. Available online at http://www.c2kni.org.uk/news/press3.htm.
15 ERNIST ICT Schools Portraits (Part C: Northern Ireland, pp. 81–114), Woerden: Zuidam and Zonen, May 2004. Available online at http://www2.deni.gov.uk/inspection_services/surveys/index.htm.
16 Details at www.faulkes-telescope.com/
17 termtalk, Summer 2005, GTCNI, Belfast.
18 Costello Report (para 5.14) 3 'Future post-primary arrangements in Northern Ireland', the Costello Report. Available online at http://www.deni.gov.uk/pprb/costello_report.htm. See also the DE pages about the Costello Report. Available online at http://www.deni.gov.uk/pprb/index.htm.
19 Library Learning. Connected (13) Summer 2005. Learning Teaching Scotland. Glasgow. http://www.ltscotland.org.uk/ictineducation/connected/articles/13/specialfeature/librarylearning.asp www.ni-libraries.net and Article on Libraries from Connected.
20 www.elearningfutures.com.
21 Anderson, J. and McCormick, R. (2006) 'Pedagogic quality: supporting the next UK generation of e-learning', in U.-D. Ehlers and J.M. Pawlowski (eds) *Handbook on Quality and the Standardisation in E-Learning*, Berlin: Springer, Section 26; and Anderson, J. and

McCormick, R. (2005) *Pedagogic Quality in Policy and Innovation in Education. Quality Criteria*, Brussels: EUN Schoolnet. Available online at www.insight.eun.org.

22 Stein, G. and Wallace, R. (2004) *Assessment for Learning in the Classroom: GCSE ICT Online*, NiEL Partnership Project, Christchurch, Cantebury. Available online at client.canterbury.ac.uk/research/case-studies/qwizdom/assess/assessment-4–learning.pdf.
23 Roulston, S. and Clarke, L. (2003) 'A-level geography decision-making exercises in a virtual learning environment', *Geography*, 88(2): 141–8.
24 Wells, M. (2006) 'Extending collaborative learning online case studies', Department of Education, Curriculum Entitlement Conference, RTU, Antrim. January.
25 Unpublished notes of Scholar Project. Dr M. McArdle, 2004.
26 'Evaluating the potential for virtual learning environments: a VLE for citizenship', DE Research briefing, March 2005
27 Extracts from video case-studies published for learning enhanced through technology: the leadership challenge, C2K, Belfast, 1998.
28 Wood, D., op. cit.
29 Black, P., Harrison, C., Lee, C., Marshall, B. and Wiliam, D. (2003) *Assessment for Learning: Putting it into Practice*, Maidenhead: Open University Press.
30 Wood, D., op. cit.
31 Wallace, R. (2004) 'Assessing online', *Times Educational Supplement*, March.

6 Connected learning for citizenship

1 Selwyn, N. (2002) 'Literature Review in Citizenship, Technology and Learning', Futurelab Report 3. Available online at http://www.futurelab.org.uk/download/pdfs/research/lit_reviews/Citizenship_Review.pdf (accessed 3 January 2007).
2 Frean, A. (2006) 'Dull lessons fail to teach pupils how to be good citizens', *The Times*, 28 September. Newspaper report based on Ofsted inspection of citizenship.
3 See for example http://www.britishcouncil.org/etwinning.htm.
4 http://www.asharedfutureni.gov.uk/ (accessed 2 January 2007).
5 Austin, R. (2007) 'Reconnecting young people in Northern Ireland: a critique of ICT and citizenship', in B. Loader (ed.) *Making Digital Citizens*, London: Routledge.
6 Niens, U. and O'Connor, U. (2005) 'Evaluation of the introduction of local and global citizenship to the Northern Ireland Curriculum', Interim report to CCEA, September.
7 http://www.deni.gov.uk/index/8-admin_of_education_pg/101–strategic-review-of-education.htm (accessed 2 January 2007).
8 Davis, N., Cho, M.O. and Hagenson, L. (2005) 'Intercultural competence and the role of technology in teacher education', *Contemporary Issues in Technology and Teacher Education*, 4(4): 384–94. Available online at http://www.citejournal.org/vol4/iss4/maintoc.cfm (accessed 7 May 2006).
9 http://www.socsci.ulster.ac.uk./education/ict_conf/index.html.
10 Hamber, B. 'Digital diversity. building peace and reconciliation through technology', www.digitaldiversity.ie (accessed 2 January 2007).
11 http://ec.europa.eu/idabc/en/document/5157/330.
12 http://www.unescobkk.org/index.php?id=496.
13 Doward, J. (2006) 'The broadband revolution', *The Observer*, 10 December, p.1.
14 Grant, L. (2005) 'Using Wikis in schools: a case study', Futurelab discussion paper. Available online at http://www.futurelab.org.uk/research/discuss/05discuss01.htm.

15 Austin, R. (2006) 'The role of ICT in bridge-building and social inclusion; theory, policy and practice issues', *European Journal of Teacher Education*, 29(2), May: 145–61.
16 www.dissolvingboundaries.org (accessed 2 January 2007).
17 Hoter, E., Shonfeld, M. and Ganayim, A. (2006)'Shake up and wake up the faculty: a model for intervention in technology diffusion', in D.A. Willis, J. Price and J. Willis (eds) *Technology and Teacher Education Annual*, Charlottesville, VA: Association for the Advancement of Computing in Education.
18 Austin, R. (1992) 'A European dimension in the curriculum: the role of satellite TV and electronic mail', *Learning Resources Journal*, 8(1), February: 8–13.
Austin, R. (1992) 'European studies through video-conferencing', *Learning Resources Journal*, 8(2), June: 28–31.
Austin, R. (1992) 'A new view of Ireland, Britain and Europe', *Head Teachers Review*, Winter: 6–8. See also http://www.european-studies.org/ (accessed 1 May 2006).
19 Martin, M. (2000) *Videoconferencing in Teaching and Learning: Case Studies and Guidelines*,. Omagh, Northern Ireland: Western Education and Library Board; and Anderson, J. 'Kore wa nan desu ka'. Available online at http://www.ltscotland.org.uk/ictineducation/connected/connected14/specialfeature/korewanandesuka.asp (accessed 7 May 2006).
20 This is true except for the period of devolved administration from 1998–2002.
21 Austin, R. (2007) 'Reconnecting young people in Northern Ireland; a critique of ICT and citizenship', in B. Loader (ed.) *Making Digital Citizens*, London: Routledge.
22 Allport, G.W. (1954) *The Nature of Prejudice*, New York: Addison-Wesley.
23 Tropp, L.R. and Pettigrew, T.F. (2005) Relationships between intergroup contact and prejudice among minority and majority status groups', *Psychological Science*, 16(12): 951–7.
24 Meagher, M.E. and Castaños, F. (1996) 'Perceptions of American culture: the impact of an electronically-mediated cultural excahnge program on Mexican high school students', in S.C. Herring (ed.) *Computer-mediated Communication: Linguistic, Social and Cross-cultural Perspectives*, Philadelphia, PA: John Benjamins, pp. 187–202.
25 Postmes, T., Spears, R. and Lea, M. (1998) 'Breaching or building social boundaries? SIDE-effects of computer-mediated communication', *Communication Research*, Special issue: *(Mis)communicating Across Boundaries*, 25: 689–715.
26 Postmes, T., Spears, R. and Lea, M. (2002) 'Inter-group differentiation in computer-mediated communication: effects of depersonalization', *Group Dynamics*, Special issue: *Groups and Internet*, 6: 3–16.
27 Sundberg, P.A. (2001) 'Building positive attitudes among geographically diverse students: the project 1–57 experience', National Educational Computing Conference, 'Building on the Future', 25–27 July.
28 Gaertner, S.L. and Dovidio, J.F. (2000) *Reducing Intergroup Bias: The Common Ingroup Identity Model*, Philadelphia, PA: Psychology Press.
29 Mollov, B. and Lavie, C. (2001) 'Culture, dialogue and perception change in the Israeli–Palestinian conflict', *International Journal of Conflict Management*, 12(1): 69–87.
30 Wenger, E. (1999) *Communities of Practice: Learning, Meaning and Identity*, Cambridge: Cambridge University Press.
31 http://www.dissolvingboundaries.org/research/apr2006.doc.
32 Leeman, Y. and Ledoux, G. (2003) 'Preparing teachers for intercultural education', *Teaching Education*, 13(3): 279–92.
33 http://www.gtcni.org.uk/.
34 *Istance, D. (2004) Knowledge Management in the Learning Society*, Paris: OECD/CERI.

Istance, D. (2004) *Innovation in the Knowledge Economy: Implications for Education and Learning Systems*, Paris: OECD/CERI.

35 McCluskey, A. (2004) *Schooling: A Sustainable Learning Organisation? ERNIST Organisational Change Study*, CTIE.

36 Austin, R. (2006) 'The role of ICT in bridge-building and social inclusion; theory, policy and practice issues', *European Journal of Teacher Education*, 29(2), May: 145–61.

Austin, R. (2004) 'History, ICT and values: a case study of Northern Ireland', in M.I. Munoz and D.P. Perez (eds) *Formacion de la Ciudadania: Las TICs y los nuevos problemas* (translated as *Citizenship Training: ICTs and New Problems*), Alicante: Asociacón Universitaria del Profesorado de Didáctica de las Ciencias Sociales, pp. 45–57.

Abbott, L., Austin, R., Mulkeen, A. and Metcalfe, N. (2004) 'The global classroom: advancing cultural awareness through collaboration using ICT', *European Journal of Special Needs Education*, 19(2): 225–40.

Austin. R., Abbott. L., Mulkeen. A. and Metcalfe. N. (2003) 'Dissolving boundaries:cross-national co-operation through technology in education', *The Curriculum Journal*, 14(1): 55–84.

37 Niens, U. and O'Connor, U. (2005) 'Evaluation of the introduction of local and global citizenship to the Northern Ireland Curriculum', Interim report to CCEA, September.

38 Report of a Survey of Provision for Education for Mutual Understanding in Post-primary School, Education and Training Inspectorate, 2000.

O'Connor, U., Hartop, B. and McCully, A. (2002) 'A review of the Schools Community Relations Programme 2002', a consultation document published by the Department of Education for Northern Ireland.

39 Cairns, E. and Hewstone, M. (2001) *In Peace Education: The concept, Principles and Practices Around the World*, Marwah, NJ: Larry Erlbaum Associates.

40 Chief Inspector's Report 2002–2004. Available online at http://www2.deni.gov.uk/inspection_services/general_pub/Chief_Inspector_Report_02_04.pdf (accessed 31 May 2006).

41 http://www.socsci.ulster.ac.uk./education/ict_conf/index.html.

42 Xchange Podcast interview with the presenters on http://xchangeblogs.com/podcasts/PGCEstudents.mp3.

43 Proposals for Curriculum and Assessment at Key Stage 3, CCEA, 2003.

44 http://www.socsci.ulster.ac.uk./education/ict_conf/index.html.

7 Special and inclusive education

1 *ICT in Primary, Post-Primary and Special Schools, 2001–2002*, Bangor: ETI, 2003. Available online at http://tinyurl.com/y8bqrb.

2 Questionnaire data from PGCE primary students collected by D. Loughrey and G. Graffin. Data collected by D. Patterson, Regional Training Unit summer school, 2005.

3 http://www.c2kni.org.uk/success/belmont.htm. http://www.belmonthouse.ik.org/.

4 Becta, 2000. Available online at http://www.becta.org.uk/page_documents/teaching/generalsen2.pdf#search='SEN%20%20%20ICT%20%20motivation'.

5 Phelan, A. and Haughey, E. (2000)'Information and advice: special educational needs and information communications technology', National Council for Technology and Education (NCTE), November. Available online at http://www.ncte.ie/images/seninfoadvice.pdf (accessed 12 January 2007).

6. Wynne, E. (2004) 'An investigation into the use of information and communication technology in special needs education in mainstream primary schools', Thesis, University College, Dublin.
7. Xchange 2006 Conference, Belfast.
8. Blamires, M. (ed.) (1999) *Enabling Technology*, London: Chapman.
9. Stradling, R., Sims, D. and Jamison, J. (1994) *Portable Computers Pilot Evaluation Report*, Coventry: National Council for Educational Technology.
10. Jordan, M. (2000) *Horizon Project: Final Evaluation Report*, Cork: Cork Institute of Technology.
11. Blamires, M. (2000) 'Recent Advances in ICT and SEN', NAAOSEN, Canterbury: Christ Church University College
12. Brown, L. and Percival-Price, N. 'My town'. Available online at http://www.c2kni.org.uk/learningninews/mytown.htm.
13. Malouf, D. (2001) 'Introduction: special education technology and the field of dream', in J. Woodward and L. Cuban (eds) *Technology Curriculum and Professional Development*, Thousand Oaks, CA: Corwin Press.
14. MacFarlane, A. (1997) *Information Technology and Authentic Learning*, London: Routledge.
15. Crook, C. (1994) *Computers and the Collaborative Experience of Learning*, New York: Routledge.
16. Ofsted (2001) *The Impact of Government Initiative – Interim Report*. Available online at www.ofsted.gov.uk/publications/1043.pdf.
17. Bonnet, M. (1997) 'Computers in the classroom: some value issues', in A. McFarlane (ed.) *Information Technology and Authentic Learning*, London: RoutledgeFarmer.
18. Lick, C.M. and Little, T.H. (1987) 'Computers and mildly handicapped individuals', in J.D. Lindsey (ed.) *Computers and Exceptional Individuals*, Columbus, OH: Merrill.
19. Underwood, J.D.M. and Underwood, G. (1994) *Computers and Learning: Helping Children Acquire Thinking Skills*, Oxford: Blackwell.
20. Ravitz, J., Wong, Y. and Becker, H. (1999) *Teaching Learning and Computing: 1998 Report to Participants*. Available online at http://www.crito.uci.edu/tlc/findings/special_report/report_to_participants_rev2.pdf.
21. Mulkeen, A. (2004) *Schools for the Digital Age: Information and Communication Technology in Irish Schools*, Dublin: NCTE.
22. Cox, M.J. (1997) *The Effects of Information on Students' Motivation*, final report, Coventry: NCTE.
23. Pachler, N. (1999) 'Theories of learning and ICT', in M. Leask and N. Pachler (eds) *Learning to Teach Using ICT in the Secondary School*, London: Routledge.
24. Perzylo, L. (1993) 'The application of multimedia CD-ROMs in schools', *British Journal of Technology*, 24(3): 191–7.
25. Gardner, H. (1999) *Intelligence Reframed; Multiple Intelligences for the 21st Century*, New York: Basic Books.
26. Becta (2000) 'Emotional and Behavioural Difficulties (EBD) and ICT', information sheet. Available online at http://www.becta.org.uk/page_documents/teaching/generalsen1.pdf (accessed 14 January 2007).
27. Pachler, op.cit.
28. Brown-Chidsey, R. and Boscardin, M.L., 'How helpful are computers? Comparison of the computer experiences of students with and without learning difficulties'. Available online at http://www.ncsu.edu/meridian/sum2001/computers/index.html.

29 http://www.inclusive.co.uk/infosite/bblack.shtml. Down's Syndrome, Computers and Curriculum.
30 Phelan, A. and Haughey, E. (2000) *Special Educational Needs and Information and Communications Technology*, Dublin: NCTE.
31 McKeown, S. (2000) *Unlocking Potential: How ICT can Support Children with Special Needs*, Birmingham: Questions Publishing.
32 Medwell, J. (1998) 'The Talking Book Project: some further insights into the use of Talking Books to develop reading', *Reading*, 32(1): 3 -8.
33 Collins, J., Hammond, M. and Wellington, J. (1997) *Teaching and Learning with Multimedia*, London: Routledge. Available online at http//www.data.org.uk/data/sen/accom_res.php.
34 European Agency for Development in Special Needs Education (2003) *Special Needs Education in Europe – Thematic Publication*. Available online at www.european-agency.org.
35 O'Baoill, N. (2006) Fleming Fulton School, XChange conference, Belfast. Creative Animations at Fleming Fulton. Xchange Case Studies. DENI, 2006. Available online at http://xchangeblogs.com/podcasts/inclusion.mov.
36 http://www.belmonthouse.ik.org/.
37 Fennema-Jansen, S. (2001) 'Measuring effectiveness: technology to support writing', *Special Education Technology Practice*, January–February.
38 Brown, L. (2006) 'Employability project', Xchange 2006 case studies document, DENI, June.

8 Enterprising education

1 Reading, V. (2002) 'Knowledge is Power', European Commissioner for Education and Culture, Extracts from the Public Service Review, European Union, Autumn.
2 Students in four representative schools were involved in this study; the results of data analysis are reported here for the first time.
3 I am grateful to my colleague Elaine Courtney for her assistance in administering this questionnaire.
4 http://dreamlablearning.com/. 'Dreamlab Learning', termtalk, January 2006, GTCNI, Belfast.
5 http://www.nerve-centre.org.uk/.
6 http://www.dcalni.gov.uk/allpages/allpages.asp?pname=creativity.
7 http://www.nesta.org.uk/nationalcollaborative/.
8 http://www.niftc.co.uk/page.asp?id=49.
9 http://www.ccea.org.uk/.
10 Fullan, M. (1990) 'Changing school culture through staff development', in B. Joyce (ed.) *ASCD Yearbook*, Baltimore, MD: Association for Supervision and Curriculum Development.
11 Crockett, M. (1998) 'Innovation and inertia', in R. Halsall (ed.) *Teacher Research and School Improvement: Opening Doors from the Inside*, Buckingham: Open University Press.
12 Leonard, D. (1996) 'Quality in education and teacher development', *Irish Educational Studies*, 15 (Spring): 1–8.
13 Fullan, M.G. and Stiegelbaur, S. (1991) *The New Meaning of Educational Change*, London: Cassel.
14 Pring, R. (1995) 'The community of educated people: the Lawrence Stenhouse Memorial Lecture', *British Journal of Curriculum Studies*, 43(2): 121–45.

15　Fullan, M. (1990) 'Changing school culture through staff development', in B. Joyce (ed.) *ASCD Yearbook*, Baltimore, MD: Association for Supervision and Curriculum Development.

9 Leadership for quality in an e-school

1　*The Becta Review*, 2006, Coventry: Becta. Available online at http://publications.becta.org.uk/download.cfm?resID=25948.
2　Becta Self- Review Framework, Coventry: Becta. Available online at http://tinyurl.com/ynxdal.
3　Collins, J. (2001) *Good to Great*, London: Random House.
4　Hargreaves, D.H. (2003) *Education Epidemic: Transforming Secondary Schools Through Innovation Networks*, London: Demos. Available online at http://www.demos.co.uk/catalogue/educationepidemic/.
5　Becta ICT Practice Awards, 2003. Available online at http://www.becta.org.uk/corporate/display.cfm?section=21&id=3224.
6　www.empoweringschools.com.
7　www.rtuni.org.
8　Dr Tom Hesketh, Director of RTU, cited in J. Anderson and B. Evans (2005) *School Leadership in Northern Ireland in Policy and Innovation in Education*, Leadership, Ed McCluskey, EUN Schoolnet. Available online at www.insight.eun.org.
9　Peter Senge in his 'Leading learning organisations: the bold, the powerful and the invisible' characterises leaders as 'those who "walk ahead"; people who are genuinely committed to deep change in themselves and in their organisations. They lead through developing new skills, capabilities and understandings and they come from many places within the organisation.'
10　An evaluation by the Education and Training Inspectorate of information and communication technology in primary schools, May 2005, Department of Education. Available online at www.etini.gov.uk.
11　An evaluation of information and communication technology in post-primary schools, 2006, Department of Education. Available online at www.etini.gov.uk.
12　North, R. (2006) An Evaluation of the School Empowerment Through ICT Project, July, unpublished, Belfast: Regional Training Unit.
13　Balanskat, A. and Gerhart, P. (2005) *Head Teachers' Professional Profile and Roles Across Europe in Policy and Innovation in Education*, Leadership Ed McCluskey, EUN Schoolnet. Available online at www.insight.eun.org.
14　McCluskey, A. (2005) *Northern Ireland Strategy. Peer to Peer Review Project*, EUN Schoolnet. Available online at www.insight.eun.org.
15　EMINENT School Portraits, EUN Schoolnet, 2004. Available online at www.insight.eun.org.
16　EMINENT School Portraits, op. cit.
17　www.anovember.com.
18　Personal email from Alan November, Principal Associate, Renaissance Learning Associates.
19　'Transforming primary practice', termtalk, Summer 2005, GTC NI. Available online at www.finaghyprimaryschool.co.uk.
20　Visscher, A. *et al.* (2001) and North, R. *et al.* (2000) cited in the *Becta Review*, 2006, Coventry: Becta. Available online at http://publications.becta.org.uk/download.cfm?resID=25948.

21 Underwood, J. et al. (2005) *Broadband Pathfinder Project: The impact of Broadband on Schools*, Becta Annual Research Project. Available online at http://partners.becta.org.uk/index.php?section=rh&rid=11082.
22 RTU's work on Extended Schools. Available online at http://www.rtuni.org/extendedschools/page.cfm/area/information/page/coll//pkey/840.
23 'Extended schools: schools, families, communities – working together', Bangor: DENI, 2006. Available online at http://www.deni.gov.uk/index/85–schools/03–schools_impvt_prog_pg/schools-sch-impvt-extschoolsguidance.htm. http://tinyurl.com/tdhfq.
24 McCluskey, A., with Hofer, M. and Wood, D. (2004) *Schooling: A Sustainable Learning Organisation? Perceptions and Forces at Play in Institutional Change in Education in the Light of the Up-take of ICT*, ERNIST Organisational Change Study. CTIE, Hunibach.
25 'Extended schools: schools, families, communities – working together'.
26 'Schools for the future: funding, strategy and sharing', the Report of the Independent Strategic Review of Education, 2006, Department of Education.
27 McCluskey, A. (2005) op. cit.
28 Gillian, K. (2003) 'School buildings design', Department of Education Research Paper, Autumn.
29 Newsom Report, 'Half our future', 1963, London: HMSO.
30 Dinsmore, A. (2000) 'Millennium High', Unpublished 'Schools of Thought' paper.

10 Global messaging

1 Cassidy, T.H. (1990) 'Data for decisions in developing education systems' Thesis (Ed. D.), Boston, MA: Harvard University Press.
2 McCluskey, A. (2005) *Policy Peer Reviews: ICT in Schools, Northern Ireland*, Brussels: EUN Schoolnet. Available online at www.insight.eun.org.
3 Wood, D. (2006) *Policy Peer Reviews: ICT in Schools, Methodology, Policy Peers and Practice. Peer Review as a Tool for Policy Development*, Brussels: EUN Schoolnet. Available online at www.insight.eun.net.
4 Ripley, M. (2006) 'The four changing faces of e-assessment 2006–2016'. Paper submitted to EUN Policy Innovation Committee. Zoetermeer, Den Haag. October.
5 GTCNI (2004) *Code of Values and Professional Practice*. Available online at http://www.gtcni.org.uk//index.cfm/area/information/page/codeofvaluesandprofessionalpractice.
6 *A Shared Future: Policy and Strategic Framework for Good Relations in Northern Ireland*, 2005 Office of the First Minister and Deputy First Minister, March.
7 An evaluation of information and communication technology in post-primary schools, 2006. Department of Education. Available online at www.etini.gov.uk .
8 Fadel, C. and Lemke, C. (2006) *Technology in Schools: What the Research Says*, San Jose, CA: Cisco Systems and Culver City, CA: the Metiri Group.
9 An evaluation by the Education and Training Inspectorate of ICT in Primary Schools, May 2005, Bangor: ETI, DENI.
An evaluation of information and communication technology in post-primary schools, 2006. Department of Education. Available online at www.etini.gov.uk.
10 Quality Criteria Dossier, ed. McCluskey, A. (2005) Brussels: European Schoolnet, December. Available online at http://tinyurl.com/zbrpm.
Anderson, J. and McCormick, R. (2006) 'Pedagogic quality: supporting the next UK generation of e-learning', in U.-D. Ehlers and J.M. Pawlowski (eds) *Handbook on Quality*

and Standardisation in E-Learning, Berlin: Springer. Available online at http://tinyurl.com/mhotb.
11 McCluskey, A. (2005), op. cit.
12 Bosco, J. (2005) (Western Michigan University) 'Is it possible to reform schools? Towards keeping the promise of ICT in our schools', Irish Presidency of the EU Conference on ICT in Education, Dublin, May.
13 Private email to authors.
14 'Evaluating the potential for virtual learning environments: a VLE for citizenship', 2005, DE Research Briefing, March.
15 Friedman, T.L. (2005) *The World is Flat*, New York: Farrar, Straus and Giroux.

Index

Adams, Douglas 38
administration: administrative structure 18; use of ICT in 43–4, 162–3, 173
alignment 170–5; of technology and policy 2, 35–6, 82, 163, 173–5
Allport, G.W. 101
assessment: of embedded ICT 79, 121; formative 15, 53, 80; of ICT in initial teacher education 62–4; integration of 2, 26, 163, 171–3; ongoing 80; online 90, 91, 92, 94–5, 162; software 42; use of ICT for 43, 83, 162–3
Austin, R. 3, 98, 99, 108; and Anderson, J. 8

Bain Report (2006) 17, 134
Baker, Kenneth 24
Barber, M. 13
Becta (British Educational and Communications Technology Agency) 40, 73, 112, 114, 122, 123, 126, 154
behaviourism 116, 118
Blackboard 54, 71–2, 137
Blamire, Roger 20, 182
Blamires, M. 113, 114, 115, 121
Bosco, James 181–2
Brown-Chidsey, R. and Boscardin, M.L. 124
Brown, Martin 21
bullying 4
bureaucratic *status quo* 4
business studies 15, 133, 134

C2K 23–4, 27–32, 35, 44, 53, 106; administration service 163; connections of schools to ElfNI 88–9; connection to JANET 135; in initial teacher education 63, 66, 68–9, 75; SEN software 122; software and hardware 46, 48, 63, 68–9
CAMOL (Computer Assisted Management of Learning) 21
Cassidy, Tom 170
CCEA (Council for the Curriculum, Examinations and Assessment) 11, 16, 32, 70, 82, 92, 109, 149; reforms 80, 109, 144

child protection 106
citizenship education 3, 63, 89, 95, 97–110
Clarke, L 71
CLASS (Computerised Local Administration of Schools Systems) Project 23, 25, 80
Classroom 2000 23, 25, 26–7, 28, 46, 140; *see also* C2K
CLDA (creative learning in the digital age) project 143–51
Clicker 125
Colleges of Further and Higher Education 7, 11, 14, 135, 138
Collins, J. 154, 156; *et al.* 126
Collins, K. *et al.* 4
community: accountability 164; building professional communities online 51–3; communal polarisation 8, 9–10, 12, 97–8, 107; e-school as an extended school 164–5; global 2, 4, 52, 104; learning community 181; of online support for student teachers 71–3; *see also* citizenship education
computer-based games 128–9
computer provision 20–1, 24–5, 30, 46; memory capacity 140
Conlon, T. and Simpson, M. 5
'Connecting Teachers' programme 46
conservatism 5, 8, 10, 48
Conservative Party 9
constructivism 102, 116, 117, 118, 120
Costello Report (2004) 134
Council for the Curriculum, Examinations and Assessment *see* CCEA
Cox, M.J. 117
Creative Learning Centres 179
creativity 6, 138–9; creative learning in the digital age (CLDA) 143–51; in Dreamlab project 139–43
Crockett, M. 148
Crook, C. 116
Cuban, L. 5
cultural affiliation 8, 9–10, 12, 107
cultural diversity 3

curriculum goals 2; under ET Strategy 26
curriculum revision 14–16, 39, 77, 80–2; alignment with pedagogy and assessment 171–3; cross-curricular IT 22, 78–80, 149; enhancing the classroom through 83–90; external agencies and 104–5; school empowerment for 82–3
curriculum setting 11

Davis, N. *et al.* 98, 104
Department for Education and Skills (DfES) 19–20
Department for Employment and Learning (DEL) 135
Department of Culture, Arts and Leisure (DCAL) 138, 139
Department of Education 11, 154, 182
de-schooling 3–4
Dinsmore, Adeline 154
disabilities, young people with 15, 114–15, 127
Dissolving Boundaries programme 64, 96, 99–100, 102–6, 108, 109, 114, 179
Dreamlab Generation 44, 138–43, 179

economy: of Northern Ireland 12–14; of the UK 12
Educational Computing Laboratory 20, 21
educational selection 5, 17; abolition of 16
Educational Technology Strategy 7, 25, 26–7, 32, 57; 'Empowering Schools' *see* Empowering Schools strategy; teacher competence with ICT 41–3
Education and Library Boards 18, 23, 27, 44, 55, 60, 66, 72, 138, 139, 157, 170
Education and Skills Authority 18, 31
Education and Training Inspectorate (ETI) 25, 26, 43, 47, 61–2, 74, 111, 112, 121, 156, 158
education policy: alignment with technology 2, 35–6, 82, 163, 173–5; 'A Shared Future' policy 15, 17, 97, 107, 174; building capacity for organisational change 53–4, 160–2; economic imperative of introducing IT 21–3; embedding ICT through the curriculum 29–30, 39–40, 73, 77–87; 'Entitled to Succeed' programme 33; goals 21–2; integrated ICT strategy 19–20, 24–7, 30, 35–6; political changes to 14–18, 100; Unesco's policies 99; *see also* Educational Technology Strategy; Empowering Schools strategy
education values: ICT application and 3, 111–15, 174; reflected in ICT and the curriculum 6
eLearning partnership 54, 65
Electronic Libraries for Northern Ireland (ElfNI) 88–9
EMINENT School Portraits 158, 159–60
employment: employer needs and enterprise education 137–8; historic basis of 12; ICT sector 12–13; ICT skills for 44, 132; preparation and competencies for 1, 15, 34; public sector 12; *see also* enterprise; workforce
Empowering Schools strategy 33–5, 37, 42–3, 57, 63, 82–3, 173; 2005 progress report 66; for employment skills 132
enterprise culture 15, 65
enterprise education: creativity and innovation 138–51; definition of enterprise 6; global messages of 151–2; ICT training and employer needs 137–8; role of further and higher education sector 134–7; use of ICT in schools for 133–7
e-schooling as a concept 1–5, 104, 164–5, 181
eTwinning programme 98–9
European Agency 127, 128
European Schoolnet 20, 158
European Studies 89, 96, 99, 102
Extended Schools Initiative 164–5, 167, 172

Fadel, C. and Lemke, C. 177, 178
Faulkes, Dill 85
Fennema-Jansen, S. 129
Friedman, Thomas 183
Fullan, M. 52, 148, 151; and Stiegelbaur, S. 150
further education 2, 7, 11, 14, 15, 16, 33, 34, 64, 82, 134, 135, 142; enterprise education 134–7; teacher training 64

Gardiner, Barry 33, 40
Gardner, Howard 118
General Teaching Council for Northern Ireland (GTCNI) 51, 61, 62, 104, 174
Global Citizenship 7, 17, 109
global community 2, 4, 52, 104
global knowledge economy 13–14, 34, 83
grammar schools 10, 11, 18, 135, 158; ICT case study in a grammar school 83–6

Hagan, M. and McGlynn, C. 17
Hamber, B. 98
hardware: access to 24, 67, 68, 75, 103, 140; deployment decisions 76, 177–8; in initial teacher education 60, 67, 68, 75; maintenance 26, 27; pupil use of 70; refreshing of 2, 68–9, 166, 177–8
Hargreaves, David 2, 40, 51–2, 57, 154, 159; on a continuum of school services 164, 178
higher education 4, 7, 11, 13–14, 105; enterprise education 134–7; teacher training 64
housing 10, 98
human resources 2

ICT employment sector 12–13
ICT infrastructure 6, 19–24, 30, 176–8; in FHE colleges 135; in Initial Teacher Education 60–1

ICT investment 2–3, 5, 77
ICT skills: employment requirements of 12; gap between teachers and taught 40–4; measurability of 39; and media skills 149–50; and multi-media skills 147; PGCE training 67; for teacher support 42; and the work place 133
ILT (Information and Learning Technology) 135–8
inclusive education 114–15, 120–9, 131; *see also* special education needs
Independent Strategic Review of Education (2006) 11, 97, 98
Information and Learning Technology (ILT) 135–8
Information Technology: cross-curricular IT 22, 78–80, 149; economic imperative of introducing 21–3; IT skills 12, 22, 78; use of ICT in 133
innovation 4, 15, 65, 89–93, 138–51, 148
Integrated Learning Systems (ILS) 117
intercultural education 104
Internet 19, 24, 30, 43, 66–9, 83, 85–8, 101, 106, 159, 161; online community 2, 51–3; online teacher support 71–3; online teaching *see* online teaching; taking teachers online 54–7; use in SEN 127–9
Istance, David 3–4, 104, 164, 175
IT *see* Information Technology
IT Insights report (2004) 12, 13

Japan 100, 106
Japanese Studies 89, 96
Joint Academic Network (JANET) 30, 135

Kelly, Vivian 55
Kenny, Jack 23
knowledge economy 13–14, 34, 83, 132

Lambe, J. and Clarke, L. 71
leadership development 58
leadership in schools 3, 153–68, 180–1; international study 160–2; leadership training 6, 155–6, 160–2 *see also* teacher development; teacher education; 'teacher-leaders' in ICT training 45–6
learning: autonomy 84–5, 148; collaborative learning online 91–3; connected learning for citizenship 97–110; and the curriculum for SEN 120–1; development of attitudes and behaviour 3; embedding ICT in 29–30, 39–40, 73, 77–87; global 52; ICT transformation of 3, 73–4, 83–90; language of 15; learner experiences of ICT use in other subjects 133–4; learning community 181; lifelong 15, 34; as a social phenomenon 101–2; sustainable learning 143; teachers as learners 47–8, 150; theoretical learning models in SEN 116–17

Learning NI 30, 115
learning resources 63, 86, 160, 168
Learnwise 54–5
Leeman, Y. and Ledoux, G. 104
Leonard, D. 150
lifelong learning 15, 34, 40, 58, 78, 96, 164, 175
literacy tools 125–7, 129

McClean, Michael 158–9
McCloskey, Bernard 92
McCluskey, Alan 2, 3, 52, 104; evaluation of NI ICT strategy 158, 166, 171, 172, 174, 180
McFarlane, A. 115–16
Mackay, Alastair 161–2
McKeown, S. 126
McMahon, Harry 21
McMullan, Tom 28, 80
Malouf, D. 115
managed ICT service 7, 20, 23–32, 140, 177
managed learning environments (MLEs) 7, 60, 98, 106, 131, 173
management information systems 162–3, 168
Meagher, M.E. and Castaños, F. 101
media skills 149–50; *see also* multi-media skills
Medwell, J. 126
MEP (Microelectronics Education Programme) 21
microcomputers 20–1, 24; *see also* computer provision
Microelectronics Education Programme (MEP) 21
Microsoft Word 123–4
Mollov, B. and Lavie, C. 101
Mulkeen, A. 117
multi-media skills 74, 133, 147, 149
multiple intelligencies 118, 163

National Council for Curriculum and Assessment (NCCA) 128
National Development Programme for Computer Assisted Learning (NDPCAL) 21
National Grid for Learning (NGFL) policy 19, 25, 26
Naylor, Richard 21
Nerve Centre projects 138–51
New Opportunities Fund (NOF) programme 3, 44–50, 157
Newsom Report 167
New University of Ulster (NUU) 20–1
NICED (Northern Ireland Council for Educational Development) 21
Niens, U. and O'Connor, U. 98, 107, 110
Northern Ireland Council for Educational Development (NICED) 21
Northern Ireland Economic Council 22–3, 78
Northern Ireland Film and Television Commission (NIFTC) 92, 143, 179

Northern Ireland's schooling system: approach to teacher development 39–40; current characteristics of 10–12; the economy and 12–14; embedding ICT in 29–30, 39–40, 73, 77–87; global significance of ICT experience 5–7, 35–7, 58, 75–6, 95–6, 110, 131, 151–2, 167–82; historical and political shaping of 8–10; political changes 14–18; *see also* schools

November, Alan 3, 6, 96, 161, 173

Number Box software 127

online teaching 30, 89–90, 95–6; collaborative learning 91–3; course design 90–1; e-assessment 90, 91, 92, 94–5, 162

Online Teaching and Learning for Educators (OLTE) 57

Open for Learning; Open for Business 26

Organisation for Economic and Cultural Development (OECD) 4

P2P project 20

Pachler, N. 118, 121

Pearlman, Bob 7

pedagogy 24, 159–60, 168, 181; alignment with curriculum and assessment 171–3; *see also* teaching practices

Phelan, A. and Haughey, E. 112, 126

political divisions in Northern Ireland 9

Postmes, T. *et al.* 101

PQH (NI) (Professional Qualification for Headship) 155

Pring, R. 150

psychological theories of education 116–18

pupil motivation 49, 111–13

Ravitz, J. *et al.* 117

Reform of Public Administration in Northern Ireland 170

Regional Training Unit (RTU) 155, 157, 159, 160–1

religious affiliations 8, 9–10, 12, 107

Republic of Ireland 12, 99, 100, 104–6, 113, 118, 138, 179; ICT in teacher education 62; Internet use 128; legacy of creation of Northern Ireland and 8–9, 10; NCCA 128; school curriculum 8; software 121–2, 125, 127, 129

re-schooling 3–4, 104, 164

resources: computer *see* computer provision; hardware; software; human 2; learning resources 63, 86, 160, 168

Review of Public Administration 15, 18

Ripley, Martin 173

Schon, Donald 51

school librarian ICT training 38, 43–8

schools: buildings 165–7; empowerment through ICT 156–7 *see also* Empowering Schools strategy; e-school as an extended school 164–5; grammar 10, 11, 18, 83–6, 135, 146, 158; leadership *see* leadership in schools; as 'learning organisations' 1–2, 51–3, 104; links between 14, 16, 98–100, 101–2, 107–9; non-selective 10, 11, 86–7, 135, 146, 160; organisational improvement 162–4; religious and cultural affiliations 8, 9–10, 12, 107; self-defining of 104 *see also* re-schooling; service integration 164–5; specialist 16, 82, 105; *see also* Northern Ireland's schooling system

schools for the deaf 105

Selinger, M. and Austin, R. 61

Selwyn, N. 97, 109

'A Shared Future' policy 15, 17, 97, 107, 174

Sime, D. and Priestly, M. 65, 68, 69, 73

Simpson, M. *et al.* 69

social cohesion 17, 35

social constructivism 116–17, 118, 120

social inclusion 2, 6, 98, 130

software: access to 24, 30; assessment software 42; asynchronous 102; in initial teacher education 60, 63, 67; refreshing of 2; SEN and 116, 118–20, 121–9; social 99; training in 38, 42

special education needs 26, 63, 72, 105, 111, 125; global messages of 131; ICT and inclusion 114–15; role of the teacher 115–16; software and 116, 118–20, 121–9; teacher training 129–30; theoretical learning models 116–17; value of ICT for SEN 111–14

Standing Conference for Teacher Education, North and South (SCOTENS) 63

Stevenson Report (1997) 19, 22, 25

Stranmillis College 21

Sundberg, P.A. 101, 107–8

sustainability 2–3, 106, 131, 152, 167, 169; of infrastructure 6, 176–8; through an integrated strategy for ICT 19–20, 24–7, 30, 35–6; through leadership development 161; sustainable learning 143, 178–9

Talking Books 121, 125–6

Talking Clocks software 123, 127

Taylor, L. 69

teacher development: beginning teachers 74–5; building capacity for organisational change 53–4, 160–2; C2K training 31; and changing teacher and learner roles 93, 150–1; connected learning 103–4; continuing professional development 6, 15, 40, 42, 74–5; coordinated approach to 2, 6; curriculum innovation and 148–9; early professional development 50–1, 60; global messages of 58; leadership training 6, 155–6,

160–2; re-schooling and 4; for SEN 129–30; of staff in initial teacher education 64–5; taking teachers online 54–7; training in ICT classroom skills 38–9, 41–3, 44–50; *see also* teacher education
teacher education: competence-based 61–2; global messages of 58; ICT training in 6; initial 6, 12, 15, 59–74, 130; modelling of ICT in placement schools 69–71; online support 71–3; religious and cultural affiliations 12; reviews 15; for SEN 129–30; structure of 59–60; student impact of effective use of ICT 65–6; student teacher use of ICT 67–9; Teacher Education Partnership 50–1; *see also* teacher development
teaching practices: enhancing the classroom through ICT 83–90; need of rapid transformations in 2; in SEN 115–20
team work 33, 35, 146, 147–8, 174
technology: alignment with policy 2, 35–6, 82, 163, 173–5; computer brand incompatibility 23; data-warehousing 164; sustainability 82, 106
Thompson, Heather 55
Topping, Gordon 27
training *see* teacher development; teacher education
Tropp, L.R. and Pettigrew, T.F. 101

Uhomoibhi, J.O. 13, 14
Ulster Polytechnic 21
Ulster, University of 55, 66–8, 69, 104; NUU 20
Underwood, J.D.M. and Underwood, G. 117
unemployment 12
Unesco 99
Universities Council for the Education of Teachers (UCET) 60
'Unlocking Creativity' initiative 138–9

video-conferencing 17, 30, 64, 88, 90, 98, 102, 106, 115, 166; global community through 2; skills for 103; use in schools for the deaf 105
virtual learning environments (VLEs) 56, 71–2, 90, 137, 173, 182
Vygotsky, L.S. 116, 118

Wallace, Richard 90, 91
Wood, D. 172–3, 178
word processing 66, 75, 123–5
workforce 12, 13, 22, 24
Writing with Symbols software 115, 126
Wynne, E. 112, 113, 115, 118, 123, 128; Wynne's study 113, 118, 121–2, 125, 127, 128, 129

Zones of Proximal Development (ZPD) 116, 118